Battle-Tested

Carrier Aviation in Afghanistan and Iraq

REBECCA GRANT

Table of Contents

INTRODUCTION

"America will always need sailors and ships and shipborne aircraft to preserve her liberty..."
– Samuel Eliot Morison, 1963[1]

Afghanistan was a turning point for carrier striking power. Never before in this kind of war were carrier-based aircraft so vital to the joint air component. Without them, there would have been no quick air superiority over Afghanistan, no rapid start to Operation Enduring Freedom, no revolution in the conjunction of airpower, special operations and the Afghan opposition forces. Without them, the hunt for bin Laden and al Qaeda could not have started when it did. Without them, Taliban-ruled Afghanistan might have remained a "safe harbor" for terrorism through the winter of 2001-2002 and perhaps beyond.

The story of carrier aviation in Afghanistan is a case study of skilled warriors meeting an unforeseen test of battle by putting recent technological and tactical advances into play under a new operational concept born of war's immediate and unforeseen requirements.

Aboard the USS Carl Vinson, an F/A-18 Hornet pilot inspects his aircraft prior to flight operations in support of Operation Enduring Freedom. U.S. Navy photo by Photographer's Mate 3rd Class Saul Ingle.

"They are a battle-tested force," said Vice Admiral John Nathman in August 2002.[2]

To be "battle-tested" means many things. It means facing the perils of combat, its hardships and sacrifices while continuing to make night traps, build bombs and spot decks. The test of battle is the test of the individual and the unit: the pilot, the aircrew, the airwing, the carrier, the battlegroup and the men and women who give them life.

But there is another test that combat poses. It is one that cannot be passed with bravery and valor alone. This is the test of tactics and employment at a higher level of joint force integration. Meeting this test of battle generally means being able to master unique combat requirements that emerge as warfare shifts.

A major shift does not happen in every conflict but it happened in Afghanistan, and the carriers rose to the challenge. The USS Enterprise and USS Carl Vinson and the carriers that deployed after them had no way of knowing that they would be tested on the new criteria of the Afghan air war: persistence, precise coordination with ground controllers, complex new targets, day and night coverage of a wide open country with divert bases hundreds of miles away and rescue and repatriation far from certain.

This 21st Century battle-tested force continued the highest traditions of the naval service. Take, for example, a similar shift that occurred during World War II. Much has been written about the fleet's experiments with carriers in wargames at Newport and off Hawaii in the 1920s and 1930s and how they laid the foundation for carrier warfare in World War II. However, the sea victories owe even more to lessons learned in combat.

Recall that the initial carrier engagements of that war, from the attacks on the Gilberts and the Marshalls and Wake and Marcus Islands to the April 1942 Doolittle raid to Coral Sea and Midway and through the battles around Guadalcanal, followed the doctrine of independent carrier operations. The pattern was altered only by the *ad hoc* attempt to keep *Lexington* and *Yorktown* together in one destroyer screen at Coral Sea. Although *Hornet* and *Enterprise* were both under Spruance at Midway, he fought the airwings separately (*Yorktown* was on its own).

Carriers in the deadly waters around Guadalcanal worked alone. Morison had this to say about the Battle of the Eastern Solomons fought in late August 1942: "As at Midway and Coral Sea, each carrier group, in a tight circle about two miles in diameter, was independent of the other."[3] For this battle, *Enterprise* and *Saratoga* were only about ten miles apart. Both were under the overall command of Fletcher but their airwings did not fight as one."[4] In fact, none other than the Chief of Naval Operations, formidable, profane, irascible Admiral Ernest J. King, forbade multi-carrier task forces after Midway.

Then for several grim weeks in the fall of 1942 the Navy rarely had a choice about how to employ its carriers. Epic sea battles around Guadalcanal between August and October claimed Wasp and Hornet and damaged *Enterprise* and *Saratoga* on multiple occasions. After *Hornet* sank on October 26, 1942 the United States Navy for a time had no operational carriers in the Pacific. As late as spring 1943 *Saratoga* was on her own while *Enterprise* was in overhaul – a situation so dire that it moved the British to lend a hand by dispatching *HMS Victorious* to the Pacific to join in two-carrier operations.[5]

1942 with its taste of victory and second helpings of defeat was not the defining year for aircraft carrier tactics. Carriers had not yet found the operating concept to bring victory at sea. As historian Clark Reynolds keenly observed: "The remaining problem at the outset of 1943 was the single carrier vs. the multi-carrier task force.

It took the success of the fast carriers to turn the tide for good.

The change to the multi-carrier task forces came with the arrival of new ships with different equipment, airwing compositions and tactics: the *Essex*-class carriers. Carriers went on to score their greatest victories by operating in packs. By 1944, the *Essex*-class fast carriers operated in task force groups of up to 15. Together their striking power packed quite a wallop. Mitscher launched 216 planes from ten carriers in ten minutes after sighting the Japanese force late in the afternoon of June 20, 1944, the second day of the Battle of the Philippine Sea.[6]

These 26,000-ton vessels, in massed task forces, did not just check the Japanese advance. They reversed it, destroyed the remains of Japan's carrier aviators and fleet, and won victory in the Central Pacific. To accomplish this task, these sailors and aviators capitalized on improved technology, tactics and equipment from longer flight decks and extra 5-inch guns, to the new F6F Hellcat. Above all was the lesson from recent engagements: new operating concepts for multiple carriers rolled together under the heading of the fast carrier task forces.

With a full deckload strike spotted aft, an Essex-class carrier invades the Gilbert Islands late in 1943, protected by its own 5-inch anti-aircraft guns (left) and those of a battleship astern. U.S. Navy photo.

Battle-tested, the Americans of the fast carrier task forces blended bravery, valor, tactics and the right operational concept.

So did they again for Afghanistan. Carrier striking power led joint operations at the start, and wartime conditions brought a new response from the fleet that met the needs of persistent, expeditionary airpower for the war on terror.

The light-speed evolution in tactics and operational concepts forged during Operation Enduring Freedom did not stop there. It led directly to an impressive, flexible role for carrier-based aviation in the build up to war with Iraq – the major combat operations phase concluded in 2003, with the stability operations and counterinsurgency phase ongoing throughout 2004 and beyond.

Innovation under combat conditions is the most powerful engine of change. The rapid progress during Operation Enduring Freedom carved out a new role for carrier aviation in the joint air component and Operation Iraqi Freedom took it even further. Those combat experiences are at the core of the Navy's new Fleet Response Plan, which reverses years of recent tradition, and the triumvirate of Sea Shield, Sea Basing and Sea Strike, where the integrated striking power of naval forces gets the doctrinal treatment it so richly deserves.

The battle-tested force with two major campaigns behind it has set a course for carrier strike dominance in expeditionary warfare. Of course, change continued as stability and counterinsurgency operations in Afghanistan and Iraq demanded more persistence and precision and have taken the air component to a new level.

The main point of this book is to trace and document the changing role of carrier striking power by examining its role in the joint air component from October 2001- May 2003. Two stories precede it. One necessary preface is the Revolution in Strike Warfare that was underway in the 1990s. That is the subject of Chapter One. Chapter Two focuses on the rise of terrorism, problems with Iraq after 1998, the tragic events of September 11, 2001, and the Navy's response both at home and abroad.

Chapter Three discusses the Afghanistan war, with carrier striking power at the center of the decision to begin Operation Enduring Freedom. Chapter Four describes how "battle was joined" as the four carriers pulled together the ingredients of persistence and linked with SOF forces on the ground. Chapter Five covers the final major victories in the fall of 2001 and the continued operations as the focus of Operation Enduring Freedom shifted to tracking down al Qaeda remnants and stabilizing Afghanistan. Chapter Six covers the single most concentrated test of battle: the delivery of air support in the intense two weeks of fighting during Operation Anaconda in March 2002.

Chapter Seven examines preparations, both diplomatic and military, for the war in Iraq. Chapter Eight analyzes carrier operations in the fast and flexible beginning of Operation Iraqi Freedom. Chapter Nine sees the carriers through the decisive combat operations phase proclaimed over on the deck of the USS *Abraham Lincoln* on May 1, 2003. Chapter Ten evaluates strategic directions for carriers and Sea Strike in the future.

Acknowledgements

I consider myself lucky to have had the chance to pull this story together and I owe thanks to many individuals. First, to my father, who took me aboard a Fast Carrier on the occasion of the decommissioning of *USS Yorktown* when I was very small. After the ceremony, I met a man whom I was told was an Indian, Admiral J.J. "Jocko" Clark. But the elderly man in his coat and tie did not seem much like an Indian to me and I'm afraid I was nowhere near as impressed by his former skipper as Dad hoped I would be. Fortunately, I have a picture taken with Jocko that day, and when I look at it now I'm thrilled I was born in time to meet one of the Fast Carrier admirals.

Later I had the opportunity to learn a lot about modern airpower and make a profession of research on it. I had not thought much about the *Yorktown*, except for an occasional visit to Charleston, until 1999 when Admiral John Nathman gave me a copy of the book *The Fast Carriers*, which he told me he had made required reading for his staff in the Air Warfare Requirements directorate.

Two years later, the carrier operations in Afghanistan in 2001 struck me as something distinct, something of great significance for the future of carriers in national defense. That impression was reconfirmed during the main combat phase of operations in Iraq in 2003. Admiral Mark Fitzgerald, who had been part of practically every significant carrier action from 1991-2002, extended me the chance to research the topic in greater depth. Admiral Tom Kilcline guided the final result. Mr. Mick Taylor, Principal Assistant for Air Warfare Plans, Analysis and Assessments (N783B) saw the project through from conception to completion.

The substance of this study comes from research and from interviews. Several men and women gave me their time, making it possible to tell much of the story in their words. My thanks to interview subjects General T. Michael Moseley, Admiral John Nathman, Admiral Tim Keating, Vice Admiral David Nichols, Vice Admiral James Zortman, Vice Admiral Mark Fitzgerald, Rear Admiral Charles Johnston, Rear Admiral Steven Tomaszeski, Rear Admiral John Stufflebeem, Rear Admiral James Robb, Rear Admiral Matthew Moffit, Rear Admiral John Kelly, Rear Admiral Anthony Winns, Rear Admiral John Cryer and Captain Patrick Driscoll. The assistance of Lieutenant Commander Ronald Stinson helped set up the major interviews.

My thanks also go to the fourteen pilots who opened their logbooks and talked specifics with me at Lemoore Naval Air Station in July 2004.

All errors of fact, judgment, analysis and typing are mine alone.

CHAPTER 1:

Revolution

"Little in Desert Storm supported the Maritime Strategy's assumptions and implications."
— Admiral William Owens, 1995[7]

Carriers in the 1980s were a long way from the level of lethality and persistence they would display over Afghanistan and Iraq.

Operational concepts had changed greatly from the days of massed carrier airpower in the fast carrier task forces. Aircraft carriers in the late Cold War trained to operate alone with their battlegroups against a lethal Soviet sea and land-based threat. "My whole background was the Cold War environment," said Rear Admiral John Stufflebeem, who was then an F-14 pilot out in the fleet, "CAPs and defending against the horde of Russian Badgers and Backfires that [would] come out to find us."[8]

U.S. Navy pilot Lt. Reggie Hamon expends flares from his F/A-18C Hornet over the Pacific Ocean during a competitive training exercise. DoD photo by Lt. Karl Rauch, U.S. Navy.

Fleet air defense was the top priority. "There were multiple targets coming out at the ship. So the defense of the carrier battle groups was a centerpiece of pretty much all of our tactics off the carrier for the first two decades that I was involved in flying off of ships," recalled Rear Admiral James Robb, another F-14 pilot.[9]

Carriers went solo in the Maritime Strategy of 1986. Chief of Naval Operations Admiral James D. Watkins and Marine Corps Commandant General P. X. Kelley described a broad global role for naval forces that depended on carriers operating alone and independently with their battlegroups even if World War III broke out. The aircraft carriers' role was to be on scene to contain and control a regional crisis or help seize the initiative in global war. The Maritime Strategy also expected naval forces to influence the combined-arms land battle in Europe and help terminate the war on favorable terms – a tactical and strategic nuclear threat perfectly appropriate to the mid-1980s. However, the heart of the strategy was rapid crisis response.[10]

OPERATION DESERT STORM

Change began with Operation Desert Storm. Naval aviators flew thousands of combat sorties from the six carriers in two operating areas and entered the precision age with laser-guided bombs off the A-6. This time, victory was a superb teacher, for Operation Desert Storm ignited a period of change that increased the lethality of carrier striking power many times over during the next decade.

Looking back at Desert Storm illustrates what a change it was. For the first time, the Navy carriers were providing air combat power as part of a joint air component, mandated by command structure changes in the 1986 Goldwater-Nichols Act. Yet the emphasis on independent operations and alpha strikes meant that the six carriers who flew combat missions during Operation Desert Storm from January 17 to March 1, 1991 were operating much as Fletcher's had in 1942.

"Desert Storm, in my mind, was sort of a classic naval aviation way of doing business. You amass a lot of firepower and then you get on this new entity called the air tasking order and you flow a whole bunch of sorties to service targets," said Stufflebeem.[11]

"The role of the airpower that we had in response to the '91 war was broken into two pieces," explained Robb. "One would have been the counter air force. You know the fighters that were doing pretty much a fighter mission, like the F-14s. And then the A-6s and A-7s that were doing the air to ground" along with F/A-18s, he said.[12]

Those F/A-18s were early block models. "We had FLIRs, but we did not have lasers," said Rear Admiral Matthew Moffit, who in 1991 was an F/A-18 squadron commander who flew combat missions from USS America. "We did a lot of general purpose ordnance delivery."[13]

Vice Admiral Mark Fitzgerald at the time was deployed with the USS John F. Kennedy, the first of the carriers to surge toward the Persian Gulf after Iraq invaded Kuwait. Carriers and land-based aircraft quickly became the deterrence and reprisal force in case the Iraqis moved across the Saudi border. What the aviators did not know was that it would be months before combat operations began – but it was time they all needed to plan and rehearse the massive joint air campaign. "We practiced the first night's strike three times," Fitzgerald said of that waiting period. "I mean, full up, all the tankers came out, everything." Early rehearsals revealed serious difficulties coordinating with the joint air component, under the command of Air Force Lieutenant General Charles Horner. "The first strike we flew was an abomination. We couldn't find tankers because we didn't understand how Air Force tankers worked, those kinds of things."

Fitzgerald was among a handful who ended up flying from the ship to visit the air campaign planners in the Black Hole, their makeshift offices in the basement of the Royal Saudi Air Force building in Riyadh.

It was a meeting of two different cultures attempting to fight under the same flag. "At the time, we were very unfamiliar with air tasking orders (ATOs)," Fitzgerald remembered. "We were doing 'ATO 101' trying to figure out how they worked."[14]

Communications from the carriers to the land-based air operations center directing the air war were "somewhat archaic," said Moffit. It affected strike planning, assessment, everything. A computer print-out of the thousand-page ATO arrived daily aboard ship via an S-3 that flew to Riyadh to pick it up. In 1991 "we didn't have these automatic parsing devices that we do now that pulled out your missions," added Moffit. "You had to go through and identify that business. So there were some long nights in preparation for the next day's strikes." Not infrequently, the ATO was late due to rolling changes in Riyadh. A late ATO was an inconvenience for land-based units who got electronic copies, a major headache for strike planners at sea who had to wait for the hard copy. In the Red Sea "we got to the point where we all shared information," Moffit said, so if one ship got the ATO, "then we'd hustle a helo over there to get a copy and bring it over."[15]

That inconvenience paled next to the frequent lack of other strike planning materials. "Overhead imagery? Not readily available," recalled Admiral Timothy Keating, who was a deputy airwing commander aboard *Saratoga* at the time. "Target planning in 1991 consisted on occasion of going down to the ship's library and pulling out a LIFE Magazine or a Rand McNally Atlas. Or photographs that were days, weeks, months, years old out of the archives," he said. Post-target analysis consisted of "watching one's HUD tape, which in the F/A-18 unfortunately was not the most visually stirring evidence," Keating said.[16]

Tankers were another problem. In 1991 the Air Force typically set its big-wing KC-135 and KC-10 tankers in 60-mile orbits. For Navy strike aircraft coming off the ship, "we were spending all our gas trying to chase down these tankers," said Fitzgerald. "You'd chase and chase and chase them down – we didn't have radars in our airplanes – and then all of a sudden, next thing you know, *whoosh*, they'd come by [and we'd head] out 60 miles the other way chasing them. Guys were just running out of gas." The Navy liaisons eventually won access to the joint campaign planners and convinced them to position some tankers in 15-mile orbits. But the bottom line was that as Fitzgerald said "it took all six months of preparation" to work out how to combine Navy, Air Force and Coalition aircraft for the Desert Storm air campaign.[17]

Tactics revolved around alpha strikes. "In some cases it was one target with four planes, doing the old wagon wheel roll-in from as high as the Hornets could get, to stay above the surface-to-air threat," Keating recalled. Early losses quickly convinced the air component commander to scrap the low-altitude ingress and pop-up tactics of the Cold War. A-6s and all other aircraft were ordered to bomb from medium altitude after the first week.

There was little true close air support or strike reconnaissance of the kind that would become so familiar a decade later. Moffit figured that "maybe once we spoke to a FAC-A of some sort. But not much. You were just given an area [and told to] go drop bombs" there, he said.[18] A killbox grid system in wide use for the first time funneled strike aircraft toward fielded Iraqi forces.

Some missions were short but others took endurance. Carriers operating in the Red Sea sent pilots on long missions that averaged six or seven hours and sometimes more. "I had a nine-hour mission across over to Kuwait one night, which was pretty interesting," Moffit recalled.[19]

By any measure, Operation Desert Storm was a tremendous success, and a benchmark for modern airpower. Yet only a sliver of the air component was truly in the precision age. Communications links were minimal. Planners still used grease pencils. Real-time retargeting was done only in emergencies (as at the Battle of Khafji when JSTARS observations caught an Iraqi force on the move and AWACS rerouted several strike aircraft from all services while airborne to meet it).

Naval aviators did all they could given the limits of their weapons systems. The experiences of the USS Theodore Roosevelt, CVN-71, were representative. CVN-71 arrived on station in the Persian Gulf with 20 F/A-18s, 18 A-6s and 18 F-14s. Over the 43 days of the war, CVN-71 averaged a sortie rate of 1.28 for the F/A-18s and stood down for only 4 days during the operation, the lowest number of days not in action of all six carriers. During the ground war peak from February 25-27, 1991, the Theodore Roosevelt's F/A-18s surged to 122 sorties for a total three-day sortie rate of 2.03.[20]

It was almost all unguided ordnance. The "lion's share of what we did was just go out with four or five Mk 82s or Mk 83s and drop those from a relatively high altitude," said Commander Daniel Hinson, who was then an F/A-18A pilot aboard Theodore Roosevelt.[21]

The results were a source of pride but they were also a signal for change. A report by the Center for Naval Analyses counted 6297 carrier sorties that flew over land and dropped bombs. The average per carrier was just 24.4 strike sorties per day.[22]

Carriers had fought the first air war of the precision age constrained by technology and by tactics. "The fleet was never forced to fight the open-ocean battles the Navy had

A Navy A-7E Corsair II is passing an old Ottoman castle built by the Turks in the mid-Eighteenth Century.

4

been preparing for during the preceding twenty years," retired Admiral William Owens later observed.[23] The late Cold War survivability challenges coloring the Maritime Strategy simply had not emerged in Operation Desert Storm.

In the aviation community, a strategy shift away from Cold War tactics was already underway. After the fall of the Soviet Union the "carrier force was trying to figure out its relevance," said Robb. Carriers got closer to shore in the littoral, brown-water environment and "the ship went from defending the battle group to power projection. You had a very clear swing of the strategy between open ocean warfare and flying power projection ashore."[24]

The mid-1990s saw the start of the tactical air neck-down with A-6s retiring and airwing composition heading for a standard deck mix of F/A-18s plus F-14s in a blended air superiority and strike role. Just as important, the dominance of the F/A-18 in the fleet created the chance to merge disparate communities. The drive to increase lethality – to create a revolution in strike warfare – was underway.

"WHERE ARE THE CARRIERS?"

What did not change as much at first were the operating concepts. To be sure, the Navy as a whole was in the midst of a tremendous shift toward littoral operations. After 1992's strategy paper "...From the Sea" the presence mission dominated.

President William J. Clinton was on board *Theodore Roosevelt* when he said on March 12, 1993: "When word of a crisis breaks out in Washington, it's no accident that the first question that comes to everyone's lips is: 'Where's the nearest carrier?'"[25]

It became the catch-phrase carrier doctrine of the decade. Senior officials repeated it regularly. The presence doctrine – emphasizing the role of the single carrier – became the pillar of carrier operations. Forward presence suited the strategic climate of expeditionary operations and quickly supplanted pure warfighting requirements as the major factor in sizing and employing the carrier force.

For the carriers, the number one operating concept was to be on station to shape the crisis until joint forces rolled in to fight the major theater war or operations other than war. That meant regular six-month deployments with a force of 12 carriers (after 1994) as a pipeline to support continuous deployment in three regions.

The 1994, Naval Doctrine Publication 1 titled 'Naval Warfare' defined both "routine presence" and "crisis response, the emergent, timely dispatch of naval forces to a specific area" as elements of forward presence.[26] The price of presence as a doctrine was that it separated carrier operating concepts from the new centerpiece of national strategy: massed striking power in regional conflicts. It also meant adhering to six-month deployments was essential, if the Navy was going to conduct the presence mission over the long haul. And that bred a reluctance to yank carriers out of their deployment cycles or extend their cruises while crises simmered.

Twelve carriers, however, could not give 100 percent presence coverage of the Mediterranean, the Gulf and the Western Pacific. The Navy began to "gap" the Med for a few months each year, with occasional gap periods in the Persian Gulf, too. Maintaining two carriers on station at any hub – for example, during a crisis with Iraq – strained the entire fleet, disrupting everything from deployment cycles to ammunition allotments.

For the time being, the potential tactical conflicts went untested, as the revolution in strike warfare made strides.

CNO Jay Johnson released the Naval Operational Concept in early 1997, summing up the Navy's capabilities. "Our ability to deliver a wide range of naval firepower and generate very high aircraft sortie rates can have a major impact on the course and outcome of a conflict, especially during the critical early period of a joint campaign, when continental US-based forces are just starting to arrive in theater," said Johnson.

Single carrier presence reigned as the main operating concept and carriers were judged by the firepower each could generate on its own.

No better example came out of the 1990s than the USS Nimitz SURGEX of 1997. The idea was to demonstrate maximum effort from a single carrier. SURGEX began on

U.S. Navy Lt. Rick Krystof watches an F-14 Tomcat hurtle down the catapult of the aircraft carrier USS Nimitz on Jan. 29, 1998. DoD photo by Petty Officer 2nd Class James H. Watson, U.S. Navy.

July 20, 1997 and in 98 hours, the Nimitz and CVW-9 generated 975 fixed-wing sorties. A total of 771 strike sorties put 1336 "bombs," mostly practice BDU-45s, on targets within 200 nm of the carrier. F/A-18s flew 79% of the strike sorties and posted a phenomenal sortie rate of 4.2. SURGEX was an endurance feat that tested the ability to conduct continuous day and night operations. Its impressive results, however, depended on several factors.

The Nimitz SURGEX was based on a scenario of intensive air support for Marines ashore in Kuwait. These were short missions. They were free of constraints of joint force tanking, target changes and airborne control. However hefty its results, SURGEX fit only a narrow band of potential real-world joint operations. SURGEX was over in four days and all of the Nimitz's 771 sorties for the exercise stayed well within a 200 nm combat radius. Persistence over the battlespace was not measured, nor was the need for dealing with long sorties, 24-hour battlespace coverage, and combat operations that lasted for months.

Although naval strategy had shifted to presence and littoral warfare, the Cold War legacy of independent operations still had a firm grip on carrier operating concepts.

DESERT FOX

The events that were to loosen that grip were beginning to take shape as terrorist activity and problems with Iraq increased in 1998. There were also two more significant carrier engagements to come before the end of the 20th Century: Desert Fox and Kosovo.

First was Operation Desert Fox. UN inspections in Iraq broke down in the fall of 1998 and CENTCOM came close to action in mid-November, calling off a planned strike with moments to spare. According to President Clinton, his national security adviser Sandy Berger received three letters from Saddam promising compliance just as "planes were already in the air" for the strike. Officials in the National Military Command Center rushed to contact CENTCOM and turn back the strike, which would have consisted of TLAM launches as well as airstrikes. Clinton later said "I was skeptical, but I decided to give him one more chance."[27]

The close call spooked Iraq's military forces. "There has been some dispersion of Republican Guard and regular army units over the last week or so," acknowledged Pentagon spokesman Ken Bacon on November 10, 1998. "That is, they've spread out over larger areas."[28] Dispersal was to become almost a trained response.

Unfortunately, it also made regional allies gun-shy. The plan for November strikes depended on land-based air as well as the *USS Eisenhower* battlegroup, which was preparing to hand-off to the inbound *USS Enterprise*.[29] When trouble brewed again a month later the Saudis declined to let bases in the Kingdom be used to strike Iraqi

The light streak of the afterburners from an F/A-18 Hornet lights up the night as Capt. Marty Chanik, commanding officer of the aircraft carrier USS Enterprise, monitors the first wave of strike aircraft launching from the flight deck in support of Operation Desert Fox on Dec. 17, 1998. DoD photo by Petty Officer 2nd Class Michael W. Pendergrass, U.S. Navy.

Lt. Carol Watts (center), an F/A-18C Hornet pilot, flies with her hands as she discusses with Lt. Lyndsi Bates (right) her night-time strike against Iraq on Dec. 17, 1998, after returning on board the aircraft carrier USS Enterprise during Operation Desert Fox. DoD photo by Petty Officer 3rd Class Tedrick E. Fryman III, U.S. Navy.

targets. US forces had "worn out our welcome," as Vice Admiral David Nichols, who was then on the CENTCOM staff, put it.[30] The end result was that CENTCOM "had an access problem," said Fitzgerald, who was also at CENTCOM at the time. The Saudis did not "want us flying any strikes out of there" and if they "started flying out of Kuwait, we [would] tip our hand," he continued.[31]

Carrier air (plus TLAMs and a few B-1 bombers) stepped in. On December 17, the US and Britain launched a series of strikes to punish Saddam for his non-compliance with the UN and to break up key pieces of his military command and control and damage weapons production capabilities.

"Our mission is clear: to degrade Saddam's capacity to develop and deliver weapons of mass destruction, and threaten the region," Clinton reiterated in his December 19, 1998 radio address, adding: "had we failed to respond it would have given Saddam a green light to rebuild his arsenal and threaten his neighbors."[32]

The operation signaled a new role for the carriers at the center of the joint air component. "Desert Fox the first day started out as pretty much a carrier-based operation," said Fitzgerald. *Enterprise* executed a majority of the sorties in the four-day operation. Striking fast was essential. CENTCOM Commander General Anthony Zinni, USMC, later said that "We prevented his [Saddam's] ability to prepare, to set SAM ambushes, to disperse his forces, to do a number of things that would have made our mission more difficult."[33]

Carl Vinson arrived on station in time to fly in the fourth and final night of Operation Desert Fox and two ships from the *Carl Vinson* battlegroup launched TLAMs. Lieutenant Todd Marzano was on his first operational deployment as a Hornet pilot in VFA-94. "Our ship pulled in the last night," he said. "We just did one series of strikes and then they stopped the campaign." He did not get to drop bombs in Operation Desert Fox, but he saw that the Hornets were already far more capable weapons platforms.[34]

The fact that Desert Fox was only a four-day operation did not obscure its value as a marker of how far carrier striking power had come. Carrier-based aircraft and TLAMs dominated the joint air component's strike mix. Precision weapons ruled the air tasking orders. This was no longer the carrier striking force of Operation Desert Storm. It was a newly lethal, flexible force, equipped with the weapons, sensors and datalinks to take air warfare to a higher level.

Brief as they were, the Desert Fox strikes made a significant impression on Saddam's military. Republican Guards headquarters at Taji were struck. Talil, a major airfield near Baghdad, had its weapons storage bunkers and maintenance facilities destroyed. Strikes hit the Ministry of Defense in Baghdad and put holes in the roof of the Ba'ath party headquarters. Military communications targets such as repeater stations were hit from Tikrit in the north to Basra in the south.[35]

Operation Desert Fox was notable in one other way that also had a touch of the revolutionary about it. Three women pilots took part in the strikes. Lieutenant Kendra Williams became the Navy's first female pilot to drop bombs in combat when she flew on the first night of Desert Fox. "I was just doing my job," she told the press. "I'm ready to do it again."[36] Lieutenants Carol Watts and Lyndsi Bates of VFA-37 later piloted F/A-18 Hornets during the strikes. A female pilot from *Carl Vinson* underscored the change when on January 24, 1999, she became the first to employ the new Joint Stand-Off Weapon (JSOW) during a routine OSW combat mission.[37]

Yet change was incomplete. The revolution in strike warfare had reshaped carrier airwings, but not their operating concepts. Policy-makers still viewed carriers primarily as presence assets. "If you don't have that presence, you have less of a voice, less of an influence," said Secretary of Defense William Cohen.[38]

KOSOVO

The lesson left on the table was that every carrier action from Lebanon in 1983 to Desert Fox in 1998 at least two carriers had been involved. Expeditionary, joint air warfare required multiple carriers.

However, the final conflict of the 1990s was to prove the exception. NATO's Operation Allied Force was a 78-day air war that hit key strategic targets, ravaged Serbian fielded military forces, introduced the concept of flexible, time-sensitive targeting on a

An F-14 Tomcat powers up for its catapult launch off the deck of the USS Theodore Roosevelt in support of Operation Allied Force on May 29, 1999. U.S. Navy photo by Photographer's Mate 1st Class Dennis D. Taylor.

wide scale and demonstrated NATO's resolve to prevent Milosevic from terrorizing and taking over the former Yugoslavian province of Kosovo.

Just one aircraft carrier, the always-busy *Theodore Roosevelt*, participated in NATO's biggest air campaign. Operation Allied Force was already three days old when *Theodore Roosevelt* sailed from Norfolk on March 26, 1999. CVW-8 engaged in the first week of April as NATO was tripling the number of strike aircraft for the campaign.

The Coalition air component soon recognized it had a much harder task ahead and needed persistent airpower over the battlespace in Kosovo to search out targets and take on the first of what became known as time-sensitive strikes. In Operation Allied Force, that airpower came from the hasty deployment of the land-based air forces, from both the US and NATO.

But it would be single-carrier operations for NATO's big air war.

In late April, *Enterprise* transited the Mediterranean on the way home from a Persian Gulf cruise that had begun with Operation Desert Fox and continued with increased activity in Operation Southern Watch. Despite the fact that US and NATO forces were still building up their strike power in theater, *Enterprise* was not diverted to join the campaign. The ship's six month cruise was nearly over and initial problems with integrating CVW-8 two weeks earlier had left the CAOC with a diminished appetite for naval assets – with the major exception of the EA-6Bs.

The CAOC couldn't get enough of the Prowlers. When operations began "we had 26 EA-6Bs in place at Aviano, and Aviano's a single runway. It's kind of like a landlocked carrier," said Rear Admiral John Cryer, who at the time was with the EA-6Bs.[39] *Theodore Roosevelt* added another squadron. Serbian air defenses were dense and their tactics were adaptive. "They were very cagey about putting any radars on and leaving them up for HARM because there was a tremendous amount of HARM in the air," said Cryer. That left significant Serb SAMs on the ground. Hence the NATO strike packages relied heavily on jamming from the Navy and Marine Corps EA-6Bs. Some key air defense targets remained off the list due to NATO politics, and pilots found the air defenses made their presence known. In this expeditionary environment, "the Prowlers did a terrific job of suppressing the radar picture that the Serbs could try to build," Cryer said.[40]

And they did it under risky conditions. Cryer described one of the missions he flew supporting an F-15E strike package targeting Pristina. Unlocated SA-6s were in the area and "as we got up there and close, we had total of six missiles in the air almost right away." Their erratic tracks against the night sky indicated the missiles were being guided toward the strike package. The F-15Es broke in defensive maneuvers as the EA-6Bs put HARM in the air and sent up an electronic wall of jamming. "We were on our back a couple times, but we kept jamming," Cryer said of the mission.[41] The F-15Es reformed and struck their targets.

Land and sea-based naval aviators participating in the Kosovo crisis had come far in the revolution in strike warfare. Strike fighters were precise and lethal. ATO transmission was electronic and parsed. Precision-equipped F/A-18s and F-14s got a taste of the new style of air warfare with CAOC controlled strikes, time-sensitive targeting of air defense sites and other valuable targets, and the process of sending strike aircraft to hunt military targets in the Kosovo Engagement Zone. A rapidly retargeted TLAM hit a parked MiG-29 in an impressive new show of flexible targeting. Other NATO allies picked up most of the air defense tasking for Operation Allied Force. Pure power projection was what NATO needed and strikes from the sea accounted for about a quarter of the Serbian fielded forces targets struck by NATO.

By 1999 the aircraft carrier had achieved a new level of lethality via the ongoing "revolution in strike warfare." "Carriers now attack many more targets with much greater precision," said Keating in the summer of 2001. "A carrier air wing can strike nearly five times as many aimpoints each day as its predecessors could in Operation Desert Storm." More lethality was on the way. Keating estimated that the deployment of full complements of F/A-18EF Super Hornets would make it a sevenfold increase in striking power.[42]

Yet the transit of the *Eisenhower* stood as a reminder that presence or "being there" as Keating called it remained the top strategic and operational task. Despite the advances underway in the revolution in strike warfare, the carriers were locked into competing demands of presence, crisis response and sustained operations.

But aircraft carriers were about to demonstrate they could perform not just as an integral part of the air component, but as its centerpiece. Persistence – "staying there" –would quickly trump presence and shaping in the next crisis: Afghanistan.

CHAPTER 2:

The Rise of Terror

"We believe that the biggest thieves in the world are the Americans and the biggest terrorists on earth are the Americans. The only way for us to defend against these assaults is by using similar means. We do not differentiate between those dressed in military uniforms and civilians." – Osama bin Laden, Interview with ABC News, June 1998

It took al Qaeda bombings in Africa to turn the spotlight on Afghanistan.

The USS *Abraham Lincoln* battlegroup was on station in the Persian Gulf on August 7, 1998, when American embassies in Nairobi, Kenya and Dar es Salaam, Tanzania were hit with truck bombs in a near-simultaneous attack.

An F/A-18 Hornet launches towards the sun from the flight deck of the aircraft carrier USS Constellation as the ship steams in the Persian Gulf on July 29, 2001 in support of Operation Southern Watch. DoD photo by Petty Officer 3rd Class George Branham, U.S. Navy.

It took little time for the US to conclude that "Osama bin Laden's network of terrorists was involved in the planning, the financing, and the execution of the attacks on US embassies in Kenya and Tanzania," according to General Hugh Shelton, Chairman of the Joint Chiefs of Staff.[43] This time the US had to respond. Due to the deepening dispute with Iraq that year, the US had doubled the number of Tomahawk missiles aboard warships ready for near-instant use against Iraq. Now the Tomahawks became the prime weapon in the retaliation against bin Laden's network. On August 20, 1998, Tomahawks struck the Zhawar Kili Al-Badr base camp, training camp, and support complex in the eastern mountains of Afghanistan. Another TLAM strike hit the Shifa chemical plant in Khartoum. The nighttime strikes were timed to minimize collateral damage.

"There can be no safe haven for terrorists," said Shelton at the Pentagon press briefing on August 20, 1998. "The international community must not tolerate such acts nor accept those nations who would aid or harbor terrorists."[44]

"The intelligence community is confident that this facility is involved in the production of chemical weapons agents including precursor chemicals for the deadly V series of nerve agents like, for example, VX," Shelton explained. "We also know that bin Laden has extensive ties to the Sudanese government which controls this chemical facility."[45]

CENTCOM relied heavily on 5th Fleet for the strikes, which Fitzgerald saw up close due to his position on the CENTCOM staff. He later described it as a major command and control exercise. "It was the first time that we'd controlled that big a space" stretching from the Sudan to Afghanistan, Fitzgerald said. One blip occurred when a submarine in the Mediterranean inadvertently caused the sudden loss of communications links to the TLAM shooters "right before we were getting ready to shoot. Everybody panics. What happened?" recalled Fitzgerald. They went to secure network email as the back-up.[46]

Osama bin Laden.

EXPLORING OPTIONS

Retaliatory strikes were one thing, but the broader issue of how to employ US military power against the threat of terrorism was quite another.

Both the CIA and the FBI began tracking bin Laden more closely. The FBI later issued an indictment against bin Laden and 16 of his associates following a multinational investigation of the African embassy bombings.[47] Also, President Clinton pressed Pakistan's Prime Minister Nawaz Sharif for help in finding bin Laden on multiple occasions in late 1998 and 1999. Attempts to work covert operations with Pakistan hit a bump when General Pervez Musharraf deposed Sharif in a coup on October 12, 1999, but by early 2000, contacts renewed, and Clinton continued to press Pakistan for help.[48]

Hunting a terrorist band was a new challenge and for the next three years US military forces were in uncertain waters.

Nichols noticed the change in contingency planning. "After we didn't get Osama bin Laden in TLAM strikes in Afghanistan, we started this game of trying to follow Osama around Afghanistan and trying to figure out how to get a shot at him," he recalled.[49] Submarines remained on call in the North Arabian Sea to conduct a TLAM strike if bin Laden turned up.[50] They knew it would be a lucky shot "at best." Contingency plans "began to develop to get Osama, and/or go in there and bust up Taliban." Pakistani sovereignty made overflight and basing difficult. None of them "were very pretty," said Nichols of CENTCOM's notional options. Another prospect was to track bin Laden "with a little special ops force," but it could not go in alone. To support it, "you start adding everything that needs to go with that. Pretty soon you got aircraft carriers, B-2s, couple hundred strike airplanes supporting 4 or 5 A-teams" on the ground, Nichols said.[51]

In the end "we didn't think that would be successful," he said of the concept. "We're conventional thinkers, I guess," he said later. The insertion mission also "smacked of Desert One and that craziness." That failed operation to rescue US embassy hostages in Tehran had cost the lives of 8 US servicemen in 1980.

Above all "there were too many policy hurdles" that stood in the way of "really having that military discussion with the decision makers." As Nichols pointed out, "shooting a missile into Afghanistan is one thing. But flying helicopters in there, and spitting out special ops guys, is a whole 'nother thing." To be sure, "there was plenty of political will on the part of the Clinton administration to get Osama," Nichols observed. "But there was also not much appetite for political and diplomatic risk...and changing the way we did business in that part of the world."[52]

Another complication was the unresolved problem of Iraq and its weapons programs. A CIA report to Congress in August 2000 revealed that after Desert Fox, "Baghdad again instituted a reconstruction effort on those facilities destroyed by the US bombing, to include several critical missile production complexes and former dual-use CW production." The CIA cited "no direct evidence" of renewed Iraqi WMD programs but hedged by saying that "given past behavior, this type of activity must be regarded as likely." The CIA then went on to describe Iraq's efforts to build short-range missiles and convert Czech L-29 jet trainers into UAVs.[53] Former UN chief weapons inspector David Kay explained in January 2001, "I think everyone that I know of in the community agrees that if the Iraqis had the nuclear material, highly-enriched uranium or plutonium, they would have a weapon in less than a year." "The explosive manufacturing and missile program has gone ahead," Kay added.[54]

It turned out that Saddam was doing all he could in these years to foster the impression that he could quickly put his finger on a deadly WMD trigger. He told interrogators after his 2003 capture that being credited with WMD possession was part of his plan to stay in power even in the face of UN sanctions. Hussein had indeed ordered the use of chemical weapons during the Iran-Iraq war and had come to believe that this barbaric move had saved his army from defeat, at the cost of 80,000 Iranian casualties. He also believed his WMD stocks had prevented a Coalition drive to Baghdad in 1991. Moreover, he believed that cultivating the impression that his rump research programs could be reactivated quickly gave him an international bargaining chip.[55]

It was a strategy born to backfire. Saddam was stalling; bin Laden's organization was plotting; and US national security priorities were about to change forever.

Tragedy in Yemen

It took two more sophisticated al Qaeda attacks to do it.

On October 12, 2000, al Qaeda struck again with a suicide attack on the *USS Cole* in Yemen. Ships transiting from the Mediterranean to Bahrain could not make the trip without refueling and the Navy was short on oilers to position in the area. For a time, Djibouti had been the routine refueling point, but "Djibouti was going south fast," recalled Fitzgerald. In contrast, "Aden had been quiet for a while" due to efforts of the Yemeni government and "it appeared that Aden was going to be a reasonable place to go" with a lower threat if only because al Qaeda did not want to risk provoking the Yemeni government.[56]

Thirteen brief fueling stops in Aden occurred in 1999 and fourteen had been made in 2000.[57] Aden was ranked at THREATCON Bravo and the *Cole* had armed sentries on deck that morning. Refueling was almost complete when the suicide boat detonated its concealed bomb.

The blast claimed the lives of 17 sailors and injured 39 more. "To those who attacked them, we say: you will not find a safe harbor," warned President Clinton at the memorial service.

Port side view showing the damage sustained by the Arleigh Burke class guided missile destroyer USS Cole on October 12, 2000, after a suspected terrorist bomb exploded during a refueling operation in the port of Aden, Yemen. DoD photo.

Devastating as the attack was, it came as a signal of continued American vulnerability – and uncertainty about what these terrible acts meant. "That could have happened in any port in the world," said Fitzgerald. "It was just a boat. They had a safe house. They had explosives. They loaded them into the boat. They brought the boat down to a local landing, launched it. Not very sophisticated and something you could probably do in just about any harbor in the world as long as you could get the explosives. And Lord knows there's plenty of explosives in Yemen."[58]

Even after the attack on the *Cole* the US found itself in the same dilemma: was it an act of war, calling for a military response? Or was the pursuit of al Qaeda an international law enforcement issue? "Treat it like a crime scene, because that's exactly what it is," the commander of CENTCOM, US Army General Tommy Franks, told a general he dispatched to Aden during the investigation.[59]

Fitzgerald saw it differently. "This was an act of war," he said later.[60]

At any rate, it was clear who was behind it all. Clinton believed firmly in bin Laden's guilt and "came close to launching another missile strike at him in October, but the CIA recommended that we call it off at the last minute, believing that the evidence of his presence was insufficiently reliable."

Fleeting intelligence and legal hesitancy ended attempts to retaliate for the attack on the USS *Cole*. "The Pentagon recommended against putting Special Forces into Afghanistan, with all the attendant logistical difficulties, unless we had more reliable intelligence on bin Laden's whereabouts," Clinton later said in his memoirs. "That left bigger military options: a large-scale bombing campaign of all suspected campsites or a sizable invasion. I thought neither was feasible without a finding of al Qaeda responsibility for the *Cole*," concluded Clinton.[61] He later told President-elect Bush that not getting bin Laden was "my biggest disappointment."[62]

The dilemma of just how far America wanted to go to counter terrorism was unresolved.

Four months after the attack in Yemen, the grey area between international law enforcement and military reprisal still caused debate. In February 2001, two men involved in the 1998 African embassy bombings were put on trial. The occasion led one expert, L. Paul Bremer, to reflect on how the US response to terrorism had evolved so far:

Every time one of these major attacks happens, the president is faced with a difficult choice: Does he consider the issue to be primarily a law enforcement issue or does he consider it to be a national security issue? And in many ways you have to go down both paths. Of course if you can get your hands on some of the foot soldiers and try them and put them in jail, that's good. But that can't be the only answer. If you look back from the time of Pan Am 103 to the present, that's now 12 years, several hundred Americans have been killed in terrorist acts and no senior terrorist has paid any price yet. We've got a few of these guys we've rounded up, these small fishes...but we haven't got any of the big guys and that's not good.[63]

"The threat that keeps me awake most of the time is this terrorist threat, because it can reach out and touch you when you least expect it," Rear Admiral Henry Ulrich, the *Enterprise* battle group commander, said in March 2001. "When you think you're the safest is when you might be in the most danger."[64]

Heightened warnings in the summer of 2001 focused on threats to Americans stationed abroad. The no-fly zones over Iraq were also active. "They are getting more and more aggressive," Lieutenant Tyler Nekomoto, an F/A-18 pilot on his first cruise with *USS Constellation*, said of three months spent enforcing the no-fly zone that summer.[65]

Rear Admiral John Cryer arrived on August 9, 2001 for a 90-day rotation as the Deputy Commander, Joint Task Force – Southwest Asia. Cryer and his boss, Air Force Major General Gary "Swede" Dylewski, worked from the Combined Air Operations Center located in the Eskan Village section of Riyadh. Land-based aircraft patrolling in Operation Southern Watch had already moved 60 miles south to Prince Sultan Air Base as a result of the 1996 Khobar Towers bombings. The CAOC, too, was making the move south under orders from CENTAF, the air component of CENTCOM, which was under the command of Air Force Lieutenant General Charles Wald.

The new CAOC at PSAB would become the hub of two major air campaigns but when Cryer first set eyes on the facility in August 2001 it looked like more than the Coalition would ever need.

From his experience with Operation Allied Force, Cryer saw what a leap ahead the CAOC had made in just two years. "I think the Air Force had a lot of frustration which came out of that [Kosovo crisis experience] and as a result of their experience they developed CAOC X." The high-priority experimental program became "the model on which they built the CAOC at Prince Sultan Air Base."[66]

The Eskan Village CAOC was "basically a portable hangar," said Cryer. "It had been operating for quite some time." Now, Cryer and Dylewski had the chance to set up something much better at Prince Sultan Air Base. "When Swede and I walked into the CAOC down in PSAB, we looked around and we looked at each other and said '*man we're never going to use all this stuff.*' Because it was huge. It was much bigger than we ever thought we would need for Operation Southern Watch."[67]

The CAOC was cavernous and it was loaded with communications. Nine-meter dishes pulled in VHF and satellite communications. The equivalent of 70-100 T-1 lines flowed data into and out of the CAOC. "Everything was bigger; everything was better; the displays were great. They had these data walls out there that were just absolutely stunning. Bandwidth for Predator got immeasurably better," said Cryer, to the point that the unmanned vehicle's video feed was "targeting quality clear." On the operations floor "all of the cells were just exactly where you wanted" them to be.[68]

Magnificent it was. High-profile it was not. Cryer remembered that in late August 2001 "there wasn't a tremendous amount of interest in what we were doing because it was still Operation Southern Watch."

Not that the skies below the 33rd parallel in Iraq were quiet. Most weeks saw four or five days of flying. The Iraqis had been sparring with the UN-backed Coalition aircraft for months and OSW had long since become a regular shooting war. Standard OSW missions were "relatively dangerous" as Cryer put it because "you just never knew" when the Iraqis would take a shot.

The Operation Southern Watch missions had already carved out some new rules of engagement that would affect the post 9/11 air wars. The "frustration with Southern

Watch of course was the rules of engagement – they were extremely restrictive," Cryer said. The Iraqis might move a mobile surface-to-air missile radar south of the 33rd parallel in violation of the UN resolutions. Surface-to-air missile batteries often took fleeting shots at patrolling aircraft. The CAOC would set up a strike, but if the target started to move, rules of engagement demanded that pilots break off the attack. "We would go in, set the strike up, and then they [the Iraqis] would discover that we had a strike coming north, and the first thing they would do is fire up the motor and as soon as that thing became mobile, you were no longer allowed to hit it. It was crazy," Cryer recalled.[69]

One of the F/A-18 pilots supporting OSW at the time was Lieutenant Melanie Lynch, who by August was drawing near the end of her first operational cruise aboard the *USS Enterprise*. "I was slated to do one or two of those but we wouldn't ever get very far and it would be cancelled airborne, just because the stuff that we were going after would move, or they would get a tip that we were coming in so the mission would basically get cancelled – we would come back to the ship," she recalled.[70]

But the Coalition had its successes, too. They "did hit several Spoon Rests that were on trucks while I was there as well as an SA-3," said Cryer.[71]

To most observers in the summer of 2001, Iraq still looked like the potential flashpoint, if there was one. Keating recalled a conversation with Vice Admiral Willie Moore, Commander, 5th Fleet. At the time, Keating ran the Directorate of Operations and Plans (N3/5) on the Navy staff, with Rear Admiral James M. Zortman as one of his deputies. They had visibility into the lingering al Qaeda threat but not its ultimate form. Of the conversation with Moore, Keating recalled: "He was in Bahrain and I was in the Pentagon. We were talking about force protection and threats. We were worried about Bahrain, the Middle East. And Willie said *'you know, I think you guys are in more danger there where you sit than where I sit.'*

"We thought that was preposterous," said Keating.[72] Three weeks later, al Qaeda attacked on September 11, 2001.

SCRAMBLE

At 0846, al Qaeda hijackers flew American Airlines Flight 11 into the North Tower of the World Trade Center in New York City.

The first response in the war on terrorism fell to two pilots sitting alert that bright, clear morning. Just six minutes earlier, controllers at the North American Aerospace Defense Command (NORAD) Northeast Air Defense Sector in Rome, New York had received notification from the FAA of a potential problem. Two F-15s from Otis Air National Guard Base on Cape Cod scrambled into the air at 0852. They were 71 miles – about eight minutes – out from New York City when the second hijacked airliner, United Airlines Flight 175, struck the South Tower of the World Trade Center.

The second strike swept away all confusion about whether the nation was under attack. The next closest jets were at NORAD's alert detachment at Langley AFB, Virginia. Three F-16s took off from Langley at 0930. Seven minutes later, the third hijacked plane, American Airlines Flight 77 roared over the Navy Annex next to Arlington Cemetery, clipping aerial antennae, and impacted the Pentagon.

Police helicopters and emergency ambulance crews stand by to aid injured workers following the crash of a hijacked commercial airliner into a section of the Pentagon on Sep. 11, 2001. U.S. Air Force photo by Staff Sgt. Gary Coppage.

A fireball burst through the southwest walls of the Pentagon. Keating and his staff had opened a new Navy command post there on Monday, September 10, christening it with symbolic "champagne across the bow."

"Tuesday the 11th we had our meeting down there," said Keating. He left to attend an office call with the ambassador from Yemen. By that time, "we knew that an airplane had hit the World Trade Center." Just after leaving the meeting downstairs in the command center, Keating saw film of the second aircraft's impact in New York. His first instinct was to "go back down to the command center because something was obviously going on," he said. "It's hard for me to realize how naïve we were. Here are two airplanes and the world trade towers and I'm going to head down to command center thinking well I guess that's where I need to go." But his meeting with the Yemeni ambassador delayed him and Keating was still in his fourth-floor office when he felt the building shake just after 0930 as the airliner hit. "We knew then, things were not good. Tried to get down to command center and couldn't," he said. The command center was destroyed with heavy loss of life.

Over the next "10, 20, 30 minutes, we tried again to get down to the command center, realized there was no way we were going to get to that part of the building."

Smoke began to fill the office. Communications were out. Keating and his staff evacuated, heading for the exits into the fresh air of the Pentagon's big interior courtyard. "Folks are streaming out running. Some of them obviously injured," he said. Black smoke was "roiling out, people are trying to get into that damaged part of the building and it's clear that it was very grim inside there."[73]

The Navy lost 42 in the Pentagon that day.

"About 20 of those who were killed worked directly for me," said Zortman, who by chance was in San Diego that morning. "Most likely, if I had been in Washington, I would have been in the command center. It was very personal to me."[74]

Keating ended up heading back to his quarters at the Navy Yard where he knew he had secure communications. The CNO had done the same. Soon they set up a secure conference in a space in the NCIS building on the yard. Eventually, they made it to the Navy Annex, then worked for weeks from a Marine Corps' command center in that complex.[75]

Keating later discovered he'd known Chick Burlingame, the captain of American Airlines 77, quite well. They'd been at flight school together and had been neighbors for a time.

"It's a small thing," Keating later said, but Chick, "he was tough. For those folks to have gotten him, they had to have been good....I just don't understand how they got away with it. But they did."[76]

NATIONWIDE CAP

NORAD's alert F-16s from Langley set up a rotating CAP over the city of Washington. Office workers evacuating government buildings from Capitol Hill to Foggy Bottom heard the sonic boom of one F-16 ordered by NEADS to make a low pass over the Mall and Pentagon, and thought there had been another attack.

A fourth hijacked jet was still in the air. "By this time, we were watching United Flight 93 wander around Ohio," recalled Brigadier General Larry Arnold, who that day was in command of First Air Force, NORAD's air component based in Florida.[77] United Airlines Flight 93, en route from Newark to San Francisco, was off course. It had turned east over Ohio then disappeared for nine minutes from the FAA's radar track before reappearing briefly.

NORAD now had clearance for the fighters to engage. The three Langley F-16s flying CAP over Washington, DC were fully armed, in communication with NORAD, and ready to intercept Flight 93 if it turned for Washington. Based on rough calculations the intercept would have occurred at about 1030 that morning somewhere west of Frederick, Maryland. The passengers of United Flight 93 made sure that never had to happen. They fought back and took the hijacked airliner into the ground in Somerset County, Pennsylvania.

At 1000, 3181 airborne tracks were in the FAA's database; by midday, the skies over America were clear of civilian traffic.[78]

THE NAVY RESPONSE, EAST AND WEST

But the threat was not gone and NORAD needed Navy help to button up continental air defenses in case more hijackers were inbound.

Rear Admiral Steven Tomaszeski was aboard USS *John F. Kennedy* in Florida that morning. His Chief of Staff, Captain Skip Wheeler, told him about the first plane that hit the World Trade Center, and then the second. "The next thing that comes in is an order from Second Fleet to sortie our ships as quickly as possible from Mayport," Tomaszeski said.[79] Sailors got the ship underway at about 1000 that morning.

It was the beginning of a sea shield for the east coast, but more needed to be done. "*George Washington* was out at sea already without any planes on board," said Tomaszeski. *Kennedy's* assigned Air Wing 7 "was on the beach in Oceana."[80]

Tomaszeski talked with Vice Admiral Cutler Dawson, Commander, Second Fleet. The decision on the air assets was to "split 'em and give us some combat capability on

The USS George Washington is underway off of the East Coast of the United States on Sept. 12, 2001, providing additional air defense after the Sept. 11 terrorist attacks in New York City and the Pentagon in Arlington, Va. U.S. Navy photo by Photographer's Mate 3rd Class J. Scott Campbell.

GW out of carrier Air Wing 7 and then send the rest of them to *Kennedy*. So we'll split the carriers, cover the east coast, get an Aegis shield up and we'll be good to go," said Tomaszeski.[81] As the F-14s and other aircraft scrambled from Naval Air Station Oceana, the carriers were linking their sea shield with NORAD. "I had orders from NORAD," confirmed Tomaszeski. Connectivity was clear, folding the Navy resources into the command and control chain. "The NORAD orders told me specifically what to do and who to communicate with so we could set up this radar shield," Tomaszeski said.[82]

Although the September 11 al Qaeda attacks hit only the east coast, those responsible for defense of the west coast thought they might be next. With the time difference, NORAD's west coast command center was alive to the possibility of attacks from inbound airliners not yet grounded by the FAA. In fact, the only airliner intercepted that day was tailed by alert fighters from Alaska's NORAD region. They teamed with Canadian pilots to intercept a Korean airliner with a suspicious squawk and escort it to a landing at White Horse, Yukon Territory, where local authorities had an evacuation of the town center in progress.

The Navy's Third Fleet Commander, Vice Admiral Michael Bucchi, called Arnold at First Air Force, and volunteered his forces. "We understand CINC NORAD is the supported CINC," Bucchi said to Arnold. "How do we support you?"[83]

Robb, who was now the battlegroup commander, sortied *Stennis* from San Diego around noon on September 11. The airwing was ashore and he "called 20 airplanes out that afternoon" to join the carrier. "Then pretty much every ship in San Diego harbor came out" and joined the make-shift battlegroup, he recalled. San Diego's airport, Lindbergh Field, was so close to the piers at North Island that Robb wondered about an attack. "We didn't know what the terrorists were going to do with regard to trying to blow up a nuclear ship," Robb said.[84]

Over 300 fighters were on ground or airborne alert by the end of the day. Combat air patrols continued in surge mode for the next several days. The Navy helped man CAPs on the west coast. "We had a mission to support NORAD in taking on airplanes that

Two F-15 Eagles from the Massachusetts Air National Guard's 102nd Fighter Wing fly a combat air patrol mission over New York City in support of Operation Noble Eagle to protect the U.S. after the Sept. 11 attacks. U.S. Air Force photo by Lt. Col. Bill Ramsay.

were left," said Robb. "Chaotic" was his word for the first day. The hastily-summoned aircraft "flew combat patrol over LA and San Diego." To contribute to the 24-hour coverage, the ship took parts of the day and land-based strike fighters covered other segments.[85]

The larger problem was radar coverage. NORAD focused on US borders only. It did not have coverage extended out to sea, nor could it track aircraft across the continental US without the FAA. Holes existed even in the dense East Coast air traffic corridors. Out west, the gaps were enormous. Communications amongst fighters and command centers were also patchy.

The Navy could and did continue to work the problem of extending radar coverage out to the sea lines of approach. AEGIS cruisers took up station to reinforce the air picture of the east and west coasts.

"I will tell you that this is being conducted as a joint operation," Clark said on September 13. "There are also air defense ships, cruisers and destroyers operating in the area with them, and all of that is being done in a joint manner."[86]

For the next several days naval aircraft became part of the mammoth air defense response. Marine reserve F/A-18s at Andrews AFB borrowed weapons from the 113 FW and the Marines flew two sorties in the CAP over Washington, DC on September 11. At sea, *Kennedy* and *George Washington* launched combat air patrols over the Atlantic approaches. "We split *Kennedy* and *GW* so they were far enough away, tactically, so we could engage anybody if that engagement was necessary," said Tomaszeski.[87]

The potential threat of terrorism had seemed to be in the future; its outline shadowy, its profile incomplete, and its likelihood uncertain. By the time the second plane hit the south tower, terrorism had a face, and that face belonged to bin Laden.

JCS Chairman Shelton was just two weeks away from retirement on September 11. His military aircraft was two hours out of Andrews en route to a NATO summit when they got word of the attacks. "I was thinking, '*This is a big one.*' It is changing the face of terrorism. It is basically bringing it to the United States," he told Larry King a few weeks later. "There was no doubt in my mind. When I heard the second plane had hit, I knew that wasn't an air traffic control problem or just a pilot problem."

Shelton ordered the plane to turn back home. "We came back right over the World Trade Center and could see, even from that altitude, the devastation, the smoke that was coming up. It was obvious it was going to be horrible," Shelton said. "There was anger. There still is."[88]

Half a world away, two carriers whose crews thought they were about to conduct a hand-off now found themselves preparing to team up for action.

Closest to the scene of action was the *Enterprise*. "I was watching CNN when I saw the second plane hit the tower," said Captain Sandy Winnefeld. "Right then I thought '*we're not going home.*' It was only a matter of hours before they turned us around."[89]

"We were going to cross the equator and have a shellback ceremony and then go around to South Africa. We were really looking forward to that port call," remembered Lynch of the *Enterprise* about-face.[90] The *USS Carl Vinson* had deployed in August and was passing the tip of India en route to the Arabian Gulf. Instead of being *Enterprise's* relief, the *Carl Vinson* steamed ahead to become a partner in the upcoming strikes.

The sailors of the carrier battlegroups gathering in the North Arabian Gulf knew that the American government and people were well-united in the desire to fight back. "Make no mistake, the United States will hunt down and punish those responsible for these cowardly acts," vowed President Bush just a few hours after the attacks. "We will make no distinction between the terrorists who committed these acts and those who harbor them," Bush declared.[91]

"Yes, we believe that acts of war have been committed against the American people," Secretary of State Colin Powell confirmed, "and we will respond accordingly."[92]

CHAPTER 3:

Afghanistan Begins

"Like 1941, this war will be a little more personal than defending our vital interests. We are defending our families and our homeland." – Rear Admiral Harry Ulrich, October 7, 2001[93]

How to respond to the al Qaeda threat after September 11 was a major strategic dilemma. Osama bin Laden's base was Afghanistan, and in less than three weeks, the decision was made to rely on carrier-based airpower to lead off a joint operation to take control of that country away from the Taliban, who had given bin Laden and al Qaeda a home base there.

The U.S. Navy aircraft carriers USS Enterprise (upper) and USS Carl Vinson (lower) meet briefly in the waters of the Arabian Gulf region on Sept. 16, 2001. Both ships are on regularly scheduled deployments in support of Operation Southern Watch. USS Enterprise was extended in the region following terrorist attacks on New York City, and Washington, D.C. U.S. Navy Photo by Photographer's Mate 3rd Class Douglas Pearlman.

However, it was not obvious on September 11, 2001 that airpower from the carriers was about to take center stage in the global war on terrorism. In fact, the US was struggling to formulate options.

On September 12, Secretary of Defense Donald Rumsfeld directed CENTCOM to start preparing "credible military options." "The best defense against terrorists is an offense. You simply cannot batten down the hatches and try to cope with every conceivable thing any terrorist could imagine to do. I mean, they've already done some unimaginable things. The only answer is to take the effort to them where they are," he said a few days later.[94]

Franks asked for a week to ten days to develop a course of action. "We had al Qaeda and Taliban target sets in Afghanistan and plans to strike those targets with TLAMS and manned bombers," Franks acknowledged. "But CENTCOM had not developed a plan for conventional ground operations in Afghanistan" or for access agreements with bordering nations.[95]

In CENTCOM's earliest discussions of ways to clear Afghanistan of Taliban and al Qaeda, the role of aircraft carriers – and for that matter, the joint air component as a whole – had not yet emerged as a lead element of simultaneous operations. In fact, employing aircraft carriers as the backbone of joint operations was anything but a foregone conclusion when planning started.

Franks' first instinct was to plan for a multi-pronged land attack into Afghanistan relying on helicopter airborne assault with Pakistan as a staging area. "I can't see conducting operations inside Afghanistan without basing, staging and overflight support from Pakistan," he told his staff on September 12.

There was just one problem. "We had no air bases on that soil or even near that soil," said Robb, who was about to take up a new job as J-5, Director of Plans, at CENTCOM headquarters in Tampa.[96]

Stufflebeem was now on the Joint Staff at the Pentagon. He monitored the early planning thrash as CENTCOM called for more troops and more aircraft to support a ground force operation. Soon there came "this painful realization that it was going to take too long and amass too many forces," he said of the planning.[97] Rumsfeld had been at a full National Security Council meeting with Bush on September 12 and he knew the President wanted to push the Pentagon to get beyond the cruise missile and law enforcement bind of the last few years. "They had yet to be challenged to think on how to fight a guerilla war using conventional means," was the way Bush later described his own view.[98] As a result, Rumsfeld cut the timeline to start and the numbers of forces in half – then he did it again.[99] A ground offensive was out.

A NORTHERN ALLIANCE

The combination of airpower and SOF operations came into the spotlight when CENTCOM decided that the key to regime change in Afghanistan was strengthening the opposition forces who had been fighting to topple the Taliban for years.

The Afghan opposition forces consisted of regional leaders in the north, west and south who cut their teeth during the war with the Soviet Union from 1979-1989. When the Taliban took control in 1996 they pledged to put an end to the civil war and to create a pure Islamic state. Instead, basic government functions withered and the Taliban enforced an oppressive code of behavior that drove over two million Afghan refugees to Pakistan.[100]

Civil war continued, as the Taliban consolidated control over 80% of the territory of Afghanistan and most of the major cities. The opposition forces were still strong in their respective regions but they were anything but a cohesive bloc. "There's a lot of competition between the groups. There's a lot of competition within the groups. The groups are basically aligned along ethnic and religious lines," a CENTCOM official later said of the Afghan opposition forces.[101]

The mountains near the old Soviet border belonged to the Northern Alliance, a loose coalition of irregular forces that had for years been under the leadership of Ahmad Shah Masood, former Afghan President Burhanuddin Rabbani, and General Abdul Rashid Dostum, leader of the National Islamic Movement, plus several other groups. Smaller resistance groups often switched back and forth between operating with the Northern Alliance or with the Taliban. "More of a shotgun wedding than an alliance," was how one of Franks' advisers described the Northern Alliance.[102] Masood – a popular hero known as the Lion of Panjshir – kept them together.

Masood's Northern Alliance had about 15,000 fighters – enough to resist a major Taliban offensive in the summer of 2000. "Masood continues to receive support from Iran, Russia and Uzbekistan," noted the prestigious International Institute for Strategic Studies, "and there appears to be no end in sight for this conflict."[103]

In fact, Masood was powerful enough that bin Laden had to get rid of Masood to secure the al Qaeda redoubt in Afghanistan. On September 9, 2001, al Qaeda terrorists posing as a news video camera crew detonated a bomb and assassinated Masood. "When I heard the explosion, I rushed into the room," said a local security commander named Raimullah. "It was a terrible scene. The windows were blown out. Everything was burning. The Arab who'd been holding the camera was on fire, by the window."[104]

Masood's death was devastating. Still, there was little choice except to put the Afghan opposition forces at the center of the upcoming operation. "There's no question but that there are any number of people in Afghanistan, tribes in the south, the Northern Alliance in the north, that oppose Taliban, and clearly we need to recognize the value they bring to this anti-terrorist, anti-Taliban effort, and, where appropriate, find ways to assist them," Rumsfeld said on September 30.[105]

The air component, and SOF forces, got the job. "Unconventional approaches are much more likely and more appropriate than the typical conventional approach of armies and navies and air forces," Rumsfeld hinted the next day.[106] With the right kind of firepower, the Northern Alliance and other

Secretary of Defense Donald H. Rumsfeld. DoD photo by R. D. Ward.

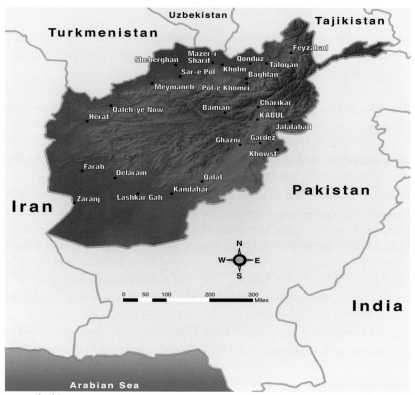

Map of Afghanistan.

opposition forces could start engaging quickly and drive out the Taliban and help hunt down bin Laden and his al Qaeda.

CENTCOM'S PLAN EVOLVES

That firepower had to come from the air component and the air component depended on the carriers at sea. "The only thing that we had was the *Enterprise*," Cryer said of those tense days. "That's all that was there. Because the Air Force didn't have the tanking capacity to bring the F-16s or the F-15E Strike Eagles from Kuwait all the way into Afghanistan" until later.[107]

Stufflebeem confirmed "we didn't have a foothold to start operations with any ability to mass firepower except for very long-range, long-endurance aircraft like B-52s."[108] Besides, CENTCOM needed complete control of the airspace so that other operations – humanitarian relief, and clandestine insertions, resupply and extractions of special forces teams – could proceed. Fortunately, the Navy had the flexibility to keep the carriers in place while CENTCOM worked planning options.[109] The presence doctrine was set aside and plans laid to mass carrier striking power.

But even with the two carriers on station, strikes could not be launched immediately. Afghanistan's forbidding geography made overflight and base access critical issues. Bordering Afghanistan to the north were the independent states of Turkmenistan, Uzbekistan, Tajikstan. China touched Afghanistan along a thirty-mile sliver of border at the Wakhan corridor. To the west lay Iran. To the east lay Pakistan, with the crucial band of coastline near Karachi providing the most direct route to Afghan airspace.

30

Nothing was going into Afghanistan without diplomatic overflight clearances. At first "we did not have ground basing agreements made with any of the 'stans, including Pakistan," noted Stufflebeem."[110]

One big advantage was the United Nations resolution condemning the September 11 attacks and calling "urgently" for "international cooperation to prevent and eradicate acts of terrorism."[111] From the global outpouring of sympathy and shared loss came the makings of a powerful international coalition that would eventually include over 60 nations.

While access and overflight agreements were in the works the next task was to "take a long hard look at what was available from a TACAIR perspective," Cryer said.[112] Here the carriers stood out. Control of the air would fall to the strike fighters of the *Enterprise* and the *Carl Vinson*. That would be enough to gain air superiority and make Afghan airspace a zone of Coalition dominance. Backed by freely maneuvering airpower, the combination of Afghan opposition forces and precision Coalition strikes under SOF guidance should overmatch the Taliban's military capabilities.

Franks briefed Bush on September 21, 2001.[113] His plan prioritized early airstrikes and a sustained campaign with SOF forces assisting the Afghan opposition. The plan had four phases: setting conditions, initial operations, decisive operations and stability operations. The carriers would guarantee air control and enough flexible, precision firepower to get the SOF forces and their new Afghan partners off to a strong start.

However, the air war ahead counted on a strategic mobility and command and control structure that was still being set up. CENTCOM "had to wait for various bridges to get built, which would be tanker bridges, AWACS bridges. The larger Air Force had to move their large forces, bed them down, and then work out their plan to get them in the air at the right places at the right time," Stufflebeem said. Support and communications would be crucial to the precise, tailored air war ahead. For the carriers on station at the beginning of OEF "it wasn't that we were held back as much as we just sort of had to wait for the others to catch up."[114]

Also, as Franks briefed Bush, he wanted to wait about two weeks to align host nation support for staging SOF and Combat Search And Rescue operations (CSAR.) "We could begin the air operation sooner," Franks said at the White House meeting on September 21. "But over the long haul, that would not be the best plan. We want air and SOF operations to be as near-simultaneous as we can get them." Tempting as it was to launch retaliatory strikes right away, Bush opted for patience.[115]

Having joint CSAR in place was essential. No one underestimated the risks. The Taliban and al Qaeda were not going to adhere to Geneva Convention procedures if they captured pilots. Air Force Lieutenant General T. Michael "Buzz" Moseley, who would take over from Wald several weeks into the campaign, underlined why a strong CSAR force was so important from the outset. "I have to be able to go pick that kid up quick. Because there was never ever any notion in my mind, anyway, that there would be Taliban POW camps that would repatriate airman," he said. "You get shot down and float down into that world and they will kill you."[116]

Over the next ten days CENTCOM refined its plan and began the process of moving more forces toward the theater. By October 1, 27 countries had granted overflight and landing rights to deploying US military forces. The air bridges were in place. A full plan for Operation Enduring Freedom was briefed to Rumsfeld on October 1, and approved by Bush the next day, along with an attack order to commence operations on October 7, 2001. Rumsfeld gave orders for US forces – primarily logistics, special operations, and support – to deploy to bases in Tajikistan and Uzbekistan on October 2.[117]

The strategic significance of naval aviation had never been more crucial and apparent. Not since Libya in 1986 had the US chosen to rely on naval aircraft as the main arm of air dominance. Perhaps not since the Central Pacific campaigns of World War II had the availability of carriers and their first-rate striking power been the core of a major joint operation.

"Having the carriers snuggled up off the coast of Pakistan and having the permission of Pakistan to just over-fly en route to Afghanistan, was probably key to being able to start this thing as fast as the administration wanted to go," said Stufflebeem."[118]

Carrier airpower was going to be the opening act of the global war on terror. Ahead lay the major test of battle.

OPERATION ENDURING FREEDOM BEGINS

Operation Enduring Freedom began late on the night of Sunday, October 7, 2001. "About 15 land-based bombers, some 25 strike aircraft from carriers, and US and British ships and submarines launching approximately 50 Tomahawk missiles have struck terrorist targets in Afghanistan," said Air Force General Richard Myers, who was now Chairman of the Joint Chiefs of Staff.[119]

An F/A-18C Hornet is launched from the aircraft carrier USS Carl Vinson in a strike against al Qaeda terrorist training camps and military installations of the Taliban regime in Afghanistan on Oct. 7, 2001. DoD photo by Petty Officer 1st Class Greg Messier, U.S. Navy.

A U.S. Navy F-14D Tomcat streaks by as it launches from the flight deck of the aircraft carrier USS Carl Vinson operating in the Arabian Sea on Oct. 10, 2001 in support of Operation Enduring Freedom. U.S. Navy photo by Photographer's Mate 1st Class Greg Messier.

The first order of business was to "remove the threat from air defenses and from Taliban aircraft," Rumsfeld said. "We need the freedom to operate on the ground and in the air and the targets selected, if successfully destroyed, should permit an increasing degree of freedom over time," he added.[120] That meant that the air component would rely on carrier-launched F-14s and F/A-18s to ensure air superiority. Without it, the campaign could not have started.

Afghanistan's surface-to-air missile defenses were not the dense, sophisticated threats of Iraq or Serbia. But they could still be unnerving. One F-14 pilot, Lieutenant Chris Gasko, still saw plenty of activity. A couple of times he watched "the string of tracers from the ZSU-23s [Soviet anti-aircraft gun] around the cities coming up. So we know we have our sanctuary but it's still like '*dude, they're shooting at us.*'" Hand-held SAMs that looked like bottle rockets came "corkscrewing up at you." Gasko acknowledged it was "a little unnerving at first, but you just kind of get used to it. Dispense your items, expendables and stuff. Go for it. Couple times we got a little bit of SA-3 or SA-2 indications but we never saw any of those kinds of launches." Gasko did see "some medium and heavy caliber AAA over Kabul and around the Bagram area. I know a couple guys saw some over by Mazar-i-Sharif as well."[121]

The F-14s and F/A-18s also carried ample air-to-air missiles at first since the Taliban table of equipment listed dozens of older Soviet jets such as MiG-21s and Su-22s. Early strikes from the *Carl Vinson* hit MiG-21 and Su-22 fighters parked at a military airfield near Shindand in western Afghanistan, an airfield at Mukurin in western Afghanistan, and the airfield at Kandahar, a Taliban stronghold in southern Afghanistan.

On one of the attacks, Captain Charles Wright, Deputy CAG aboard *Carl Vinson*, was assigned the airfield at Kandahar as the target for his F-14. He and his wingman each pickled a GBU-12 on two parked MiG-21s along the runway apron.

"When they blew, they blew big," Wright said. "You could tell they were full of fuel and ammunition because the explosions were pretty significant."

Satisfying as it was, the F-14 crews would have relished a chance to take on the MiG-21s in the air. "We would have liked to have seen them airborne," Wright said. "It would have been a professional satisfaction to have shot one down in the air. But they weren't in the air. Blow 'em up on the ground, blow 'em up in the air, that's the way it goes."[122]

The priority targeting reflected Washington's concerns. Few thought there was a viable or even flyable Taliban air force but Washington was concerned about it anyway. Plans called for helicopters, tankers and transports to operate in Afghan airspace and even a lucky shot from the Taliban was unacceptable.

Carrier air superiority enabled CENTCOM to start SOF positioning and humanitarian airdrops right away. "Initially there was a big fear about the Afghanis flying to try to shoot us down. And so everything would have to go with fighter cover," Stufflebeem explained.[123]

Staff Sgt. "Pete," a loadmaster on board one of two C-17 Globemaster III cargo planes, tosses the symbolic one millionth humanitarian daily ration out the rear of the aircraft as it flies at high altitude over Afghanistan Oct. 31, 2001. Photo by Staff Sgt. Jeremy Lock.

That included two Air Force C-17s that flew humanitarian airdrop missions over Afghanistan on night one of the campaign.

Seven million Afghanis were believed "to be at risk of loss of life as a result of conditions inside Afghanistan," Franks estimated.[124] He wanted the Afghan people to "know that we are not attacking them, but that our war is with al Qaeda and the Taliban."[125] For the C-17s, it was a 6500-mile mission from Germany, requiring multiple aerial refuelings. Careful mission planning plus protection from strike fighters such as those launched from the *Enterprise* made it feasible. "The Taliban is not happy about that," said one officer aboard the *Enterprise* said of the humanitarian missions. "We're hearing reports that the Taliban is threatening anyone who picks up food."[126]

With cargo and SOF aircraft operating all over Afghanistan, CENTCOM remained concerned about the pre-war MiG count long after the CAOC and the pilots flying the strikes sensed Afghanistan's air defenses were out of business. "I will say that there was some discussion with the CINC on this big point because they had the air order of battle for Afghanistan and they wanted a head count of all the MiGs that we'd destroyed," recalled Cryer. Many of the MiGs had been towed five or ten miles down the road from their airfields and parked. The MiGs might be intact but they had nowhere to take off. Not surprisingly, "they never did fly against us," noted Cryer.[127]

"I think that we can fly pretty much where we want in Afghanistan without fear of the Afghans being able to keep us from flying there," said Wright on day four of OEF, October 11.[128]

THE FIRST DAYS

Air superiority was well in hand but solidifying air support for ground attack was another task altogether. The first several days included numerous pre-briefed strikes against fixed military sites with high payoff and low collateral damage predictions, such as airfields and air defense sites. "My first assessment is that we've been successful in terms of going after the targets we've been assigned," said Rear Admiral Thomas E. Zelibor, commanding the *Carl Vinson* battle group.[129]

The critical targets for degrading the Taliban ran the gamut from fixed sites to emerging battlefield targets. As OEF began, one of the first areas targeted was the "front" on the open plains north of Kabul. As many as 5,000 to 10,000 Taliban were gathering there in garrison and some were on the front lines "arrayed with heavy weapons in revetments in covered and concealed positions to some extent," a CENTCOM briefer explained.[130]

As a result, the pilots flying off the *Enterprise* and the *Carl Vinson* had their hands full eliminating a substantial number of pre-assigned military targets. However, they were also being diverted to emerging targets. Lynch flew several illustrative combat missions during the two weeks the *Enterprise* remained on station after October 7. Her missions consisted mainly of pre-assigned targets although there were a few times when "higher priority targets would come available."[131]

One of those was a classic – and very dramatic – military target. On this October 13 mission, "somewhere during the tanking evolution we got different coordinates. We wrote them down, typed them in. They were for JDAM. My lead aircraft coordinates were different than mine, so we each had different targets." Lynch and her flight lead headed north toward Kandahar. Once over the target area they "put up the FLIR" but "we didn't really see anything down there." They rechecked the coordinates and then set up the strike. The F/A-18s "went in and did a pass where I stayed as wingman on him and he went and dropped his JDAM. He had a good hit. Got FLIR footage of it, good explosion there so definitely a good hit. And then it was my turn," she said. They came back around and she made another pass for it and dropped the 2000-lb. JDAM. Suddenly the target began exploding and "it just gets bigger and bigger and bigger. Amazing – there's just this huge fireball down there and you could see secondaries coming out and exploding and it was huge."

"*What did you hit, Sable?*" asked her flight lead.

"When we got back that night and landed on the ship, I went down to the CVIC [carrier intelligence center] and I wanted to know what information they had about my target. And they didn't know," she said. After checking the target a few days later one of the intelligence officers informed her she'd hit a large underground ammunition bunker.[132]

Laser Mavericks also came into play. Lynch recalled flying missions toward the end of her deployment using laser Mavericks instead of JDAM. For these missions, the F-14s did the buddy lasing for the Hornets. "The Tomcats would launch ahead of us, they would go into the area and they would find tanks within a specific area, and then we would come on station, we would start communications with them," said Lynch. Then "we would just basically do a coordination between them as to what direction we were coming in, when we were getting set up to actually be ready to drop for the laser Mavericks." To complete the strike the F-14s trained a laser spot on the target while the F/A-18's laser Mavericks picked up the spot and hit home. "That was actually a lot of fun," she added.[133]

THE *USS KITTY HAWK*

Before long the air component's tougher job would be to find ways to match its sophisticated power with special forces and their Northern Alliance partners on the ground.

In this task, a carrier, the *USS Kitty Hawk*, was about to take on a most unusual role. Franks was eager to insert special operations forces into Afghanistan as soon as possible. The map showed that many of the Taliban and al Qaeda strong points would be within range of SOF helicopters flying from a ship off the Pakistani coast. Amphibious carriers did not have enough deck space for what Franks had in mind. "I needed a steel lily pad – a Forward Operating Base – just off the coast of Pakistan and I needed it soon," Franks said.[134]

Scott Smith was one of the F/A-18 pilots of Airwing 5. They were in Japan on September 11, but it soon became clear they were working up to deploy somewhere – or at least some of them were. He was picked to join a mixed group of Hornet pilots from multiple squadrons – "mostly junior officers, mostly lieutenants and below. We had three O-4s, and our DCAG was the senior member of the crew out there," he said.

Kitty Hawk was to leave most of CVW-5 in Japan and take on SOF forces. "We came up with what we thought would be a representative aircraft sampling of what we would need" for the mission of providing a sea base for the SOF forces, said the DCAG, Captain

The crew of the forward-deployed USS Kitty Hawk displays their patriotism with a flight deck "spell out" of the word "FREEDOM" on Dec. 18, 2001. U.S. Navy photo by Photographer's Mate Airman Lee McCaskill.

Patrick Driscoll. The detachment had to keep some helicopters for SAR and S-3s for tanking. The E-2s stayed home in case the main body of CVW-5 deployed elsewhere.

"On October 1 we actually took our little contingent out on the *Kitty Hawk* to head over toward the Gulf," Smith said. The detachment "knew we were going to be an afloat forward staging base" for special operations forces, "but we didn't know exactly what that meant at the time."[135]

Soon *Kitty Hawk* had a deck full of "a bunch of black helicopters parked everywhere" and some special operators who "were pretty tight-lipped" with the curious aviators. There was a bit of aviator shop talk – but nothing touching on missions or capabilities. The SOF forces kept their equipment cordoned off and their plans to themselves.

Since the SOF mission had priority, the CVW-5 detachment pilots had been told not to get their hopes up about flying combat missions. According to Driscoll the "issue became could you fly fixed-wing while you're flying rotary wing." If something went wrong with the flight operations the worst case would be "a guy coming back having a ramp strike, for instance, and clogging the flight deck for 6 or 7 hours" and "then having the SOF guys come back and not have a place to land. So they said, we're not going to take that risk. But we planned on flying. And just in case we integrated into the ATO process. We did all the preps."[136]

CHANGES

From the start of OEF it was evident that the air component was doing business in a different way – and not just because one carrier had strange aircraft on its decks.

First was the emphasis on preventing collateral damage. Collateral damage estimates or "bugsplats" for key targets debuted on a wide scale in Operation Allied Force in 1999. In that war, NATO governments wanted tight control over airstrike targets in Belgrade and other civilian areas. Planners appended slides to target files showing projected civilian casualties for anticipated blast patterns, and NATO government heads had to approve the target selections.

For Afghanistan, collateral damage was an issue because the mission was to wage war against the Taliban and al Qaeda – not the Afghan people. CENTCOM wanted selected targets hit accurately and hard. But minimizing collateral damage was also a top priority. For that reason, few bridges, or other infrastructure targets were on the Coalition's strike list. Difficulties arose when a key target – be it a fixed site, or a moving leadership target – was in an urban area or near other civilians and infrastructure.

Guidance on collateral damage became a standard briefing item. Aboard the *Carl Vinson*, CAG Bennett said he preached to his aircrews: "Make sure you know what the hell you're dropping on. Just don't go in there cowboying, slinging bombs in Afghanistan."[137]

Other major changes lay with the CAOC itself. It was joint, busy, and able to see across the battlespace and reach more deeply into the execution process than ever before. The new CAOC in PSAB was of course the nerve center for the air war. The atmosphere at the CAOC was joint from the start despite the fact that the command center was predominantly manned and commanded by Air Force personnel. "There were no Air Force-only discussions," said Cryer and no "parochial atmosphere inside the CAOC combat operations. It just didn't exist."[138]

Pre-planned fixed target strikes with high-value assets were also going to end up with a limited role in this air war. OEF made quick use of prime strategic assets then counted on manned strike fighters with flexibility and persistence.

That meant only a brief role for B-2s and TLAMs. For night one, the B-2 stealth bombers flew from the continental United States and released 16 independently-targeted 2000-lb. JDAMs on targets such as airfields and air defense sites. They landed at Diego Garcia, switched crews without shutting down their four engines, and returned home to Missouri.

TLAMs launched from ships in the North Arabian Gulf targeted air defense sites such as radars, along with other vital targets. Powerful as these strikes were, the CAOC needed more versatile and sustainable contributions of carrier-based aircraft for the sustained phase of the campaign. "We used TLAM and we used the B-2s for the first couple of days. There was some discussion about keeping B-2s in theater at first," said Cryer. After the first few days, the air component decided the B-2 just was not needed. "It was nice to have the asset," Cryer said, because of its 16-JDAM capacity, "but on the other hand we just didn't need the stealth capability and the tail was enormous to bring them aboard" with deployment to a forward location.

Much the same thinking held true for the TLAM after its initial strikes. "After the first two nights there was just no need for a stand-off weapon of that caliber because we really had pretty much destroyed every single radar. There was nothing emitting in the country any more after the second night," Cryer explained.[139]

What the CAOC could not get enough of was a continuous supply of strike fighters, backed up by small contingents of B-1s and B-52s based in theater. That meant 24-hour operations.

To keep up the rhythm, the *Enterprise* was on night operations while the *Carl Vinson* took days. They'd made the switch shortly before Operation Enduring Freedom started. Lynch, aboard *Enterprise*, said "we were all bummed out that we had to do

An aviation boatswain's mate performs a preflight inspection as part of the aircraft launch procedures on Nov. 24, 2001 in the Arabian Sea. U.S. Navy photo by Photographer's Mate Third Class John E. Woods.

the night" since it meant a complete shift in the schedule. Night launch times varied, though, and sometimes missions were long enough to grant a daylight recovery. If "it was a really late launch, like 1 or 2 o'clock in the morning, generally [we were] back for a day trap, which was a bonus. But there's times when we'd launch at 10 or 11 o'clock and come back at 3 or 4 in the morning and it's a night recovery." To Lynch, "night combat was alright, actually. But coming back then for the night recovery, that was no fun."[140]

TIME-SENSITIVE TARGETS

Another characteristic of the OEF air war was pursuing time-sensitive targets – such as top al Qaeda and Taliban leaders. This was new territory for most aircrews and CAOC directors alike and it was a massive priority. Unlike the hide-and-seek SAMs of Serbia, these time-sensitive targets were often individuals that had to be identified, tracked and found at locations where attacking them would not create heavy collateral damage. At the same time, each attempt represented huge efforts to combine intelligence and strike assets.

"We'd never really done TSTs the way we were doing them," said Cryer of the Afghan air war.[141]

Central to it all was the hunt for bin Laden, Mullah Omar, and other senior al Qaeda and Taliban. The CAOC had Predator video and feeds from numerous other assets, including some from the CIA, monitoring compounds and safe-houses where top al Qaeda leadership might appear. The CIA had been operating Predators for several years and their small fleet included Predators armed with Hellfire. Hellfire and Predator were a slick combination. Hellfire was highly accurate and its relatively small 250-lb. warhead damped down collateral damage, allowing more shot opportunities in close quarters. Yet this advantage was also a drawback when it came to hitting bulkier targets such as buildings when 500-lb., 1000-lb. and 2000-lb. precision munitions were much preferred to the relatively light Hellfire warhead.

Predator unmanned aerial vehicles, like this one, have been used to increase battlefield awareness at operating locations in support of Operation Enduring Freedom. U.S. Air Force courtesy photo.

Almost immediately, two facts became apparent. First, political sensitivities were such that senior commanders – Franks included – would on many occasions have little choice but to insert themselves into the process. Second, CENTCOM found it needed much more than Predator video. It needed the CAOC to combine the surveillance feeds from orbiting Predators and other assets with strike assets from the carriers in order to complete the kill chain.

One early example illustrated both facts. On October 8, 2001, Tampa time, Franks started watching a CIA feed of an armed Predator tracking a three-vehicle leadership convoy near the city of Kandahar. Adrenaline ran high in the command center. CENTCOM's lawyer stood with Franks to approve the changing targets in the Predator's view. Afraid to risk a miss if they expended the Hellfires on a moving convoy, the commanders in Tampa watched the Predator track the targets for hours, hoping for it to stop and offer a decent shot. The convoy halted at a building and the passengers went inside. Then came discussions between the CAOC, Tampa, the Pentagon, the CIA at Langley and the White House as to whether or not the building they saw in the Predator's video was a mosque. Franks personally directed Predator to blow up one of the parked vehicles. People came out of the suspected mosque, jumped in the remaining vehicles and headed to a walled compound.

Two F/A-18s vectored in by the CAOC used GBU-12s to take out the compound while Predator returned to its base.[142] Later reports indicated this Predator hunt may have just missed Mullah Omar.

No doubt these targets were time-sensitive, but they could also take hours to execute. Cryer quickly found that as a CAOC day shift director working the time-sensitive targets "was ongoing and it occupied a tremendous amount of my time in the CAOC."

First came tracking and assessment. The mix of CIA and military surveillance assets put multiple players in the picture. Tight rules of engagement mandated by the White House to prevent collateral damage often ended up requiring even Franks to check in with Rumsfeld or Bush on some targets and inserted inevitable time delays.

Preparing to execute a strike added more layers. The CAOC never knew where a time-sensitive target might appear. Cryer described the flow of a typical TST strike as it unfolded over a period of hours. "We were watching a safe house, vetting a target through a variety of different sources," he said, "until it was determined that yes, this was the site that we needed to hit. Then it would be our job in the CAOC to go ahead and tee up the strike."[143]

Cryer described one TST event where he had "a division of Hornets out up northeast of Kandahar" which he needed to bring up to Kabul for the strike. That took tanking, plus transit time figured into the calculation. "You worked the problem in terms of what it's going to take to get them up there" and then "brief them up on the target." Next, the CAOC director and staff had to "come up with a lasing source." The F/A-18s Nighthawk FLIR was fine for military targets out in the open. On the other hand, with a target in downtown Kabul came collateral damage risks of hitting houses and civilians, and the need to keep the Hornets at a relatively high altitude, impairing the sensor even more. "There were times when if you brought the Hornet down low enough, you could do it" within the collateral damage boundaries, Cryer said. Generally, though, the CAOC "wanted to keep them pretty high."

While this was going on, Tampa many times had to approve strikes on certain targets because of the nature of the target or because it was close to civilian infrastructure. Those at the CAOC chafed at getting a little more "help" from Tampa than they would have liked. At the same time, Cryer explained that given the nature of OEF it was understandable that headquarters sometimes "felt compelled to inject themselves." Also, he stressed "I can't remember any target that really wasn't fully our responsibility for shooting. At the end of the day it was Wald's or Moseley's call." Frequently, TST execution fell to the pair of one-star and two-star admirals and generals directing the CAOC's day or night shift.

While Tampa worked the final approvals the CAOC "would tee up the strike using GBU-12, for example, out of a Hornet with a 25 millisecond delay on the fuse, which mitigated collateral damage as much as we possibly could. Then we'd set it up, if we were either buddy lasing from one source or another, maybe a Tomcat." As clearance came through "we'd go ahead and...execute the strike drop and you'd watch the survivors come out of the building." If survivors tried to flee in their vehicles "we would follow them with Predator and then we'd stay after them until we got every one of them." "This was fascinating," Cryer said.[144]

But there were many downsides, especially at first. For those in the cockpits over Afghanistan prosecuting TSTs could mean a long wait. Pilots loitering with bombs were on the whipsaw end of the chain. They were also seeing a strange small object in the target airspace. Until it started making headlines during the Afghan air war, the CIA ownership of Predator and the Predator with Hellfire combination had been shrouded in secrecy. Questions from the carrier air wings came fast. "Basically, they were not briefed on some of the things that they needed to be briefed on. Predator was one of them. We had aircrews up there that didn't know what the heck this thing was," said Cryer. The CAOC solved the problem and briefed the carrier aircrews as best they could.

Not much could be done about the vectoring and loitering needed to keep the strike aircraft and their valuable GBU-12s on station while Tampa and the CAOC worked the TST chain. Cryer realized the pilots' "frustration there because they just didn't know what was going on. They were being asked to orbit over Kabul, way the heck away from the carrier" with "no idea when they were going to get a Charlie time" and "nobody's telling them anything."[145]

For Cryer, on dayshift in the CAOC just as for those in Tampa, "the most frustrating thing about the TSTs was the command and control." It made everyone question whether this new war with its rules and reach-back was violating every sensible tenet of decentralized execution and combat operations sacred to airmen for decades. Cryer remembered: "There were times that we were doing TSTs [and] I was on the phone to the guy in Tampa, who's looking at Predator at the same time I was, and I'm wondering why in the world I'm talking to him, considering that I can see it and we're here." It was classic discomfort but what it meant for the CAOC was that "we had to have some certainty that what you were pulling trigger on was no kidding a vetted target." If that meant some targets slipped away, so be it.

From the CINC's perspective, as Franks made clear, the tight command and control was necessary. "It was his show to run," Cryer said firmly. Spectators watching the Predator feed were another issue, but one Franks soon resolved by ensuring they were not in the execution loop. From the CAOC side, Cryer attested that the TST process stayed within the chain of command. "We weren't taking guidance from the Pentagon," he said.[146]

A SHIFT BEGINS

Finally, OEF marked a seismic shift in air war execution as aircrews went from hitting pre-planned targets to striking emerging targets. "There are pre-planned targets, and there's also the ability to handle targets that might emerge," Myers said as early as October 8.[147] "By the end of the first week, the pilots didn't know what targets they'd be striking when they launched," said Vice Admiral John Nathman, Commander, Naval Air Forces.[148]

The full force of the shift from pre-planned to emerging targets took time to register but when it did, it set a whole new tactical concept for airstrikes. Emerging targets – whose coordinates were not known to aircrews when they launched – were either TSTs directed by the CAOC, or early efforts by ground controllers to direct air strikes to soften up Taliban strong points.

Prosecuting these targets was a chore that demanded aircrews keep their heads in the game. At first, CIA personnel were in various locations across Afghanistan but no full-up SOF teams were in place until October 19. Carrier pilots struggled with targeting during these early OEF missions. "It was extremely frustrating at first," said Driscoll, flying missions from *Kitty Hawk*. Initially the ground controllers he encountered sounded like they were either "non-military" or at best, inexperienced. "I spent a couple of hops just trying to find targets that were not being properly marked or properly talked on," he recalled.[149]

One case stood out. "Controllers were very hesitant to expose their positions at all," Driscoll said. One controller was "in a mud village" and trying to talk Driscoll onto an enemy "element up in the foothills." It just wasn't working.

"I put an orange tarp on top of my roof," the controller told Driscoll. Driscoll circled, trying to spot the tarp without going below the 10,000 foot hard deck. "We just could not see from 10,000 feet," said Driscoll.

Then Driscoll asked: *'do you have a laser?'*

'Oh, I've got the laser,' the ground controller replied.

'Turn the laser on and start pointing it,' Driscoll instructed him.

"Sure enough, the laser came on, but by then it was too late to get a good talk on and get to the target so we didn't drop any bombs that time," Driscoll finished.[150]

"We learned very quickly what sort of things that we wanted the FACs to be telling us and what they needed to hear from us," said Smith. For "the first couple of flights it was sort of painful, but then after that we were able to work through it and got a good idea of how we wanted to work things."[151]

These were the first tremors of a seismic shift in expeditionary air warfare: launching, ingressing, and working with the ground controllers or waiting on station for new coordinates from the CAOC. And it would turn out to be just what CENTCOM needed to make its concept of operations for Afghanistan work.

MOVING AHEAD

Fixed targets still accounted for a number of sorties. Typical targets for the weekend of October 13-14 included "terrorist camps, military training facilities, airfields, air defenses, and command and control facilities," said Myers, along with "surface-to-air missile storage sites, garrison areas, troop staging areas, and al Qaeda infrastructure.[152]

The *Theodore Roosevelt* arrived on October 15. "The war started on the 7th, we got there the 15th," said Fitzgerald. "*Enterprise* stayed for another week."

Now three carriers were operating together in the strike role. Fitzgerald was delighted when Moore told him to have his aircrews ready to go the first night they arrived. "We didn't think the Afghanistan thing was going to go so fast. We knew that we were probably going to drop bombs on somebody. In fact we thought it was going to be Iraq. We were surprised," he added – but pleasantly so. *Theodore Roosevelt's* aviators rushed into combat as soon as they were close enough to launch.

Fitzgerald found that there were only enough tankers planned for the two carrier battle groups already in action. To fly the first missions to the Kandahar area the *Theodore Roosevelt* had to fall back on its own resources for organic tanking.

"That got really dicey because you were doing blue-water tanking," said Fitzgerald. Like Mitscher's Hellcats at the Philippine Sea, they were heading for battle without enough fuel to recover. "We were launching them, sling-shotting them up there, knowing that coming back they wouldn't have enough gas, so we had to get gas up to the them

Aboard the USS Theodore Roosevelt, an F/A-18 Hornet makes its approach for a carrier arrested landing following a strike mission over Afghanistan on Nov. 15, 2001, while an aircrew observes the landing from an F-14 Tomcat as they await their own launch instructions. U.S. Navy Photo by Chief Photographer's Mate Eric A. Clement.

coming the other way," Fitzgerald said. To recover them "we were taking our tankers, launching them up, gassing them, tankers would land, get pumped, turn right around and go back up airborne and catch them coming back."[153]

"That's not something we like to do," said Fitzgerald. Emergency divert bases were available in Pakistan but "we weren't crazy about landing there," he said.

As sorties continued, all eyes were on the ground situation. Progress was hard to measure. "The Taliban come and go every day," one refugee told a *New York Times* reporter. "Now that the Taliban has reinforced here, their forces are believed to outnumber alliance forces by three to one," speculated the reporter. "An alliance assault that is not backed up by heavy American bombing would probably end in thousands of casualties and failure," he predicted.[155]

In fact, the main thrust of the campaign – supporting SOF and Northern Alliance maneuver against Taliban-held cities – was still ramping up.

Commentators and critics were not sure what to make of OEF. "We're making some progress in our efforts to create the conditions for sustained anti-terrorist operations inside Afghanistan," Rumsfeld assured them at mid-month.[156]

An early stray bomb that hit a civilian facility in Kabul made air war critics bristle. Myers put the incident in perspective. "I want to note that we have used hundreds of munitions in the first week of our visible military operation," he said on Monday, October 15, 2001. "Saturday, of course, we had an unfortunate case where we missed the target near the Kabul airfield. Our planners, in fact, do everything they can to avoid such mishaps, but sometimes these things, unfortunately, happen. Operations continue."[157]

OEF had gotten off to a fast start due in no small part to the ability of the massed aircraft carriers to provide air superiority, hit fixed and emerging targets, and begin the process of TST strikes and direct support to ground forces. For now overall results were hard to assess. But persistent airpower was about to change all that.

CHAPTER 4:

"Battle Was Joined"

"These were real effects. This was not about a point paper in the Pentagon. Our pilots were kicking somebody's butt." – Admiral John Nathman, 2002[158]

It took nearly a month for the ground piece of the operation in Afghanistan to begin to show results. "It was a slow start," said Driscoll. "But it picked up steam pretty quick." By late October, the aircraft carriers were at the center of a new type of war.

Two factors set OEF rolling toward decisive combat operations. Aircrews worked out how to provide precision and persistence; and on the ground, a critical mass of well-trained controllers started to use the carrier-dominated air component to astonishing effect.

In the skies over Afghanistan on Oct. 31, 2001, two 500-pound Laser Guided Bomb Units (GBU-12) (left) and an AIM-9 Sidewinder short-range air-to-air missile are visible on the wing of an F/A-18 Hornet from the USS Carl Vinson. U.S. Navy photo by Lt. Steve Lightstone.

SOF MOVES IN

From the start, Franks was eager for "American boots on the ground" to engage the Taliban and al Qaeda. "The sooner we had the teams' combat air controllers designating Taliban and al Qaeda targets for the bombers, the quicker Northern Alliance troops could climb out of their World War I-style trenches and advance on the enemy," he said.[159]

SOF forces played a small role in Operation Desert Storm hunting Scud sites and spotting for air attack. Commanders toyed with the idea of SOF operations in Afghanistan after 1998 and drew up plans for bringing them in to track enemy targets during Operation Allied Force in 1999, although NATO political sensitivities ultimately ruled out the use of ground forces. Now, for Afghanistan it was "absolutely imperative here that you start with people on the ground" who could assess the military situation, identify targets, and most of all, and work with the Northern Alliance.[160]

Franks' plan called for a force of about 200 SOF to team with the Northern Alliance and conduct initial combat operations. Even though airpower was available, the Northern Alliance was not instantly ready for coordinated air and ground offensives. Building the teamwork was an individualized process of matching SOF teams to each opposition leader. It took time, money and more. Secretary of State Colin Powell explained it perfectly: "You had a first-world air force and a fourth-world army and it took a while to connect the two," he said.[161]

Teams from "other government agencies" such as the CIA were making contact with the Northern Alliance leaders by late September. But the main combat effort would come from SOF teams dispatched to work with the leaders of the Northern Alliance and direct their operations in the field. Most important of all, the SOF teams would have highly trained air controllers with them – individuals who knew exactly how to make the best use of the GBU-12s, GBU-16s and 2000-lb. JDAMs coming in under the wings of strike fighters.

Aboard the USS Theodore Roosevelt on Oct. 20, 2001, a pilot and ordnanceman run checks on a computer control group for a laser guided bomb carried by an F-14 Tomcat. U.S. Navy photo by PHAN Amy DelaTorres.

Getting the prime teams into Afghanistan proved tougher than anticipated. Part of the problem was an initial desire to insert them via old Soviet Mi-17 helicopters in US possession. Franks later said the thinking was that the Mi-17s would not attract as much ground fire since the Taliban used Soviet-era helicopters, too, primarily Mi-8s. Dust storms and snow on landing sites caused problems. Furthermore, the CIA advance men needed time to set up liaison arrangements with all the Northern Alliance leaders. It added up to what Franks called "ten days of hell" after OEF began on October 7 as they waited for insertions to begin in earnest.[162]

The SOF forces centered around Task Force Sword, commanded by Major General Dell Dailey, and Task Force Dagger, commanded by Colonel John Mulholland, who would operate from the airbase at Karshi-Kanabad in Uzbekistan. Main players among the Afghan resistance leaders included General Rashid Dostum, who had a predominantly Uzbek militia ready to press Mazar-i-Sharif in the north. Hundreds of miles west, near Herat, Ismail Khan was the principal warlord. Tajik General Mohammed Fahim had taken over after Masood's death and held the key to putting pressure on Kabul. Hamid Karzai's band was on the move in the south. Each warlord had to have its own specially trained SOF team in order to make a decisive move. Only then could the next phase of the campaign roll forward.

The "hope was that we were going to be able to energize the Northern Alliance against the Taliban and get them to take the initiative. And we wanted to use airpower to accomplish that. So, it very quickly became obvious that our SOF guys, working with the Northern Alliance commanders, could really make a huge difference – *if* we were there to support," said Cryer.[163]

INGREDIENTS OF PERSISTENCE

Thus, the plan for Afghanistan would succeed or fail depending on persistent airpower. The air wings were finding out what it took to provide persistence.

Tanking. Top of the list was tanking. The long sorties and multiple refuelings made pilots connoisseurs in their preferences among the array of US and Coalition tankers. By far their favorite was the familiar S-3. According to Lynch, "tanking behind

Maintenance personnel dispatched from the U.S. Navy aircraft carrier USS John C. Stennis remove a refueling basket, which became disconnected from a U.S. Air Force KC-10 during in-flight refueling, from the refueling probe on an F/A-18 Hornet strike fighter on Feb. 1, 2002. U.S. Navy photo.

49

The flight deck of USS Carl Vinson teems with aircraft, ordnance and flight deck Sailors late into the night of Oct. 11, 2001 as the aircraft carrier conducts flight operations in support of Operation Enduring Freedom. U.S. Navy photo by Photographer's Mate 3rd Class Saul Ingle.

the S-3 is fairly easy in that it's got a nice, long, very forgiving refueling hose. We just did it so often that it was easy to do, like riding a bike," she added.

The Air Force's KC-135 and KC-10s awaited the carrier pilots over Afghanistan's deep airspace. Most had much less experience with the big wings, especially under combat conditions. As Lynch explained, "although I had some experience with it, I didn't have a whole lot of it at night under an increased workload." Tanking behind the KC-135 was perhaps the worst. Pilots nicknamed this Air Force stalwart the "Iron Maiden" for its hard-locking, solid extender boom. As Lynch described the KC-135, "it's not a flexible boom and it is very difficult to tank off of. You have to have very fine skills to do it right and not do any sort of damage to the probe," said Lynch. "There were a couple people that came back to the ship from Afghanistan with the KC-135's refueling probe or basket still on their probe, because it's not as forgiving as an S-3."[164]

24-hour operations. Next came blending the air wings to sustain 24-hour operations. Here multiple carriers were vital.

Not that 24-hour operations were new in themselves; as Fitzgerald said, "during Desert Storm we had kind of done that in that we operated 24 hours, but we just did two alpha strikes." Afghanistan "was continuous, we were doing push-CAS so it was cyclic ops for 12 hours," he said. The *Theodore Roosevelt* was "running between 70 and 80 airplane launches a day."[165]

Still, 24-hour operations by the paired carriers did not quite yield 24-hour battlespace coverages. The distances and intricacies of the missions were just too great. The CAOC

50

knew it and worked to funnel air support where and when it was needed most. "It was impossible to get 24-hour coverage," said Cryer, "so we contracted with the SOF forces" to provide strike aircraft in set increments. Ideally, SOF teams would use the aircraft available to them in assigned time periods. However, the contract also had a worst-case clause. The CAOC promised "we could get somebody to them within four hours if [strike aircraft] were not overhead," said Cryer. Yet all recognized it was far from perfect. "In other words the worst case scenario is that if you get in trouble we can get somebody to you in four hours. Now that's pretty awful if you think about it. I mean if you're out there alone and come under phenomenal attack by the Taliban or Taliban and al Qaeda and it's going to take four hours before the cavalry arrives, that's a problem. But that was really the very best we could do," he said.[166]

Command and Control. There was also the command and control piece, often affected by spotty communications as well as the vagaries of the CAOC's targeting or ground controller's requests. "The real clunker in the whole Afghanistan operation was the link between the CAOC and the AWACS," said Fitzgerald. "The link between the CAOC and the AWACS was an analog one. It was voice. So you had all these great sensors out there in the airplanes...[but] there was no way of getting what they were seeing back other than by voice to the AWACS, who then translated voice via SATCOM to the CAOC."

This limitation was part of the reason everybody fell "in love with the UAVs, not because they were any better sensor than we had in the airplanes, but because they had their own link back and people could look at a picture and look at what they were seeing." The net effect was a "lot of frustration on the pilot's part, because they would find something out there, a tank or a helicopter or whatever and it would take an inordinate amount of time to get clearance," sometimes up to 4 to 6 hours, by which time the target had long since become the responsibility of another section or division.[167]

Deconfliction. Dealing with the variety of controllers on the ground was also a new experience for most of the aircrews. The CAOC tried its best to keep tabs on the locations of the SOF teams and other government agency teams, but the ground picture was far from perfect.

Pilots were well aware of the need to deconflict with the controllers transmitting targets to them. "I don't know where they were – that's just it," Bennett said of the ground controllers directing the strikes. "I think Special Operations Forces – SOF – is also Special let's-not-tell-anyone-what-we're-doing Forces, and that's fine. These guys are trained professionals and they go in and do their thing."

But double-checking the coordinates, particularly for the JDAM strikes, was *de rigeur*. "You certainly don't want to hit any of your people," he said. "So maybe if you get asked to drop a bomb, you just ask one more time – you ask for clarification."

"We're reading back and confirming the coordinates instead of one-way receiving them, so there's a definite confirmation that you heard and entered into your computer correctly the right coordinates," Bennett explained. "With the air superiority we've achieved in Afghanistan, we have the luxury of doing that."[168]

Munitions. Airwings also altered the munitions mix for the long haul. Almost immediately, the carriers began to run low on preferred munitions. All had deployed long before anyone knew they'd be in a sustained shooting war.

An Aviation Ordnanceman pushes a 2000-pound GBU-10 laser guided bomb through the hangar bay of the aircraft carrier USS Theodore Roosevelt on Oct. 17, 2001. U.S. Navy photo by Chief Photographer's Mate Johnny Bivera.

Fitzgerald felt the pinch as soon as the *Theodore Roosevelt* battlegroup arrived. "When we got over there, the *Enterprise* had dropped so many [bombs] that the supplies were down to almost none. We didn't have any 500-lb. All we had were 2000-lb. and some 1000-lb.," he said, "so we had to make a swap with the Air Force."[169] From land-based stocks came hundreds of JDAM kits. "The LGBs came out of Navy stocks in the Med," said Fitzgerald, but it was not an easy trade. EUCOM did not want to release LGBs from stocks at Souda Bay for fear of running low on its own warfighting requirements. Despite "a flurry of phone calls" the *Theodore Roosevelt* headed through the Med without the needed munitions. Eventually, a deal was cut, and EUCOM ended up having to fly the LGBs out to the region.[170]

When ground controllers and the CAOC could not get strike fighters to targets they often had to jettison ordnance to meet the weight limits for recovery aboard the carrier. Unexpended 2000-lb. JDAMs often put strike aircraft over the designated bring-back weight. Dropping scarce 2000-lb. JDAMs into the sea was not optimal. The solution was to switch to recoverable loads whenever possible. A saving grace was that not every sortie called for dropping every bomb – that was the nature of this new air war. Coverage and persistence counted most.

Filling the gaps. A final boost came from a small contingent of land-based F-15Es and F-16s flying from Persian Gulf bases. Even with two carriers and the *Kitty Hawk* detachment, the CAOC needed more coverage. Simple math of the transit times "created some gaps in coverage that we really legitimately could fill with a very good asset," said

F-15E Strike Eagles from Royal Air Force Lakenheath, England, line up on the taxiway preparing for takeoff for a mission supporting of Operation Enduring Freedom. U.S. Air Force photo by Staff Sgt. William Greer.

Cryer. The F-15E had "a phenomenal FLIR" and carried twelve GBU-12s. The CAOC was happy to have even a small number of F-15E sorties – "we just didn't have it as often as we probably would have liked," Cryer said, due to the basing and distance constraints.[171]

ONE MISSION

Ultimately it was up to the aircrews to deliver the persistence the CAOC demanded and overcome whatever unexpected challenges tried to get in the way. Smith, aboard the *Kitty Hawk*, described what it took to make it from the launch to bomb release to recovery.

"I think the shortest mission I flew was 3 and a half hours, and that's really not that bad. Because you're staying busy the whole time."

The long ones were another matter. Smith specifically remembered one mission where "we essentially met our tanker" and "followed him all the way up to Mazar-i-Sharif. Their procedures at the time were that they had to go around the mountains for surface-to-air [missile] considerations. So they would take the long route around all the way to the west, kind of by-passing the mountains and then all the way up to the north. It was a really long flight."[172]

The tanker routing reflected Washington's ongoing concern with pop-up air defense in Afghanistan. As Rumsfeld said toward the end of October: "The air campaign has done a very good job of reducing down the threat from the ground – it has not eliminated it, we know that there still are Stingers and we know there are probably still some SAMs and we know there are probably still a few MiG aircraft and some helicopters" in Afghanistan.[173]

The circuitous routing left the jets low on fuel again. "Once we got all the way up there, we'd fill up our tanks again, and try to talk to the AWACS, but if they weren't close enough then we couldn't hear them," Smith continued.

An F-14 Tomcat and an F/A-18 Hornet aircraft assigned to the aircraft carrier USS Enterprise complete air-to-air refueling operations with a U.S. Air Force KC-10 Extender on October 5, 2001. U.S. Navy Photo by Commander Brian G. Gawne.

That meant contacting a FAC or trucking south again "to try to get in radio contact" with AWACS. "Most of the time they were hanging out down around by Kandahar," Smith said. "They'd give us a new frequency, a new area to go to, they'd have to coordinate all the new tanking for us and everything then a couple of occasions that actually happened where we had to go all the way up to the north, realize that the FAC wasn't there or wasn't talking to us, come all the way back south again go talk to a new FAC in a totally different location.

"That's what we had to do to get our bombs off," Smith summed up.[174]

ON THE GROUND

As with many a joint campaign the impact of persistence in the air over Afghanistan was to be measured by effects on the ground.

It would take SOF forces with the right equipment and specialized training to link Afghan opposition fighters with the full force of American airpower.

The first SOF team hit the ground by October 19, 2001 and was in action the next day.[175] The CIA "had done an excellent job preparing the battlefield," commented one senior commander. USSOCOM's "operational detachment alpha" or ODA teams of highly trained soldiers, sailors and airmen were trained for infiltrating into hostile territory, coordinating air strikes and close air support, conducting strategic reconnaissance, handling emergency airstrip operations, directing resupply efforts. The SOF teams had what it took to give Afghan opposition forces the advice, support and resources to fight the Taliban.

US Special Forces troops ride horseback as they work with members of the Northern Alliance in Afghanistan during Operation Enduring Freedom on November 12, 2001. DoD photo.

By the time SOF teams went in, "some budding relationships" were established and the teams "rapidly assimilated."[176] The initial 12-man team joined Dostum in the north following a "dress code" of beards, long hair and native garb that let them blend in with the alliance – as long as they wore one prominent, regulation uniform item such as desert camouflage trousers.[177]

Part of the job was convincing the Northern Alliance leaders what the airstrikes could do for them. They were not experienced with the direct impact of precision airstrikes on enemy fielded forces. "These guys were not believers, they were not believers at all," said Cryer. "They didn't know what a beauty asset they had in TACAIR."[178] Persistence showed them.

Army Rangers airdropped in to Objective Rhino with its paved airfield on October 20. That same day, the *Kitty Hawk* launched special forces helicopters in an operation designed to occupy Mullah Omar's compound.[179]

Powell made a statement of cautious optimism. "The Northern Alliance is on the march in the north toward Mazar-i-Sharif, and I think they're gathering their strength to at least invest Kabul, or start moving on Kabul more aggressively," he said on October 22.[180]

Special Forces controllers began to call in more emerging targets. On October 23, for example, over ninety strike aircraft hit five planned targets in Afghanistan, to include terrorist training camps, Taliban command-and-control centers, armored vehicles, and maintenance and warehouse facilities.[181] Then strike sorties shifted emphasis from pre-planned targets to emerging targets in special zones and engagement areas identified by SOF teams on the ground. Three teams were in Afghanistan by October 26, with five more waiting in Uzbekistan.[182]

Rumsfeld later summed up why it had taken several weeks to get to that point. In his words, "part of it was that we needed to get them staged in an area near the country [Afghanistan]. Second, it required having some liaison on the ground prior to their arrival. Third, we had some very bad weather and there were days that things were canceled. Fourth, we had to deal with opposition forces that from time to time were not sure they wanted our Special Forces...in with some of the people that they had less than perfect relationships with."[183] By late October, the logistics were in place, the rivalries were largely set aside, the bombs were falling in the right place, and the campaign on the ground was about to take off.

Aircrews saw it as a change in target types and taskings. "What has changed is that we've transitioned . . . to artillery and tanks along Taliban positions, and taking out some of their big guns," said Bennett of the *Carl Vinson's* air wing. "They have a lot of artillery and tanks out there that are mobile," said an F-14 radar intercept officer also aboard the *Carl Vinson.*

"These tanks and artillery were firing, so I'm assuming there were people around them," Bennett added. "Whether those were massive troop concentrations, I don't know, but [the weapons] weren't just lying about, they were being actively used."[184]

Tactics were changing so fast that it was almost impossible for those beyond the CAOC to track the new impact of this air war.

A U.S. Navy F/A-18C Hornet descends to the flight deck of the aircraft carrier USS Carl Vinson on Oct. 10, 2001. U.S. Navy photograph by Photographer's Mate 1st Class Greg Messier.

"It's been said that those who expect another Desert Storm will wonder every day what it is that this war is all about," Franks said. "This is a different war. This war will be fought on many fronts simultaneously."[185]

Speaking to al-Jazeera on October 31, Myers explained in more detail the tactical concept for the phase of operations that was now well underway. "For several days now we've had US troops on the ground with the Northern Alliance," he said. "Their primary mission is to advise [and] to try to support the Northern Alliance with airstrikes as appropriate. They are specially trained individuals that know how to bring in airpower and bring it into the conflict in the right way, and that's what they're doing. We think that will have a big impact on the Northern Alliance's ability to prosecute their piece of this war against the Taliban."[186]

"Battle Was Joined..."

Between late October and early November the shift to emerging targets set the conditions for progress on the ground. "I still firmly believe that we're watching this battle move rather slowly on the ground. They're still exchanging artillery. We are still attacking their forces. We know we're having an effect on their forces based on what we see from pilot reports that are coming back," said Stufflebeem on October 24.[187]

"We feel that the air campaign has been effective," Rumsfeld reiterated on October 28.[188] The next day he elaborated:

> We're now able to supply ammunition and various other supplies. We're able to get considerably better targeting information from the ground today than we had been previously. We're able to provide support to the forces that are opposing the Taliban and al Qaeda in a manner that is considerably more effective than had been the case previously when the targeting information was either lacking or imprecise.

Rumsfeld suggested that any critics step back and think: "well, three weeks, not bad to have accomplished those things and to put in place that capability for the period ahead."[189]

With better forward air controllers now on the ground, Northern Alliance operations picked up, and the pace changed. "Battle was joined," Driscoll recalled.

Franks was certainly pleased with the results of the air war so far. "Linking combat

Capt. Danny Stout, an air liaison officer and B-52 pilot, travels with an Army unit to call in close-air support missions against enemy troops in the mountains of Afghanistan. U.S. Air Force photo by 2nd Lt. Rebecca Garland.

Following early morning bombing missions, an F-18 Hornet flies in the post-contact position during an aerial refueling mission with a KC-135R on Oct. 26, 2001. U.S. Air Force photo by Tech Sgt. Scott Reed.

air controllers to flights of fighter-bombers and B-52s orbiting high above the battlefield had proven even more lethal than military theorists could have imagined," he later said of this time.[190]

Little wonder, for the Northern Alliance forces were ready to tackle the front line defenses of Kabul, as Franks learned when he conferred with Mohammed Fahim Khan, Massood's successor as military leader of the Northern Alliance on October 30. According to Franks, several million dollars also changed hands.[191] It might have been the fastest deal ever in the history of US foreign military assistance.

Fahim Khan briefed him that the Northern Alliance's immediate objectives were the key northern towns of Taloqan, Kunduz and Mazar-i-Sharif. "Your air force should concentrate its bombing to allow our forces to take these cities," Fahim Khan told Franks. "Then I will move south to Bagram," he said, referring to the old Soviet airbase, and on to Kabul.[192]

Mission intensity increased. Northern Alliance and Taliban forces were fighting in closer contact. Now, "instead of being three canyons over, they're coming up the mouth of the canyon," he said. Close air support got urgent.

Driscoll described one sortie flown by Smith and a flight lead. They "got an urgent call" to check in with a controller in Mazar-i-Sharif where Northern Alliance forces were under extreme pressure. "They were in a little salient there and they were being pushed back. They were surrounded and they had a couple of ZSUs, anti-aircraft guns, that they had rotated down and were using to great effect to fire on the northern alliance guys." Added to that was a thousand foot overcast leaving "no chance of getting down and doing close air support [and] besides, we weren't allowed to go below ten thousand feet."

What Smith and his flight lead did have was the 2000-lb. JDAM. The ground controller gave them GPS coordinates – but rules of engagement specified CAOC approval since these were not mensurated coordinates. That injected a big delay as the pilots contacted AWACS, awaited clearance, and met up with a tanker for refueling so

Pilots and aircrew brief a plane captain Oct. 17, 2001 on the performance of an F-14 Tomcat after completing a mission over Afghanistan. U.S. Navy Photo by Photographer's Mate Airman Lance H. Mayhew, Jr.

they could return to execute the strike. "It took about an hour and a half evolution for these guys to get permission to drop these GPS. Well, low and behold, he gave them good coordinates. They wiped out the anti-aircraft guns. They killed a bunch of the Taliban that were fighting there and it was a great success," Driscoll summed up.

Later at the debriefing Driscoll queried the CAOC. He learned that if the ground controller carried a certain type of highly reliable gear, the coordinates were good enough for the CAOC.

This "bellweather change" as Driscoll termed it rippled through the air component. "B-52s, F/A-18s, anybody that could drop JDAM could drop through the weather," he explained. "And now we're doing close air support through the weather, which is a huge change for naval aviation," he said.[193]

Myers ran videos of strikes from October 26 with "hits of deployed Taliban forces" near Mazar-i-Sharif. Strike video one was "a hit on an armored vehicle seeking cover in a wadi." Said Myers: "This vehicle is part of the Taliban Fifth Corps that is attempting to defend Mazar-i-Sharif from Northern Alliance attacks." The second strike video showed a tank and an anti-aircraft gun emplacement. These were emergent engagement zone targets and "from the explosions, it appears AAA was damaged, while the tank was destroyed," Myers said.[194]

CONTROLLING AIR SUPPORT FOR EMERGING TARGETS

Striking the targets created a mini-revolution in warfare. The role of XCAS – the CAOC's shorthand for immediate airborne close air support – grew exponentially as emerging targets became the bread and butter of the Afghan air war.

XCAS required the CAOC's daily ATOs to schedule strike fighters and bombers over the battle area with specific vulnerability periods – periods when their ordnance was available for tasking from the CAOC or ground controllers. A Navy four-ship of F-14s might have a "vulnerability" period of two hours over target areas in Afghanistan. A B-1 or B-52 might be on call for four to five hours, for example.

Sometimes that was enough time to get the job done, and sometimes it wasn't. The success of particular missions depended first and foremost on coverage. Then came the process of identifying targets – which were plentiful during the hot action around Mazar-i-Sharif. The principal limitation came in communications and battlespace awareness.

The system in place was like nothing seen before in doctrine or exercises. Requests for airstrikes came from SOF team controllers and were relayed back to the CAOC through a short, informal chain. Air Control Elements (ACE) were manned by a few individuals from Special Tactics Squadrons (STS) and attached directly to the SOF Task Forces working at various locations across Afghanistan. SOF controllers who needed airpower contacted their ACE. The ACE then called the Special Operations Liaison Element (SOLE) at the CAOC at Prince Sultan Air Base. As Lieutenant Colonel Kenneth Rozelsky, Commander, 682nd Air Support Operations Squadron, described it, the way to do close air support was "via chat...to the SOLE." At the CAOC, the "SOLE would get up and walk across the room and say, 'Hey, we have this request.'" Operations directors on the CAOC floor then passed the SOLE request on to AWACS, callsign "Bossman," whose crew of battle managers vectored strike aircraft to the targets. Sometimes they put the strikers in direct contact with controllers.

The ad hoc system worked well enough given the nature of the fight. Only a few hundred Americans were on the ground in Afghanistan. The CAOC's biggest challenge for other types of targets – knowing where the SOF forces were – did not become an impediment when a request went through the SOLE. Wide geographic separation helped, too. The teams were scattered all across Afghanistan. Controllers

A forward-deployed E-3B Sentry airborne warning and control system (AWACS) crew prepares the aircraft for a mission at an operating location in support of the U.S. Central Command execution of Operation Enduring Freedom. U.S. Air Force photo by Tech. Sgt. Marlin G. Zimmerman.

working around Kabul in the northeast did not have to worry about deconflicting aircraft with fellow controllers calling strikes around Kandahar three hundred miles to the south. "Rather than a linear fight, it was a bunch of guys on lily pads floating around shark-infested waters," commented Rozelsky.[195] When "there were three flights in Afghanistan and four or five ODAs out at any one point, there was never a real need for prioritization," he continued.[196]

In this phase the air war "actually was quite effective because you have large land mass, a lot of air space, little bitty airplanes with a lot of bombs. Everybody's a bad guy; everything's basically a target. With very small US forces, it's a wonderful way to do it," commented Colonel Mike Longoria, Commander, 18th ASOG, the air support operations group attached to 9th Air Force. "There are no restrictions to air whatsoever. All of the airspace control measures that you would normally have to worry about in terms of air/ground relationships are not there. All you basically have to worry about is that airplanes don't run into other airplanes. AWACS does a great job of that."[197]

Denser battle conditions, more ground troops and more ground controllers would be another matter for the joint force – but that was a lesson yet to come.

Despite some rough patches, Afghanistan's air war pressed on successfully under this new style of operations. Sorties averaged about 500 per week. Air support thrived on a system tailored to a widely distributed ground battle, dominated by special operations using air interdiction as fires and Northern Alliance forces as maneuver.

TURNING THE CORNER: THE FALL OF MAZAR-I-SHARIF

Throughout the first week of November, airstrikes concentrated on Taliban and al Qaeda forces and military equipment near Mazar-i-Sharif and farther south, near Kabul. Mazar-i-Sharif was a significant first objective because it controlled land routes to Uzbekistan, needed for bulk military or humanitarian supplies, and because the Taliban and al Qaeda massed to try to defend Mazar. By doing

Aviation Boatswain's Mate 3rd Class Krystol Koos directs a F-14B Tomcat to the bow catapults aboard USS Theodore Roosevelt on Dec. 31, 2001. U.S. Navy photo by Photographer's Mate 2nd Class Jason Scarborough.

so they created a lucrative target for air. CIA Director George Tenet characterized Mazar-i-Sharif as a limited, achievable objective, worthy of concentrated effort.[198]

On November 1, for example, 65 Coalition aircraft struck nine pre-planned targets, plus dozens more in engagement zones.[199] This was the shift in air warfare that would lead to victory. Operational statistics confirmed the change. At Mazar-i-Sharif the number of pre-planned targets struck gave way to unfragged targets – targets selected by ground controllers and delivered by XCAS. By early November, strike aircraft were reporting more weapons drops on unfragged targets than on pre-planned targets.[200]

Best of all, the emphasis on emerging targets was working.

"We know we're having success," Stufflebeem briefed on November 2, 2001 "and putting severe stress" on the Taliban.[201] Fitzgerald, aboard *Theodore Roosevelt* sensed the change, too. "You could tell that it was starting to turn," he said. "You started to see in the intelligence reporting, different things changing over" and signs of success as the airstikes took out more Taliban military targets.[202]

"In one month, since October 7th, our pilots have flown more than 1800 strike aircraft and bomber sorties. They have broadcast over 300 hours of radio transmissions, and delivered more than 1.25 million rations to the starving Afghan people," Rumsfeld praised on November 6.[203]

The Northern Alliance was positioned to roll up territory on the ground. "If the Northern (Alliance) is feeling emboldened or ready to make moves, then that means that it (the bombing) has had the intended effect," said Stufflebeen on November 6.[204]

On that day, Northern Alliance forces had captured villages around Mazar-i-Sharif. The town of Shulgareh fell on November 7. Dostum and Attah were less than 10 miles short of their objective on November 8, according to reports from the SOF teams operating with them.[205] The next day, November 9, the Northern Alliance claimed Mazar-i-Sharif itself.

An Army Special Forces team member on the ground at the fall of Mazar-i-Sharif reported via email on how it had been done. "We rode on begged, borrowed and confiscated transportation," he said. "While it looked like a rag-tag procession, the morale [going] into Mazar was triumphant. The locals loudly greeted us and thanked all Americans [with] much waving, cheering and clapping, including from the women."[206]

Yet it wasn't a pushover. These same Afghan resistance forces had been trying for years to dislodge Taliban control of key areas, with no success. The difference this time was the rapid delivery of airstrikes.

For example, the special forces operator also described what happened when his men "came under direct artillery fire ...less than 50 meters away" just before Mazar-i-Sharif fell. "When I ordered them to call close air support, they did so immediately without flinching. As you know, a US element was nearly overrun four days ago but continued to call close air support and ensured the 'muj' [mujaheddin] forces did not suffer defeat."[207]

Stufflebeem in Washington watched it all closely. "I got very focused on the special operations forces, because I knew what the plan was and how they were intending to do it," he said. "I had access to the daily intentions of movement of the SOF forces as they would hook up with their counterparts from the various other coalitions, the Northern Alliance folks and Pashtun tribes in the south."[208] Monitoring the daily reports made him think: *"wow, we're taking a lot of risk in doing some of these operations. But obviously it's paying off."*

For the SOF teams fighting with the Northern Alliance and other opposition forces "there were also a lot of surprises," Stufflebeem noted. "We were surprised how agile the fighters were. We were surprised at how resilient the Arab fighters were. We found out that the Afghan fighters weren't resilient at all. As soon as it got hot, they just took off their black turbans, put on white turbans and said, 'what can we do to help you?' You know then the next day they could put on their black ones on and take potshots at us."

The Arab al Qaeda were different: "dedicated, tough, fight to the death. But also very resourceful," said Stufflebeem. "I know that was frustrating for ground forces who would say, hey we got these guys cornered, we got them captured, and you go in there and you'd kill 5 to 10 of them and all the rest of them are just evaporated. And you find out there's little tiny holes, they crawled in, they went through tunnels, they had ways to get out of these little traps."[209]

Aircrews cursed the missed opportunities when targets got away during the battle. On one occasion during the fall of Mazar-i-Sharif, retreating Taliban created "this flood of people and vehicles pouring out of there heading down south," said Fitzgerald. FLIR pictures showed it plainly but the fleeing vehicles crossed into a grey area under CENTCOM's rules. As a result, "the CAOC didn't want to go in there and bomb the vehicles because they didn't know what they were. They couldn't see what they were." Although to the pilots it was "clearly Taliban fighters bailing out" the best the CAOC could do was tell them something like "okay, bomb the road ahead of them to slow them down so we could try to figure out who they are. Bomb the cliff on the side of the road so it falls down on them." According to Fitzgerald "we missed a lot of opportunities like that because the sensor information from the airplanes couldn't be verbally transmitted back to the CAOC." That pointed out real shortfalls in the ability to push digital information," concluded Fitzgerald.[210] Fleeing Taliban and al Qaeda forces created problems on the ground, too – and would come back to haunt later stages of the campaign.

For now, there was no denying that the fall of Mazar-i-Sharif was the first triumph on the ground for Operation Enduring Freedom. Pakistan's leader General Pervez Musharraf put it in perspective when he said on November 11: "Mazar-i-Sharif falling, it has certainly – it has very big military and political implications, so I would say now it [the war in Afghanistan] has turned the corner."[211]

A NEW ARCHITECTURE

The first weeks of OEF put in place a new architecture for air warfare. Persistence and precision were its products. However, it was not only the strike aircraft who found their tactics changing over Afghanistan. The EA-6Bs, E-2s, S-3s and P-3s providing the supporting architecture for the air war also shifted to new ways of doing business.

"We used the Prowlers in Enduring Freedom during the first three days of combat operations in Afghanistan in exactly the traditional way that we have always used the Prowler," said Cryer. "That is, survivability" for other joint aircraft. In 72 hours there "was not a single emitter" in Afghanistan and the EA-6Bs shifted to a new mission: jamming Taliban and al Qaeda communications. Cryer explained that the Taliban

An EA-6B Prowler circles USS Theodore Roosevelt for its final approach on Dec. 4, 2001. U.S. Navy photo by Lt. Cmdr. Dave Adams.

had "a phenomenal reliance on rudimentary communications that we were capable of working over" with the EA-6B's jammer. Static on the radio had "a pretty debilitating effect" on the Taliban forces over time.[212]

E-2s were assisting with airspace deconfliction over southern areas of the country. The S-3s were a force multiplier as well as a pilot favorite.

Likewise the P-3 was projecting its unique capabilities over land and setting new operational precedents in the process. Rear Admiral Anthony Winns flew aboard the P-3 for some of the OEF missions. In the electro-optical and infrared mode the P-3 could position its orbit to identify targets in coordination with JSTARS. EP-3s gathered threat and warning indications "to let JSTARS know there was something out there," said Winns. The versatility added to the CAOC's ISR picture. On one night flight, said Winns, the P-3 was "imaging friendly helos flying in and out of the various areas. I recall imaging the AC-130 gunship firing."[213]

Taken together, the new architecture for OEF illustrated what the air component could do by projecting strike power from sea bases. Strike and support aircraft alike identified the ingredients of persistence and strove to make it happen. Granted, land-based tankers, bombers, fighters and command and control aircraft formed important parts of the network. Stufflebeem gave the bombers plenty of credit, too. "The level of effort aircraft were the B-52s, who could carry huge numbers of [JDAM] and loiter forever," he said.[214] But on mission after mission carrier aircraft took on and executed important tasks. The primary battlespace coverage for flexible, multi-role effects – from air superiority to XCAS to TSTs – came from the carriers in the North Arabian Sea, and the CAOC knew it.

Sailors from crash and salvage standby as an F/A-18 Hornet and an S-3B Viking launch from the flight deck of USS Theodore Roosevelt on Dec. 18, 2001. U.S. Navy photo by Photographer's Mate 3rd Class Angela Virnig.

"The Navy has generated a fantastic number of sorties, both F-14s and F/A-18s, and also their E-2s and EA-6Bs," said Moseley, who took command of the air component in early November.[215]

ON TO KABUL

The fall of Mazar-i-Sharif on November 9 began four impressive weeks that ended the Taliban control of Afghanistan.

"It would be correct to say that there is fighting going on throughout most of the country," said Stufflebeem that day.[216]

The Northern Alliance was now moving fast. "We are not there in a position to advise them when to go," cautioned Stufflebeem on November 9. "We're not there to advise them how they should undertake their particular tactics. We're there responding to their requests. We're there providing targeting for our aircraft, for a matter of precision."[217]

Rapid XCAS and XINT – immediate airborne interdiction – delivered on the instructions of SOF controllers kept the Afghan forces on the move. Driscoll recounted a typical mission north of Kabul, near Bagram. "We worked that area a lot because that's where a big battle line had formed as they were trying to go down and take the capital," he said. By this time nearly every mission ended up focusing on emerging targets. "We'd never go where we were supposed to go," Driscoll said. They studied targets "like we always do and never went there." Instead, they were handed off while over the battlespace. Procedures were much smoother. The "first thing we'd want to do is get coordinates for JDAM," he continued. The JDAMS could be launched from about 20 miles out "and that thing would sail in there" to hit the ground controller's chosen spot.

The JDAM explosion then served as a tactical marker – something that could be accomplished with laser technology, too. "Now you've got a spot on the ground," said Driscoll. "You see a hit. Everybody's eyeballs are on that. And the guy [controller on the ground] gets his laser out and says, 'from that mark, I'm going to work a ridgeline'.... You'd drop your LGBs and he would sit there and lase and it was just like calling in mortar rounds or artillery." With this "airborne artillery" the F/A-18s could "take out tank after tank after tank that was up on the ridge shooting down on these guys."[218]

Over the course of a week, the alliance, with its on-call American airpower, took town after town. The air component attacked trench lines outside of Taloqan – center of a major battle in summer 2000 – on Saturday, November 10. "It was important for these trenches, and others like them, to be cleared to open the way for the Northern Alliance to advance," Myers explained.[219] Taloqan fell on November 11. In the west, opposition forces heralded the liberation of Herat on November 12.

The morning of November 12 also saw the beginning of the end for the Taliban's control of Afghanistan's capital city. B-52 strikes pounded Taliban lines around Kabul in the morning. By late afternoon, Northern Alliance armored forces were moving down the Old Road toward the city with infantry sweeping through former Taliban positions. Fleeing Taliban fighters discarded their equipment and their dead and ran. The airstrikes around Kabul also killed bin Laden's deputy Mohammed Atef.

On November 13, the Northern Alliance's forces took control of Kabul and began to set up police control of the city. Rumsfeld announced US Special Forces teams were already in Kabul to work with them. "Every day the targeting and effectiveness has improved, and that has clearly played a critical role in killing Taliban and al Qaeda troops," Rumsfeld said on November 13.[220]

An F/A-18 Hornet from the USS Carl Vinson carries a strike payload consisting of an AIM-9 Sidewinder missile and JDAM ordnance on Nov. 4, 2001. U.S. Navy photo by Lt. Ken Koelbl.

"The Taliban appear to have abandoned Kabul and some Northern Alliance forces are in the city," Myers declared on November 13. "Last Friday the Northern Alliance controlled less than 15 percent of Afghanistan," he said. "By Monday morning they had fundamentally cut Afghanistan into two areas of control, but we must keep in mind that pockets of resistance do remain," he added.[221]

Some Taliban fled south toward the sparsely populated, mountainous areas controlled by Pashtun tribes. "Where we can positively identify Taliban as such, we are pursuing them," said Stufflebeem on November 14. However, Stufflebeem admitted that it was "difficult in the southern part of Afghanistan, west of Kandahar, to be able to positively identify what may be southern Pashtun tribes versus Taliban troops that may be on the move."[222] Northern Alliance forces were in no mood to give chase.

However, nothing changed the fact that taking the capital was a major victory. "We in fact have the initiative," Franks declared on November 15. He recalled that all along "we have said that it's all about condition-setting followed by our attaining our objectives. The first thing we did was set conditions to begin to take down the tactical air defense and all of that....the next thing we did was set conditions with these Special Forces teams and the positioning of our aviation assets to be able to take the Taliban apart or fracture it."[223]

The tactics of persistent air coverage and precisely controlled strikes had worked. As Army Vice Chief of Staff General John Keane later said, "those population centers toppled as the result of a combined arms team: US air power and a combination of Special Forces and Afghan troops."[224]

Cryer reflected: "The success of the Northern Alliance commanders in my view, and the reason it rolled up so fast, is because we were using airpower in ways that nobody really could've quite imagined. When you're on horseback and you're facing kind of an armed fortress of Taliban and these guys are scoffing at you – and [then] suddenly out of the clouds comes 15 or 20 JDAMS or J-109 penetrators and just absolute utter destruction."

The impact on the Taliban defenders was devastating. "They couldn't fight. They had no appetite to do that," Cryer concluded.[225]

The sustained operations with their unpredictable sortie times and emerging targets broke the mold of previous carrier strike operations. It was "a big mental and cultural change for the Navy," said Stufflebeem. "I think that the Navy had always intended and trained to go it alone. Maybe we're the door kicker. And the air forces would come in, once they got all their basing issues and their forces flowed and they'd pick up the bulk of some kind of campaign," he surmised. "Naval aviation used to be very much closed-minded to new ideas. We would show up as Navy guys and say hey this is our fight, this is the way we fight and we don't want it screwed up by the Air Force or coalition forces."[226]

In Afghanistan it was different. The carriers were in it for the long haul.

CHAPTER
OEF Continues

"The Taliban is not destroyed as an effective fighting force from the level of one individual man carrying a weapon until that individual man puts down his weapon."
– General Tommy Franks, November 15, 2001[227]

As Taliban rule in Kabul collapsed, the US-led Coalition still had major goals to pursue: tracking down the remaining Taliban and al Qaeda and finding out more about their shadowy network by raiding caves and other sensitive sites. Those tasks would take several months and require constant air support from the carriers. "What I can't allow to happen is to let the air wing get on some emotional

U.S. Navy Lt. John Greer (right) and Aviation Systems Warfare Operator 3rd Class Mandy Florez brief the mission plan to crew members on Oct. 27, 2001 prior to leaving on a routine patrol flight in support of Opera-tion Enduring Freedom. U.S. Navy Photo by Master Chief Photographer's Mate Terry Cosgrove.

roller coaster about 'Holy Cow, maybe we won,'" Bennett warned.[228] The percentage of strike sorties with ordnance drops dipped gently but generating sorties was still just as important, and other battles lay ahead.

Kunduz and Kandahar were next on the list. Airstrikes also hit preplanned targets such as cave complexes and in far greater numbers, immediate targets such as a Taliban tank near Kandahar on November 15 and an armored formation near Kunduz on November 18.

Fighting at Kunduz was intense. Franks estimated there might be 2,000 to 3,000 Taliban and al Qaeda fighters in the fray, and described Kunduz as "heavily infested... with some of the more hard-core people."[229] "The situation in Kunduz and Kandahar remains the same, which is ... a standoff," Stufflebeem reported on November 20, although he likened it to the situation just before the fall of Mazar-i-Sharif.[230]

Then came a new twist. The Taliban contingent at Kunduz petitioned the Northern Alliance to arrange a surrender and safe passage for foreign fighters. Mirroring their concern, President Musharraf of Pakistan made it known he wanted Pakistanis fighting with the Taliban to be allowed to return home. The Northern Alliance halted operations at Kunduz to allow three days of negotiations. The air component backed off, too.[231] Most of the forces were Afghan Taliban and Franks later said he opted to leave it to the discretion of the opposition forces as to whether they wanted to take their "enemies" into the fold. They "have taken them in willingly in a number of instances. And it's not for me to second-guess that," Franks stated.[232] As it turned out, the negotiations worked – at least in the short term. Over 1000 Taliban fighters surrendered to the Northern Alliance. Six days later, Kunduz was occupied.

A Steady Pace

Moving the battle south was not the only major change in operations in Afghanistan.

CENTCOM was widening the hunt for Taliban and al Qaeda remnants and preparing to bring in several hundred more ground forces. Stufflebeem explained: "We still have the job of finding and getting al Qaeda. We still have the job now of finding and getting at Taliban – leadership, specifically."[233] The hunt was not easy. Rumsfeld had already anticipated that the Coalition's efforts "will be shifting from cities at some point to hunting down and rooting out terrorists where they hide. This is difficult work," he cautioned.[234]

Franks explained why some Taliban and al Qaeda were getting away. "They can go across a border and wait and come back. They can drop their weapons and blend into the communities. They can go up in the mountains in the caves and tunnels. They can defect – join the other side – change their mind, go back," Franks reflected at the end of November.[235]

Ground forces would also be searching for sensitive sites – including those with potential WMD activity. "At the baseline, what we believe is that they have a crude chemical and possibly biological capability. And if there's any nuclear capability, it is liable to be more radiological than fissile," explained a CENTCOM briefer in October.[236] One major requirement was to investigate "sensitive sites" such as terrorist hide-outs,

Crew men of the USS Enterprise line up to receive an Advanced Chemical Protective Garments issued for protection against chemical, biological, or radiological attack on Oct. 7, 2001, during Operation Enduring Freedom. DoD photo by Airman Apprentice Lance H. Mayhew Jr., U.S. Navy.

weapons caches and locations that had a suspicious look. Franks spoke to the latter from Tampa in late November. "We've identified more than 40 places which represent potential for WMD research," he said. "Of those, a great many are currently under opposition leadership control. And we're very systematically going about our way of visiting each one of those....we'll continue to visit them until we've gone through all of them and performed the analyses that we need to perform to assure ourselves that we do not have evidence of WMD."[237]

With soldiers and Marines on the way, CENTCOM stood up a formal land component for Afghanistan in mid-November. It was the first time a Combined Forces Land Component Commander (CFLCC) had been appointed since the 1980s Goldwater-Nichols reorganization. Operation Desert Storm was fought without one, and Operation Allied Force did not employ ground forces. CFLCC headquarters was at Camp Doha, Kuwait with Lieutenant General Paul T. Mikolashek as its commander.

The new phase of OEF meant changes for carrier strike operations as the CFLCC became the "supported" component commander. This major joint doctrinal designation replaced the SOF and air component arrangements in play since OEF began, where often the SOF forces had been the *de facto* supported force. Not that this arrangement had been perfect. "There were all kinds of coordination problems in the beginning," said Nichols, who rotated in as a CAOC director when Cryer's stint ended. Most were "beginning to be cleared up about the time I got to the CAOC in late November," he said. One such problem was coordination with the SOF component. SOF commanders

A safety observer gives the "thumbs up" signal to launch an F-14 Tomcat from aboard USS Theodore Roosevelt on Dec. 19, 2001. U.S. Navy Photo by Photographer's Mate 3rd Class Michelle L. McCandless.

were prone to calling up the CAOC and asking for specific packages to strike targets in an hour or two. What "we defaulted to – and it worked pretty well – was pre-planned packages with capability that went where the fight was," Nichols said. It "was essentially on-call CAS. Ready to go if the guys on the ground needed them, and they did, most of the time."[238]

The major feature of the Afghan war was "integration of the air cover to be in complete support of very small numbers of folks on the ground," said Robb. In contrast to OSW, where fixed target strikes were the only game in town, "Afghanistan's all about having a guy on the ground. Not only is he on the ground, but you were in direct support of him and you can't leave because he's there. As long as he's there you have to have somebody there."[239]

Even after weeks of success, deconfliction with SOF and other government agency operations still had its moments. "The phone would ring, and it would be some CIA guy and he'd say, 'hey a helicopter's flying here to here. It's a Russian Mi-17. Don't shoot it.'" It would turn out the covert operations helicopter "was just lifting off," Nichols recalled, giving the CAOC minimum time to react. "It's those kind of things that we never really had to deal with before in a planning process," he said.[240]

Afghanistan's rapidly evolving air war and informal component arrangements had worked so far because there were few crises to challenge component coordination. CFLCC forces now had top priority but they were moving into a very different environment that bore no resemblance to traditional CAS.

As a result, one major issue for the newly-formed land component was simply understanding just what the air and SOF team had been doing so successfully for over six weeks. The OEF battlespace was very different from the phase lines, corps boundaries and fire support coordination lines of a doctrinally-conventional battlefield. Old doctrinal concepts of control lines and area ownership had given way to JSOAs and engagement zones. Off-limits "sites of interest" and constant unknowns about friendlies – like the ex-Soviet helicopters – created a jigsaw puzzle of battlespace control measures.

For the moment, OEF remained a war of air plus SOF. The small land component forces numbered under a thousand and were spread out over multiple locations from Uzbekistan to Qatar. Still, the lines of control were becoming tangled – but it would take months for the consequences to show.

FLEXIBLE AIR SUPPORT

The second half of November saw *Carl Vinson* and *Theodore Roosevelt* continuing to split the shift to sustain high sortie rates and long missions. The *Theodore Roosevelt* was still "the night carrier," said Fitzgerald. Fatigue was a concern but not yet a factor in the operations. "We monitored that very closely to see how they were doing," Fitzgerald said of his aircrews. So far they were doing fine. "I would tell you that yes, they were hard missions, they were long missions, but we didn't see any adverse effects," he said.

An F/A-18 Hornet prepares for launch from the flight deck of USS Theodore Roosevelt on Oct. 27, 2001. U.S. Navy Photo by Photographer's Mate 2nd Class Jeremy Hall.

There "weren't guys that did stupid things. There weren't long recoveries at the ship because the guy kept boltering," he said. Nights had their advantages. In a way, "we were actually on the right cycle because the first launch of the day was at midnight, and so the guys flying long ops would be coming back at sun-up, and then we'd be finished flying by noon time, so most of the landings for the guys flying the really long cycles were in the daytime."[241]

The aircrews were now covering a mix of missions: air support for the ground FACs, fixed target strikes on key areas such as Jalalabad, and of course, continuing prosecution of time-sensitive targets.

Emerging targets dominated more and more. Myers said in late November: "Increasingly the majority of our strikes, about 90 percent, have been against emergent targets by aircraft operating in what we call engagement zones, or by aircraft conducting close air support for opposition ground forces."[242]

By now, OEF had institutionalized three major changes in the execution of the air war that impacted carrier strike operations. One was the seismic shift to emerging targets. Another was refinement to the time-sensitive targeting process, and a third was recognition of a shift in how the air war was controlled and executed.

TSTs were still taxing because of the approval process and the narrow ROE. In the CAOC, the intelligence, surveillance and reconnaissance division used Predator and other assets as they worked continually to "maintain SA [situation awareness] and develop targets. Most of the targets [developed this way] were targets of opportunity, emerging targets, [and] we had to get permission from CENTCOM to bomb."

"We had this big 'mother may I' process that went all the way to CENTCOM," said Nichols. "We couldn't decide to pull a trigger in the CAOC. So we're sure there's a bread truck full of Taliban but because it doesn't fit this narrow description of ROE, we have to go through the routine with CENTCOM and it drove CFACC and me crazy. And we lost shot opportunities because of that. Significant opportunities were lost."[243]

Nichols attributed the tight leash in part to the fact that mistakes were made. "Remember we bombed the Red Cross warehouse twice," he said. But he believed the underlying reason lay with cultural factors and a long, institutional history of Army mistrust of air component commanders, regardless of who they were.[244] Whether it was lack of trust, lack of understanding, or lack of familiarity, few disputed that coordination among the joint components was not all it could be.

What it boiled down to was an unprecedented degree of centralized control over execution of the air war. That increased the demands for persistence in the battlespace. Aircrews still got frequent retasking. "The biggest frustration the air crews had was flying up there not knowing where their target area was going be. They were pushed around the whole country" as requirements funneled by the CAOC demanded. They had to be ready for anything and know the locations of extra tankers and keep a constant eye on fuel states, divert times, and of course, the carrier's landing cycle. In essence, the aircrews "had to basically have a contingency plan for the entire country. That was really hard. Guys were carrying whole ATOs with them," Fitzgerald said of this time.[245]

It "all depended on what the load was. We were dropping anywhere from 0 to 20 bombs an hour up there," he added.[246]

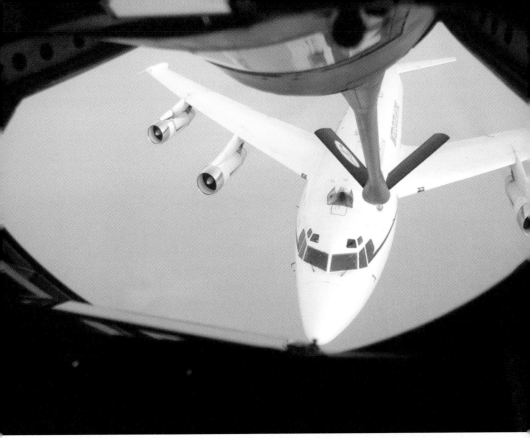

A RC-135V/W Rivet Joint reconnaissance aircraft receives 30,000 lbs of fuel from a KC-135R Stratotanker during an air refueling mission in support of Operation Enduring Freedom. U.S. Air Force photo by Staff Sgt. P.J. Farlin.

However, this persistence was just what CENTCOM needed. Mild frustration in the cockpits yielded major operational flexibility. "Really, the mission's not necessarily to make the guy in the cockpit happy," pointed out Robb at CENTCOM.

Those on the ground were also the ones taking the biggest risks, for the most part. In Operation Southern Watch, the pilots and aircrews were "the people most at risk." The burden shifted in Operation Enduring Freedom. "In Afghanistan, those folks running around on the ground were the burdened individuals who were at greatest risk," Robb said.

In fact, the aircrews were feeling the difference as the situational awareness of the CAOC began to counterbalance and outweigh that of the aircrews and the controllers on the ground. Much of that was due of course to the tight political restraints on operations – an emerging fact of life in the global war on terrorism. Technology also played a role. Not only was this CAOC joint – it was also equipped with a wealth of communications links. The undeniable net result was that the CAOC had much more visibility into the battlespace.

"There was so much situation awareness in the air operations center that included the political issues...and you could see the whole battlespace," Robb commented.[248]

With visibility came control. Situation awareness – especially in the midst of political and operational constraints – was shifting away from the cockpit and the ship to the CAOC and the command center, forward or rear. "I was land-locked, I sure would have liked to have been on the carrier, but frankly I had better SA than the guys in the battle group," said Cryer of the start of OEF.[247]

Robb set up an analogy with Vietnam. In that conflict, those in the airplanes "really were the smartest people on earth about what was going on in that battlespace. And people who were back on the ship or wherever didn't have that much situation awareness." Technology changed that. "The situation awareness that we have today on the screens is pretty incredible," Robb said. The "decisions need to be made wherever there's the most situation awareness. And I think that more and more over time, the greatest situation awareness is actually at higher levels. And the guys in the cockpit are becoming farther and farther separated from the decision process. That becomes frustrating, because you always want to support those that are in the battlespace who are at risk." At the same time, the overall goal is still "trying to shape decision-making in such a way that it moves the mission forward. So the decision to drop and not drop becomes ever more complicated."[249]

Those complications added up to an increased workload for the aircrews. Unfortunately, distance deprived them of one of the best means of making it more efficient: the E-2. For targets in the middle, north and west of Afghanistan the carrier pilots relied on the joint air component infrastructure of tankers and battlespace command and control. That meant the F/A-18s and F-14s worked communications and targets themselves. In this war, the E-2s could not help them as much because they were limited in the mission times and penetration distances. According to Fitzgerald, "the capability of our E-2 was marginalized because we didn't have the tanking capability" for that aircraft. Onboard fuel allowed the E-2s only "4.5 hours of flight time which got them up into Pakistan, but not into Afghanistan, and so we were not able to really utilize our E-2s like we would like to use them. They ended up pretty much managing the tanker orbits and when the AWACS went to tank, pick up the southern part of the battle for 20 to 30 minutes, that kind of stuff."

THE FALL OF KANDAHAR

As November drew to a close, it was time to focus on Tarin Kot and the main objective of Kandahar. The city was the last part of Afghanistan with substantial Taliban forces. As a CENTCOM briefer put it earlier, taking Kabul was a good thing, but the Afghan opposition forces "have not eliminated the Taliban as a significant political and military force until they've hit Kandahar."[250] The battles leading up to the occupation of Kandahar marked another three weeks of intensive air support from the carriers enabling maneuver on the ground.

SOF teams with the "southern tribal elements" had been edging closer since the middle of November. Among them were the forces of Hamid Karzai. Karzai was both scholar and battlefield leader and at the end of the year he would take on the task of serving as Afghanistan's interim president, then win full elections in 2004. Now, in late November 2001, he impressed Franks as "just the right Pashtun leader" to build a force to fight the Taliban and act as a political counterweight to the Northern Alliance's mix of ethnic Tajiks, Uzbeks and Hazaras.[251]

Hamid Karzai (left) meets with Secretary of Defense Donald H. Rumsfeld (right) at Bagram Air Base, Afghanistan, on Dec. 16, 2001. DoD photo by Helene C. Stikkel.

Karzai decided first to take the city of Tarin Kot, capital of Uruzgan province, 70 miles north of Kandahar. Tarin Kot was the heart of Taliban country and one of the controllers working with him, Captain Jason Amerine was skeptical. "I thought it would be a long time before we were ready to take Tarin Kot," he said. But Karzai "was very confident that he could just walk into the town and it would be his."

Karzai sent word to supporters in Tarin Kot and they started a revolt in the town. Karzai's forces, and Amerine's team with them, piled into a convoy and drove right into the town on November 17. Then came warning that "the Taliban had launched a massive group of people" from Kandahar to retake Tarin Kot. Amerine's team set up an observation post. Early the next morning, the Taliban convoy approached and the team called in airstrikes. "They completely mauled that convoy," Amerine said. "We saved that town." The ability to turn back the convoy with airpower greatly impressed the Pashtun tribes. The team directed more airstrikes on other stray Taliban units for the next week, while Karzai continued to talk to supporters and arrange defections.

Over 300 US Marines from the USS *Peleliu* and the USS *Bataan* helicoptered in to an airfield near the city on November 25. "They are not an occupying force," Rumsfeld

15th Marine Expeditionary Unit Special Operations Capable AH-1W Super Cobra helicopters launch from the Navy amphibious assault ship USS Peleliu's flight deck on Oct. 13, 2001. USMC Photo by Lance Cpl. Matthew J. Decker.

U.S. Navy pilot Lt. Ewain McDowell flies his P-3C Orion on a surveillance flight in support of Operation Enduring Freedom on Oct. 30, 2001. U.S. Navy photo by Master Chief Photographer's Mate Terry Cosgrove.

assured Pentagon reporters. "Their purpose is to establish a forward base of operations to help pressure the Taliban forces in Afghanistan [and] to prevent Taliban and al Qaeda terrorists from moving freely about the country," he said.[252] The 15th Marine Expeditionary Unit (MEU), Special Forces under Task Force 58, Seabees – the Navy's rapid-response construction crews – and Australian Special Operations Forces all had to move swiftly into the Kandahar airfield now designated Forward Operating Base Rhino. Up to 1,000 Marines would soon be on the ground and preparing for new tasks.

Rumsfeld described their missions the next week. "What they've been doing thus far is providing force protection for a forward operating base and then moving outside of that base for the purpose of being available to interdict lines of communication and roads."[253]

The Marines at Kandahar quickly put dedicated P-3s to good use. P-3 AIP support "provided the eyes in the sky to the ground operations" and gave the task force "time sensitive reactive surveillance...throughout southern Afghanistan." "We know we can rely on the P-3s to quickly react to emerging requirements and changing mission tasking," concluded one Marine.[254] Quick reaction was especially valuable for loitering and re-looks at sites of interest. At a time when ISR assets in general were just beginning to move off their defined mission planning lines, the P-3 was at the forefront of providing the new type of ISR support: persistent, but flexible.

On December 1, Karzai's forces moved forward to a town thirty miles from Kandahar. There, the Taliban put up a fight at a bridge over a dry riverbed. For two days, airstrikes dropped bombs on the Taliban concentration. Amerine's SOF forces got into "a pretty heavy firefight" at one point. "We pushed forward with my guys, bringing in airstrikes as necessary," he recalled.[255]

The next day saw the air component again delivering peak levels of support. It was another major push for the carriers. "We used about 110 strike aircraft, including about 90 tactical aircraft launched from sea-based platforms, 12 to 14 land-based tactical aircraft, and between 8 and 10 long-range bombers," reported Stufflebeem at the Pentagon.[256]

Opposition forces south of Kandahar were also closing in on the city. Stufflebeem released a video of airstrikes hitting Taliban tanks south of Kandahar. What would happen to the Taliban and al Qaeda in the city was uncertain. Some reports suggested that up to 5000 fighters had once manned this last stronghold of the Taliban. Stufflebeem did what he could to clarify the situation. "Southern opposition groups both north and south of the city are consolidating power. These opposition leaders are in contact with some of the Taliban factions and are still negotiating the release of the city to the southern opposition groups," he said on December 2.[257]

Karzai's forces were in position to assault Kandahar itself when an errant bomb killed three of the team and wounded Amerine and several other Americans and Afghans. Karzai had his face cut by shrapnel. Despite the tragedy, the team had done its job. A new team replaced Amerine's, and Karzai's forces approached from the north on December 4.

"We have captured the two districts just north of Kandahar," Karzai announced. [258] Soon this city, long known as the spiritual home of the Taliban, was in Coalition hands.

Strategically, the fall of Kandahar ended the Taliban's political control of Afghanistan. Hamid Karzai would take

The plane captain of this F-14 Tomcat looks for further instructions from her flight deck crew aboard USS Theodore Roosevelt on Dec. 17, 2001. U.S. Navy photo by Chief Photographer's Mate Dennis D. Taylor.

over as interim ruler in Kabul just sixteen days later, on December 20, 2001. Operationally, challenges remained. Many Taliban and al Qaeda had fled. "I think that we have seen anecdotally the instances where there were a lot of Taliban forces in Kandahar, and when they actually capitulated control of Kandahar, there weren't that many forces to be found," Stufflebeem later said during a Pentagon briefing session. "And so you can make a pretty good assumption there that there was some coordination done with individuals who would pay for their escape," he added.[259]

No Lull

As a result, the wave of success did not mean a stand-down for the carriers. The *Theodore Roosevelt* was in the midst of logging 159 days underway, nearly all of them with combat air launches.

The *USS John C. Stennis* was inbound to relieve the *Carl Vinson*. The air wing and crew of the *Stennis* had been getting ready to deploy early since right after September 11. Robb had started the process, and when he left for Tampa, he turned the battlegroup over to Zortman, who would take the *John C. Stennis* to war.

79

An Aviation Boatswain's Mate "Shooter" and a "Trainee" launch an S-3 Viking from the flight deck aboard USS Carl Vinson on Oct. 11, 2001. U. S. Navy Photo by Photographer's Mate 3rd Class Kerryl Cacho.

Stennis was the fifth carrier slated to join the Afghan air war, and Zortman ensured that the battle group took full advantage of training and transit time to prepare. Good satellite connectivity, video teleconferencing and data transfer – all part of the Navy's move to net-centric operations – paid off now in pre-combat preparations. "Our planners were involved in the daily monitoring of the ops and the planning that was going on, so that by the time we arrived in theater, we had been part of the planning process and daily execution monitoring process for three weeks," Zortman said.[260] To Zortman, the missions for the air wing looked like they would be more about armed reconnaissance than traditional close air support. Training emphasized the new tactics developing for Afghanistan, with "a lot of emphasis on disciplined execution." Air wing planners also tried to give aircrews some understanding of the ground maneuver scheme, which was not easy given the number of irregular forces operating in that terrain.

The *Stennis* battle group had two can't-miss port calls to make en route: Hong Kong and Singapore. Hong Kong was an especially important diplomatic gesture that let the People's Republic of China show support for the global war on terrorism. The Chinese government was "not only welcoming, but somewhat insistent" on having *Stennis* stop over in Hong Kong, said Zortman.[261]

Once underway again, the crew was eager to join in the fight. "These guys have sat around for two months with a rage building up inside them," said the CAG, CAPT R.C. Thompson just before *Stennis* departed San Diego on November 12. "Finally, they get the chance to go out and do something about it." "We're much more focused because we know there's a mission out there for us," echoed Marine Captain Jon Ohman, of

VMFA-314, embarked with *Stennis*.[262] "It's not like you want to get revenge, but you want to make sure justice is done," said Lieutenant Mike Croker, an F/A-18 pilot.[263]

The *Stennis* arrived in theater on December 15 and picked up duties as the "night" carrier. *Stennis* was the third ship to tackle the circadian hurdle. That was just fine with Marzano, who was now a lieutenant commander on his fourth operational cruise. Once the aircrews made the adjustment beginning on December 11, being the night carrier had its benefits. According to Marzano, "it actually ended up being the shift that we all appreciated the most because although you launched at night on a lot of these missions, most of them would last upwards of 4 and a half to 6 and a half hours." That meant all but the first launches of a cycle "would typically result in a day trap aboard the ship, which was a lot easier after a long demanding mission, to come back and land on the carrier during the day than it is at night."[264]

Of course, being the night carrier did have its drawbacks. One of them was permanent confusion about the time. "Even right up to the day that we switched back, you could get into a discussion about what shift someone worked, or what times the ship's store was open," said Lieutenant Mike Clapp, an E-2C aviator. "And trying to keep track of what day it was also took a lot of thought. You wake up in the middle of the evening, the date changes, the sun comes up, now go to sleep." On the other hand, he agreed that with the advantage of more daylight traps flying "actually became a little easier."[265]

Sleep experts attested that those working in sunshine on the flight deck right before their late morning bedtimes got a double whammy. Sunlight naturally tried to prod them awake, whereas the carrier's rhythm dictated 1100 was actually bed time for most

After an early morning round of flight operations, an F/A-18 Hornet awaits the next round of combat flight operations aboard the USS John C. Stennis on Dec. 18, 2001. U.S. Navy photo by Photographer's Mate 3rd Class Jayme Pastoric.

A plane captain uses lighted wands to direct the pilot of an E-2C Hawkeye on board the USS Enterprise on Oct. 7, 2001, during Operation Enduring Freedom. DoD photo by Petty Officer 3rd Class Stefanie A. Schap, U.S. Navy.

of the crew. More serious were the dangers of spotting aircraft at night. Limits also had to be placed on drills such as hose handling.[266] Yet the night shift carrier – whichever ship it was – stood out through OEF as one more sign of the flexibility and persistence that was so important to the battle.

TORA BORA

The next major application of carrier airpower was not to take a city but to rain down destruction on a prime al Qaeda strong hold at Tora Bora. Robb characterized this time as a period of transition. Once "the major battles for Kabul, Mazar-i-Sharif, and Kandahar had completed," he said, there was a sense of "okay, what do we do now?"[267]

Osama bin Laden had not been seen in public since around November 10. The hope was that he might be holed up at Tora Bora and vulnerable to an air attack and sweep by Afghan forces on the ground. On November 27, 2001, Franks acknowledged that there was a "very interesting" hunt for leadership going on in "the area between Kabul and Khyber, to include the Jalalabad area and down toward Tora Bora."[268] "General Franks has articulated he believes that the leadership of al Qaeda may be in the area south of Jalalabad, and that's why and where we've been concentrating our efforts there," said Stufflebeem on December 2.

Attack preparations began in late November with stepped-up surveillance on the ground and from air and space platforms. Franks said "we have worked through all of the intelligence capabilities that we and our coalition partners have involved in this effort; we have been able to watch a variety of terrain and undertake review of a whole variety of imagery and talk to an awful lot of people over time," and all signs pointed to paying "very close attention" to Tora Bora.[269]

Speculation on the number of enemy forces at Tora Bora "ranged from a few hundred to a few thousand," said Franks. He had only about 1,300 soldiers, marines and Special Forces in Afghanistan at the time, and they were spread across 17 locations. The Afghans would therefore be the main body of the attack, as they had been in the major battles of November. "It was Afghans who wanted to attack the Tora Bora area," Franks later said. "We had Special Forces troops with those Afghans, to be sure."[270] Blocking escape routes to Pakistan was another major challenge. "It's impossible to seal the border. It's too big. It's traditionally too porous," Stufflebeem explained. However, he said US forces were doing everything they could "to stop those lines of communications that would allow for easy access back and forth."[271] As operations intensified, Pakistan also stationed troops on their western border at prime exfiltration points in an attempt to block al Qaeda and Taliban who might attempt to escape into Pakistan.

SOF and CIA teams worked their way into Tora Bora and began to call in airstrikes.[272] On December 10, 2001, local Afghan time, coalition forces began their attack. CENTCOM's plan called for "an approach up two parallel valleys, with blocking forces at the ends of those valleys." "As the Afghan forces moved to contact, they encountered al Qaeda and residual Taliban elements up in there," Franks recounted. Afghan forces began cave-to-cave searches.[273]

U.S. Marines assigned to the 26th Marine Expeditionary Unit (Special Operations Capable) deploy to an undisclosed location within Afghanistan on Dec. 14, 2001 aboard a CH-46E Sea Knight. U.S. Navy photo by Chief Photographer's Mate Johnny Bivera.

Now the CAOC brought its prime ISR assets to bear to increase the firepower. Among them was Global Hawk, a new Air Force long-endurance UAV which had arrived in theater in mid-November 2001. Global Hawk's new orders from the CAOC were "to go VFR direct straight up to Tora Bora and start taking pictures. That was a complete change," said Air Force Major David Hambleton, one of the Global Hawk liaison officers at the CAOC. The Global Hawk team worked 50 to 100 new targets that night alone and generated a rich feed of SAR and IR data for the waiting strike aircraft.[274]

From November 25 through December 16, the air component dropped over 1600 bombs, most of them precision JDAMs, on the Tora Bora mountain area.[275]

"We have gone into this battle with the intent of eliminating the al Qaeda leadership, eliminating the Taliban leadership, and leaving behind an Afghanistan that is free from terrorists operating in their territory. There is still work to be done in that," said Pace.[276]

Few doubted that some Taliban and al Qaeda were escaping from the fight. "There are multiple routes of ingress and egress," Pace said on December 12, "so it is certainly conceivable that groups of 2, 3, 15, 20 could [be] walking out of there."[277] Control on the Afghan side of the mountains was not watertight. Stufflebeem pointed out that "allegiance can be bought."[278] Pakistani soldiers did capture a total of about 300 fleeing al Qaeda and Taliban.[279]

Osama bin Laden did not turn up during the Tora Bora operation. Reports suggested he might have left Tora Bora on December 16 and crossed the mountains into Pakistan. Ultimately, Rumsfeld insisted reports of bin Laden's presence at Tora Bora were simply "not verifiable."[280]

"A few days ago, we believed that he was in that area," explained Stufflebeem on December 17. Then the intelligence picture faded. The Coalition was now "getting scraps of intelligence from all kinds of sources: open press, interrogation of detainees, people who walk in and provide information, other intelligence-gathering sources." "And now we're not as sure because we don't have the same intensity of the level of traffic for us to monitor" bin Laden's location.[281]

Results from Tora Bora were hard to measure. As Franks later put it, the "pounding we put into that area, the numbers of caves and compound complexes that were closed...make it virtually impossible to know how many were killed." He believed it was "hundreds" and added while he could not say he was satisfied with the operation, he was satisfied with the decisions made to let the Afghans, rather than US forces "go to work in the Tora Bora area."[282]

Rumsfeld was satisfied with the operation but added a note of caution. "I would think that it would be a mistake to say that the al Qaeda is finished in Afghanistan at this stage," he said on December 19, 2001. "They're still in pockets. They're still fighting, in some cases."[283]

"AIRBORNE INSURANCE POLICY"

Aviators aboard the *Theodore Roosevelt* and *John C. Stennis* were well aware of it. On *Stennis*, CAG Thompson said on December 24 "there are still cells of Taliban and al Qaeda on the ground. "I want [Taliban and al Qaeda] always hearing jet noise," he added. "I want them to know if they poke their head out of their cave, they're going to get whacked."[284]

An F-14 Tomcat is launched from the bow catapult of the USS Theodore Roosevelt on Jan. 2, 2002. U.S. Navy photo by Photographer's Mate 2nd Class Jason Scarborough.

Zortman called it an "airborne insurance policy."[285] Taskings changed, and the total number of sorties where strike aircraft dropped bombs diminished after the operational spike of Tora Bora. Mid-January 2002 saw the graph of intensive daily air strikes in OEF taper off to consistently lower levels. Still, the number of Coalition troops on the ground was on the increase and the air component remained their main source of on-call firepower.

The newly arrived aircrews on *Stennis* fell into a rhythm. Lieutenant Eric Taylor was on his first operational cruise with the VF-147 aboard *Stennis*. "We flew once a day if we were doing an OEF mission," Taylor recalled. "Or sometimes twice a day if it was a non-OEF mission, just around the boat" for CAP or training. "You could expect, once every three days, going in country for OEF." Air operations were continuous but weapons employment was intermittent. Even the in-country OEF missions were usually "a lot of time just on station," he said. "We weren't really dropping at that point in time. Tora Bora had pretty much wound down and the B-52s were doing most of the work up there. At that point in time we were just being sent to talk to ground FACs, not really [to] employ anything for the first couple of months."[286]

Each section carried a mix of munitions tailored to give ground controllers the variety needed for targets and weather and to maximize recoverable loads. One strike fighter per section often toted a 2000-lb. JDAM while others carried a typical mix of two GBU-12s, two Mk 82s, plus full guns for all. The air threat was so minimal that the F/A-18s now generally carried just one AIM-9 apiece.

While there was enough going on to keep aircraft on call, the chance to drop bombs came only now and then. As Marzano described it, "it was occurring regularly but by no means was it something you did on every mission. It was maybe every couple days someone would come back and they will have dropped." Marzano himself did not get the chance to employ weapons until March. He and the others flying repeated strike missions "were just there to support on a case by case basis if [ground controllers] needed a little bit of CAS, here and there," he said.[287]

The long missions and frequent tanking from a variety of Coalition aircraft continued to be a challenge. "I had no experience with big-wing tanking prior to this," acknowledged Taylor. Like others before him, it went smoothly enough, but he remembered the feeling of searching for tankers in the weather then joining up and tanking "in the goo" with "turbulence and everything else."

Now and then the Coalition aircraft brought happy surprises. "The British were the greatest," said Taylor. Pilots recalled that they often made a special effort "to drag you down south to get you closer to the aircraft carrier with more gas, or they would come and meet you somewhere...and drag you wherever you wanted to go while you were getting gas." That wasn't all the British tanker crews had to offer – especially if it was "a slow day over Afghanistan." On one mission with Marzano as his lead, Taylor joined up on a British tanker "and basically hung out on their wing." To pass the time the F/A-18 pilots played "the British version of 'Who Wants to Be a Millionaire?'" over the tanker's boom frequency. "We got to ask the flight engineer and polled the flight deck crew on any questions we weren't too certain about," he said.[288]

"THE *JACK* IS BACK"

Even with occasional slow days the pace of operations in OEF was approaching record levels. By January 17, 2002, the *Theodore Roosevelt* had been at sea for 122 days straight. The crew was holding up well. "You didn't see a big morale problem," reported Fitzgerald. "I spent a lot of time roaming around the carrier," he said, "and I never saw that [fatigue] set in, which was very surprising. I'd been on other cruises that were not nearly as long where mid-cruise you start to have fistfights on the ship and you start to see tempers flaring. This operation had none of that." The carriers got constant visits from newspaper reporters and celebrities that left the crew in no doubt as to how important the mission was. "They're seeing themselves on CNN constantly," remarked Fitzgerald. It was part of "an esprit de corps that kept everybody going."[289]

That esprit de corps of the *Roosevelt* crew would be vital for many more weeks. On January 15, 2002, the Navy announced that their scheduled replacement, the *USS John F. Kennedy*, would not deploy on time. Carrier rotation became a major issue when *Kennedy* failed an INSURV inspection held December 2-7, 2001. The Navy Board of Inspection and Survey conducting the exercise found major problems with ship systems from its main engines to its catapults and fire-fighting systems.[290] *Kennedy* had been the first carrier to surge after Iraq invaded Kuwait in August 1990 but since that time, the ship had spent years in a partial reserve status without full funding or standard deployments. *Kennedy* was now back as part of the main fleet yet the period had taken its toll.

The ship's troubles could not have come at a stickier time. Plans called for *Kennedy* to leave two months early, in mid-January, to relieve *Roosevelt*, much as *Stennis* had done for *Vinson* the month before. *Kennedy*'s commanding officer was relieved and the crew took on extra work over the holidays under the guidance of Captain Johnny "Turk" Green, who stepped in as temporary commanding officer.

On February 13, Captain Ronald H. Henderson took command of *Kennedy* as the ship headed for war. Green summed up the crew's achievements as he handed over command. "Look at this," he said. "The *Jack* is back."[291]

LOOKING BACK

"There have been battles fought in Afghanistan for centuries," pointed out retired Vice Admiral Arthur Cebrowski, who was serving as Director of the Pentagon's Office of Force Transformation. "I don't think any of them have seen the speed, results, and the speed of effect that we have here."

For carrier aviation, the impact came in several areas.

First was the unique ability of the carriers to establish air superiority over Afghanistan and so permit other operations – from SOF insertions to humanitarian relief airdrops – to proceed quickly.

Second was the effect on the Northern Alliance. Given the time it took to set up SOF operations and the worry it caused Franks in early October, a delay in marshalling airpower would have been intolerable. Fortunately the carriers could ensure there would be no gap in bringing flexible firepower to bear. That gave the Northern Alliance a quick tutorial in precision airpower and what it could do for them. "I really think that things could have gone otherwise for the Northern Alliance. It was, as much as anything else, a psychological thing – how much can you support us? How much are you going to be there? And I think they realized we really were there," Cryer said later.[292]

The Northern Alliance was neither a cohesive nor an effective military force on September 11, 2001. Nor did they have the ability to take on Taliban forces that outnumbered them by 2-to-1. The success of Operation Enduring Freedom was a long shot until persistent airpower got added to the mix. All the money in the world could not have broken the trench lines at Kabul or protected opposition forces from counterattacks en route to Kandahar. That was a job for the air component. "It was amazing to see the carrier aviation come in and do what it did," said Cryer. He remembered setting up a strike on a field of moving Taliban tanks, agonizing about whether they were going to get away. "And then we had F/A-18s that came out [and] *boom*, I mean, we just watched this tank field start exploding as these guys handled each one of the targets."[293]

Cryer noted how crucial the timing of early carrier operations was. "There was no possible way that we would have seen the [speed], in fact we may not have ever gotten a victory in Afghanistan the way we did if we weren't able to act as quickly as we did."[294]

Third, the carrier aircrews proved that they could form the flexible backbone of joint air component operations. During an after-action briefing with Admiral Clark, Cryer told the CNO that from his perspective at the CAOC it was the "phenomenal team effort" that stood out in his mind. "I said, this is not about...how phenomenally great the Navy is and much better than the Air Force. But the fact that we really are starting to get it in terms of the joint force." The integrated joint operations extended from command center to cockpit. Both pilots and controllers learned new ways of doing their jobs. "In this war, we're all adapting," said Wright. "Everybody has had to throw out the parochial thinking that they may have come in with."[295]

An EA-6B Prowler lands aboard USS Theodore Roosevelt on Dec. 18, 2001. U.S. Navy photo by Photographer's Mate 3rd Class Luke Williams.

The airwings had made superb use of their organic assets – EA-6Bs, S-3s and E-2s – to extend combat reach into southern parts of Afghanistan. As a result, in Afghanistan, the Navy proved it could supply the air combat muscle and augment the joint team's supporting architecture for the air war.

Fourth was the lesson of persistence. "This was a completely different requirement" for carrier aviation, said Robb. Operation Enduring Freedom in 2001 was never a large-scale air war. Daily strike counts averaged between 50 and 100 sorties. The total sortie count from October 7, 2001 through the defeat of the Taliban in December was half of the tally for the 78-day Operation Allied Force in 1999, and nowhere near the massive effort of the Gulf War in 1991. Yet the measure of effectiveness in this campaign was not the total numbers of sorties – it was the persistent coverage of naval strike aircraft over the battlespace. Having strike aircraft with different weapons made it possible for the CAOC to run TSTs and supply ground controllers with LGB or JDAM strike options.

Robb bluntly summarized the impact on the aircrews. "It's not like you're going to take off, go drop a bomb, come back. You're going to take off, go stay a long time, live in the battlespace, maybe not drop your bomb, maybe, maybe not," he said. Aimpoints struck was not the main metric. The mission's value rested on "whether or not you could be on call." To him it was a "pretty big difference" from the alpha strikes of the 1970s, 1980s and 1990s.[296]

With all the new lessons came some old ones, too. This new war contained at least a few lessons that would have been just as familiar in the Marianas in 1944 or in Libya in 1986 or in Desert Storm in 1991. "Everything said and done, the most challenging thing that we ever do is to try to come back and land on the ship, especially at night," reiterated Marzano.[297]

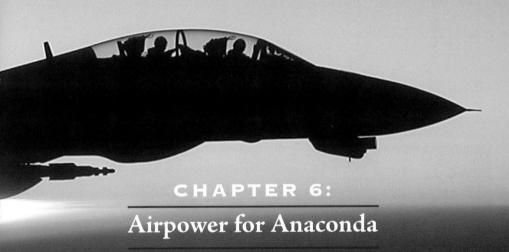

CHAPTER 6:

Airpower for Anaconda

"Thank goodness for the bravery of those soldiers that we were able to take the fight to the enemy and be successful here." – General Richard Myers, CJCS, March 10, 2002

"The snow will be gone from the mountain passes soon," Franks briefed President Bush and the National Security Council on February 7, 2002. "And we will go in from several directions on the ground while simultaneously inserting air assault forces into the objective."

An F-14 Tomcat conducts a mission over Afghanistan in support of Operation Enduring Freedom on Aug. 8, 2002. U.S. Navy photo by Capt. Dana Potts.

The objective Franks was talking about was a "remaining al Qaeda redoubt in the mountains south of Kabul"[298] in the Shahi Kot Valley.

For now, the brief mention of impending operations was part of an Afghanistan update before Franks turned to this high-level meeting's true purpose: reviewing preliminary thinking on a campaign plan for Iraq.

Within days that assault plan would take on the name Operation Anaconda and turn into the biggest conventional land battle waged by US forces during Operation Enduring Freedom. From March 2-16, 2002, just over two thousand American military forces on the ground engaged in prolonged and bloody combat in extremely difficult mountain terrain. Eight American Special Forces died in Operation Anaconda and 80 soldiers were wounded.[299] The light forces were inserted without their own artillery. Their supporting Apache helicopters suffered so much battle damage on the first day that all but two of them were temporarily out of commission. Any help these soldiers received would come from their own tactical ingenuity and above all, from the JDAMs, LGBs and Mk 82s of the joint air component. More than thirty SOF controllers, Army controllers and Coalition special forces air controllers were calling in strikes in a battle area that averaged less than 64 square miles: "not much more than the size of North Island," as Zortman said.[300]

In this crisis it was the two carriers off Pakistan that provided the bulk of the fighter sorties – an average of about 32 strike sorties per day penetrating deep into eastern Afghanistan.

Operation Anaconda was the final exam: the biggest test of battle for the ability of the carriers to provide sustained airpower in Afghanistan.

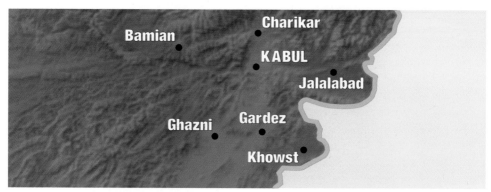

Map of Afghanistan, Khowst-Gardez region.

THE KHOWST-GARDEZ REGION

The Khowst-Gardez region was a natural collection point for al Qaeda fighters and Taliban remnants moving south from Kabul in the fall and winter. Khowst province jutted 50 miles east into Pakistan. Its capital city of Khowst, a relatively flat watershed with three main roads, gave easy access to the border, and the large refugee camps filled with Afghan nationals. Western neighbor Gardez, in Paktia province, lay 75 miles south of Kabul and was the intersection point for all major roads leading south from the capital.

About 15 miles south of the city a series of foothills ranging up to 10,000 feet formed the Shahi Kot Valley – the focus of Operation Anaconda. Villages there were reported to be sympathetic to the Taliban.

It quickly caught CENTCOM's eye. On January 1, 2002, a threat estimate from CENTCOM moved the Khowst-Gardez region up the list of remaining major concentrations of Taliban and al Qaeda. According to this assessment, there might be hundreds clustered in the Khowst-Gardez region.

SOF teams began to keep closer tabs on the situation.[301] In early February, they also drafted an initial plan for operations to clear out the Khowst-Gardez region. The al Qaeda and Taliban "started to get together in a place where they could have enough mass to be effective," Myers said of the situation. "And we've been following that, allowing it to develop until we thought it was the proper time to strike."[302] With luck the al Qaeda cluster might even include bin Laden or those close to him. At any rate, the numbers alone made it a compelling target for operations. Some estimates put the number of "foreign fighters" in Khowst-Gardez at up to 1000.

That number became a pivot point as plans for the Operation Anaconda developed fast in the period from early to mid-February 2002.

Component coordination problems also reared their heads. SOF planners handed off overall execution of the plan to Task Force Mountain, composed of 10th Mountain Division soldiers at Karshi Karnabad. The plan was briefed to the 10th Mountain Division Commander, Major General Buster Hagenback, and his boss, the CFLCC, Lieutenant General Paul T. Mikolashek, on February 17, 2002. Three days later Task Force Mountain signed out an order calling for Operation Anaconda to commence at the end of the month.

"Anaconda was probably the first major conventional action we took in Afghanistan," recalled Robb.[303] SOF teams – from the United States and six other nations including Australia – would be in position on several ridgelines around the valley and at other key points in the mountains. One Afghan force of a few hundred under the command of Zia Lodin was to move into the Shahi Kot Valley from the north. Two other Afghan forces under the commanders Zakim Khan and Kamil Khan would block southern exit routes leading to Pakistan. Helicopters would then insert teams of soldiers from the 10th Mountain Division and the 101st Airborne Division into the Shahi Kot Valley to take up several blocking positions on the mountain slopes above the three villages of Marzak, Sirkankheyl and Babukheyl, designated Objective Remington. According to the plan, al Qaeda and Taliban forces would be trapped between the Afghan forces and the US soldiers manning the blocking points who "could put a fishnet around all four sides," said one officer involved in the planning.[304] After that, it would take just a few days to round them up. Decisive combat operations should be over in 72 hours.

"We knew for some period of time that there was planning for an ongoing operation" in the Khowst-Gardez area, recalled Zortman, on station with *Stennis*. For some reason, no one gave the air component formal notification of Operation Anaconda until late February. Zortman described it as "a real reluctance on the part of the ground component commander to involve the air component commanders in the planning."[305]

"I believe there was a body of effort ongoing at Bagram that did not inform CFLCC and that planning effort at Bagram therefore did not inform the Battlefield Coordination Detachment (BCD), so there was no formal vehicle for the movement of that information into the CAOC or to us to plan," Moseley, the air component commander, later said.[306]

What caused the slip? The land component was flowing more conventional forces into Afghanistan and Hagenback was in the midst of transferring his headquarters from Karshi Karnabad to Bagram. "Anaconda happened right at the point at which this flow was beginning," said Robb from his vantage point at CENTCOM.

But the operation was far from risk-free. As Robb pointed out, "the operation was right on the edge of the logistical envelope. The assault itself had to bring in all the helicopters that were being used by air and then all the fuel that they were going to use had to be brought in by air and we were bringing in bags to put the fuel in at Bagram. We only had about 80,000 gallons on the field," he said, not enough to support the full assault. C-17s wet-winged in more, landing at Bagram, off-loading fuel into the bladders, then taking off to transfer more fuel from waiting tankers overhead and repeat the process.

Also, the plan was "really air assault with no artillery," said Robb. "Everything you bring in you got to bring in on helicopter. We're at 14,000 feet." 155 mms were out of the question and "that's going to mean that most of the artillery-like effects have to come from the air," Robb said. "Plus the precision of the airpower...was pretty appealing," he added.[307]

Logistics, air-to-ground coordination, planning to optimize JDAM: as Robb characterized it, "Anaconda was kind of a reach in all those areas in terms of being essentially the artillery of the ground assault from the air, which is something we're going to do more and more of, [and] doing preplanned strikes in a small number. But then having this large volume CAS environment where you're going to be called on to bring to bear a large number of weapons in a very tight space, [with] very complicated C2."[308]

For Operation Anaconda, Task Force Mountain – Hagenback's force – was going to have a whole lot more forces engaged on the ground than ever before in the Afghanistan war. It made for a series of unknowns. In a way, Nichols pointed out, the previous months of keeping packages in the air to respond to three or four parallel, but uncoordinated SOF fights at a time "also set us up for Anaconda." What had "evolved really was an inefficient use of airpower" caused in part by the lack of an integrated planning process of what the SOF guys were going to do" and in part by "the fluidity of the battlefield, which was not necessarily predictable." At times that meant "we were struggling like hell in the CAOC to keep up with all that, and make sure that they got the right capability in the right place and time. Generally, they did," he said.[309]

If Operation Anaconda was as swift and simple as TF Mountain's operations order said it would be, the system still might work.

That was not to be. Somewhere in the planning process, a serious flaw crept in. The final ground plan significantly underestimated the size of the enemy force they would face and guessed wrong about the most likely enemy courses of action. Among

Flight deck crewmembers look on as an F/A-18 Hornet readies for launch from the flight deck of USS Theodore Roosevelt on Jan. 7, 2002. U.S. Navy photo by Photographer's Mate 3rd Class James K. McNeil.

the forces lying in wait were well-equipped Arab and Chechen al Qaeda with crew-served weapons, sniper rifles, and mortars. Most important, CENTCOM estimates continued to peg the number at several hundred or a thousand *in the Khowst-Gardez region*. Hagenback's order placed the number of enemy at 125-200 *in the Shahi Kot Valley*. TF Mountain had for some reason narrowed its focus to counting enemy fighters in a smaller geographic area. A year later Hagenback would admit: "we only probably had about 50% of the intelligence right – locations, and more importantly, the enemy's intent, which was to stand and fight."[310]

For now, instead of a seven-to-one overmatch of US to al Qaeda and Taliban the battle would be nearly even – and the al Qaeda and Taliban already held the best terrain.

COMPONENT COORDINATION

An equally serious problem was brewing at the operational level. The land component had not coordinated plans for Operation Anaconda with the air component. At the CAOC, the 126-slide OPORD from the Joint Operations Center for Task Force Mountain at Bagram came as a surprise to senior leadership. Staff in the CAOC's BCD used the slides to brief their airmen counterparts on Febraury 21, 2002. Guidance for the air component was minimal: provide CAS, conduct resupply missions, dedicate intra-theater airlift to build up Bagram. Air Force Major General John Corley, the CAOC Director, first learned of Operation Anaconda during a routine conference on February 22. "I was horrified to discover that by the time I

had been briefed, the OPORD had already been published without what I thought was the CFACC's knowledge," he later said. Moseley was traveling in the region and did not get back to the CAOC for his first formal brief on Operation Anaconda until February 25.[311]

By then, CAOC staff had already begun routine planning. One topic was the possible gap as the *Theodore Roosevelt* handed off to the *John F. Kennedy*. If necessary, the CAOC could request more bombers to plug the hole. The CAOC was rightly confident that it could supply plenty of Navy strike fighters and a total of about 60 strikes per day from the sea and land-based aircraft in the region.[312]

What to do with them was another matter. Airpower, OEF-style, was used to much more elbow room. The Operation Anaconda area was tighter than anything yet seen on the 21st Century battlefield. For example, in 1991, a 30 nm by 30 nm killbox in Desert Storm was controlled by one airborne FAC. For Operation Anaconda, thirty or more Coalition SOF, US SOF and TF Mountain controllers would be working in the 8 nm by 8 nm box less than one-tenth the size of a standard killbox. They would also be dealing with mountains and valleys that caused line-of-sight visual and communications glitches.

TF Mountain's conventional land forces, which were relatively new to the theater, appeared to be all but unaware of the problem. The 18 special operations teams taking part in Operation Anaconda had highly-trained and well-equipped controllers, and the CAOC and the SOF teams had honed their cooperation in Operation Enduring Freedom. The SOF teams would be with the Afghan forces and in other strategic overlook locations. TF Mountain was also sending in a dozen or more tactical air control parties with the teams seizing blocking positions above Objective Remington. They were not all equipped with the latest gear or training, a worry to the air component. The success of close air support for Operation Anaconda would depend not only on delivering sorties but on funneling them into an extremely tight battlespace.

The plan was briefed to General Franks on February 26 during a video teleconference. "Love it," he told his commanders. Commanders who were present for the conference discussed their outstanding concerns, but the intent to wrap it up in three days categorized Operation Anaconda as a relatively low-risk undertaking. Before Franks signed off he prodded them to be sure to work closely together.[313] Bad weather slipped the start date to March 2, 2002.

Airlift requirements, fuel for Army helicopters staging the operation out of Bagram, close air support procedures, pre-strike targeting and other essential items of support were left to the very last minute. Some requirements were never formally defined. Moseley had the air component "scrambling just to figure out how to get the airplanes into the airspace" over the Shahi Kot Valley so they could deliver on-call firepower to the lightly-equipped ground forces.[314] Also, there was not enough information available from TF Mountain to put together a "collection deck" and get the full benefit of scans by ISR assets before the operation. That was a particular loss, since thorough mapping with infrared sensors might have given a better reading of the true numbers of al Qaeda lying in wait. Advance preparation was minimal. Less than ten fixed targets were approved for airstrikes prior to Operation Anaconda.

IN THE DARK

The carriers were in the dark on the impending operation. "We knew the Army was going to kick up something, but nobody really knew anything of what was going on for Anaconda," recalled Taylor aboard *Stennis*. He pointed out one of the crucial differences that would affect Operation Anaconda. "The Army had just taken over in theater from the Marines," Taylor said of this time. "The Marines were pretty good about informing everybody of what operations they had so that we could support that. But the Army basically tried to operate on their own. And from that we had no forewarning except for the fact that they were starting a big offensive. That was it."[315]

For Fitzgerald, who was getting ready to take the *Theodore Roosevelt* home, there was little indication of a major battle in the offing or what his airwing needed to do to prepare. "We

An S-3 Viking is readied for launch from catapult number two on the flight deck of the USS John C. Stennis on Mar. 22, 2002. U.S. Navy photo by Photographer's Mate 3rd Class Jayme T. Pastoric.

didn't have a clue what they were going to do," he said. They "knew Anaconda was coming, but we had no clear idea of specifically where, we knew it was up in the Tora Bora area, but that was about all we knew. We didn't know what their scheme of maneuver was; we didn't know how many people they were putting in there." There was "no definition of how this is going to work. The comm plan was 'well, *talk to your FAC on a normal frequency.*' It was a typical SOF operation where they plan it in a vacuum, they get it all self-contained, and when we get in extremis we'll call in the other guys. It was not an integrated operation by any means."[316]

Officers at the CAOC discussed the potential carrier gap as planning for Operation Anaconda unfolded but ultimately they made no changes to the carriers' schedules. There was no sense of urgency and no call from high levels for a massing of airpower. On *Stennis*, Captain McDonnell had already told his crew on February 18 that they were most likely staying past their projected six-month point. "We haven't been ordered to do that, and nothing has been approved, but this is my best guess," McDonell said publicly on February 25. "My personal assessment is that the requirement is not going to diminish," he added.[317]

In the end, the *Theodore Roosevelt* made its scheduled port call in Bahrain on February 28 after 159 consecutive days at sea then returned to station. *John F. Kennedy* stopped in Souda Bay that same day on the way to the North Arabian Sea.

With *Kennedy* due, the crew of *Stennis* gave up nights and planned the switch back to day operations for March 2, 2002. They had already "offered to up the sortie count" said Zortman and been told "that was not necessary."[318] CENTCOM raised no objection when *Stennis* took herself out of the action for the first day of the operation.

"Oddly enough, the first day Anaconda kicked off our ship had a no-fly day," said Marzano. To help the crew switch back to a daylight schedule *Stennis* showed movies and shut down the flight deck for the barbecue and games of a "steel beach picnic" on March 2. Word came in "that there was a lot of action going on, guys are getting shot at, and there was a lot of frustration on the carrier, well why are we having a picnic today," said Marzano. It was a sign of how poor the land component's pre-Anaconda coordination with the air component had been. "So obviously the coordination wasn't there at that level," he continued, "although they had other assets that were able to support. There was another carrier out there. There were also obviously ground-based bombers that could help. So it's not like we're the only show in town. But when you're up there you want to help out and participate as much as you can." For the *Stennis* pilots, "the first day was a no go."

OPERATION ANACONDA BEGINS

Operation Anaconda began the morning of March 2 and hit trouble right away. Trucks carrying Zia Lodin's 450 Afghan troops plus US and Coalition Special Forces toward the Shahi Kot Valley took the lead. Suddenly the convoy came under heavy fire. One American soldier was killed by an off-target AC-130 gunship, although at the time, all present thought they had been hit by al Qaeda mortar rounds. Lodin's attack stalled.

Soldiers air-assaulting in on the ridgeline blocking points from the CH-47 Chinook helicopters came under fire at once. Al Qaeda were positioned above and around them in numbers far greater than predicted. Some sheltered in the cave system while

Soldiers from Bravo Company, 101st Airborne Division (Air Assault), prepare to move out after being dropped off by a CH-47 Chinook helicopter in the battle zone in eastern Afghanistan during Operation Anaconda. U.S. Army Photo by Sgt. Keith D. McGrew.

others occupied prepared positions on the mountain ridges. As Coalition forces later found, the strongpoints were well supplied with weapons brought in over the preceding months.

"They were supposed to be the blocking force," one senior official later said. "And all of a sudden, they found themselves at the bottom of a valley with fire raining down on them from these guys in entrenched positions on a mountainside. They [al Qaeda] basically had them pinned down for 18 hours."[319] South of Sirkankel, a small detachment from the 101st Airborne also met fierce opposition. Their commander, Colonel Frank Wiercinski, said, "We survived three mortar barrages during the day and at one point we had nine or ten al Qaeda coming to do us, but instead, we did them."[320]

Apache helicopters joined the fray, taking multiple hits from RPGs and small arms. They limped back to Bagram with battle damage so heavy that six of the eight were not combat-ready by the end of the day. An immediate request went out for Marines on the USS *Bonhomme Richard* to send five AH-1 Cobras to TF Mountain for the fight.

Command Sergeant Major Frank Grippe – who was later wounded by shrapnel – described the first day of the fight. "We just kept the enemy fixed all day and kept the CAS [close air support] coming, and any time we could actually visibly see a target, we'd eliminate that al Qaeda element," he said.[321]

Throughout the day air controllers flooded the command cell at Bagram with requests for airstrikes. Fighters and bombers held in tracks offset a few miles from the battlefield while the CAOC directed them onto targets in sequence. Major Pete Donnelly, an Air Liaison Officer with the 10th Mountain Division, was with the small air support cell at Bagram, struggling to track and prioritize the ground controllers' requests. "It was nuts," he said of the activity the first day. "It was non-stop and it went for about 24 hours. A lot of our guys, the ones who hit *Ginger*, were in close combat for about 18 hours. We pushed them everything we had."[322]

It would take every ounce of persistence to support the deteriorating ground battle. On day one of Operation Anaconda, the precision weapons (JDAM and GBU-12s) delivered for immediate CAS averaged out to over six bombs per hour, or one every ten minutes. Actual drops ebbed and flowed with the ground situation but continued day and night. Afternoon was the peak time with 64 precision weapons released by bombers and fighters from 1300 to 1800 local time. The situation was so desperate that controllers called on two F/A-18Cs from the *Theodore Roosevelt*, Scarface 73 and 74, to strafe enemy firing positions, making three passes and delivering 400 rounds of 20mm cannon apiece just as darkness closed in. That night, AC-130 gunships attacked targets with 40mm and 105mm guns and passed coordinates onto other strikers.[323]

A pilot and radar interceptor operator (RIO) sit in an F-14 Tomcat aboard the USS Theodore Roosevelt on Mar. 1, 2002 awaiting instructions from the flight deck crew to move into position for launch, while an F/A-18 Hornet strike fighter approaches the ship for an arresting landing after returning from a mission. Navy photo by Photographer's Mate 3rd Class Stacey Hines.

"No plan ever survives the first encounter with the enemy," one senior officer commented, "and this plan changed 180 degrees."[324] It took concentrated airpower and smart tactical decisions by the soldiers on the ground to hang on.

As in the opening days of Operation Enduring Freedom it was the F-14s and F/A-18s from the carriers providing the bulk of the sorties. "As Anaconda cranked up we increased sorties to what the tanker flow would support," said Zortman. By "about the third or fourth day... we couldn't push more up there because the tankers were pretty much maxed out."[325] Operation Anaconda tested the persistence of the carriers to the limit. Flying a 1+30 cycle gave strike fighters about a four and a half-hour mission. That meant just 30-45 minutes over the target area. A six-hour mission carved out two "vul" periods for strike fighters to work with ground FACs, Predator pilots or AWACS and JSTARS to prosecute targets.

The air component made some immediate changes. "Day one or day two, I'm not happy now with what we're seeing," Moseley recalled. Moseley and Mikolashek quickly conferred on areas of mutual concern, including the "absolute requirement" for better target ID and target coordinates, generating additional strike targets, prioritizing CAS, and the problems caused because not all GFACs had the equipment to determine precise target coordinates. CJTF Mountain extricated teams in grave trouble, and then committed the theater reserve to beef up blocking positions.

For fifteen days the air component became Operation Anaconda's steady source of firepower. Navy strike sorties were at the center of the battle.

Marzano thought he'd log his first bomb-dropping mission the day after the *Stennis* steel beach picnic, on March 3. But it was not to be. Like others flying the first emergency close air support missions, getting clearance to drop during the time on station was difficult. "There was a lot of chaos down there those first few days of Anaconda," he said. "The initial plan that they had constructed for the grid system overhead the target area for organizing the flow of aircraft in and out was somewhat disorganized and it was hard to work the target area and deconflict with other aircraft out there."[326]

Ground FACs wanted air drops but procedures made it difficult to brief pilots on the targets before their vul periods ended. The confusion cost Marzano a chance to drop during the vul period for his first three missions. His F/A-18 was loaded with GBU-12s and Mk 82s – an ideal mix for the requirements of Operation Anaconda, which saw heavy use of both. On this day, however, the "FAC we were talking to was not able to clearly convey the target that he wanted us to hit." Marzano encountered just what Moseley worried about: uneven training and equipment among the FACs. Combat congestion in the airspace provided another shock. The "thing that sticks out most in my mind on that mission is we had a fairly close pass with a B-1 that went directly underneath us and dropped a string of bombs down the whole Whaleback [mountain] right where we thought we were the only ones in the target area," said Marzano. At that moment "I realized alright, this is not organized the way I thought it was and we're going to really have to kind of keep our head on the swivel and play a little more defense out there."[327]

One of the biggest challenges was preventing mid-air collisions. The Operation Anaconda battlespace was "a pretty small piece of sky," said Robb. The air planners had "the challenge of getting air into that battlespace stacked up with enough volume to respond to the effects...with enough ground FACs to coordinate those effects."[328]

The CAOC shared his concerns. At times the CAOC had "B-52s at higher altitudes dropping JDAMs; B-1s at lower altitudes; unmanned vehicles such as Predator flying through there; P-3s, aircraft contributing to the ISR assets; helicopters down at the ground; fast-moving aircraft, F-14s, F/A-18s, F-16s, F-15Es; tanker aircraft that are flying through there. So you begin to see and sense the degree of difficulty of deconfliction," Corley explained.[329] High above it all, added Moseley, "we had three civil air routes opened up," for Afghan airliners flying Muslim pilgrims to Saudi Arabia for the Haj.[330] The air component was also lifting all the Army's fuel, ammunition, cargo and personnel into Bagram. "We gathered up every available flying resource that we could in that part of the world," said Corley, including some of the Vice President's C-17s being used for his trip to the region and Marine KC-130s.[331]

The CAOC had a steady supply of strike aircraft all during Operation Anaconda. With the carriers, now including *Kennedy*, leading the way, supplying thirty or more strike sorties per day was not a problem even with the distances and mission times involved. Directing the combat aircraft traffic was still the limiting factor. On March 5, Marzano and Taylor launched from *Stennis* as the sun was setting. It was dark by the time they reached the battle area. On this occasion, AWACS put them in contact with a Predator UAV – or rather, with its pilots on the ground in the Gulf region.

The two Hornet pilots were already very familiar with Predator because they constantly had to watch out for it. "Initially, the Predators were flying about the same altitude that we were so sometimes you'd have fairly close passes with the Predator," Marzano said. Soon the F/A-18s and Predator were assigned different altitude blocks. But the pilots knew it was out there and they had to be on the lookout for it – especially when they had to roll in on a target and "be descending through multiple altitudes." They "always had to kind of keep track of where the Predator was so you could avoid it."

Predator nonetheless became a great favorite with the strike pilots because it found them targets. Predators snaked up valleys and ravines to find al Qaeda vehicles and personnel where controllers on the ground might not be able to see them. Predator flew courtesy of a constant satellite feed, and voice communications amongst the UAV, the strike pilots, AWACS, the CAOC and even Tampa flowed easily. For Marzano and Taylor on this mission, the problem was that Predator was already busy feeding "an A-10 monopolizing the area," Marzano quipped. The Predator pilots were describing their craft's view of the target area to the A-10 with Marzano and Taylor listening in as the Predator tagged targets via infrared. They were next in line to strike, but soon had to break off and return to the carrier.[332]

A flight deck director helps guide an S-3 Viking into launch position on the flight deck aboard the USS Theodore Roosevelt on Jan. 7, 2002. U.S. Navy photo by Photographer's Mate 3rd Class James K. McNeil.

Deconfliction and the potential for hitting friendlies forced the discipline. "They made some really good decisions about when not to drop," Zortman said of the aircrews in the overall Anaconda effort.[333]

Mission three on March 6 "was probably my most memorable non-drop mission," remembered Marzano. The "plan was for the first time ever to drag two JDAM up there, the 2000-lb. variant. That was a non-recoverable load. So we knew that going up there that we had to get rid of these, and it was also very heavy and draggy to drag all the way up there and then bring all the way back home. It was a fairly long mission, six and a half hours, and the weather was actually fairly bad that night, too."[334]

Mission planners had guaranteed them they had pre-determined coordinates ready and waiting for the big JDAM. Deconfliction again ruined the deal. "Right as we're approaching the target, just moments from release, we got an abort call," he said. Either a B-52 or a B-1 was "coming in at the same time and they had to deconflict so they broke us off, [and] let the bomber come in," he continued. After orbiting another 15 minutes with the JDAM primed, AWACS told them to break off and hit the tanker, where they were sent back to the ship. It was just too tough to coordinate with other assets coming in. "So after all that effort and a lot of planning," Marzano said, "we had to transit all the way back home."

The adventure was not over. The target area delay put the mission behind schedule and one of the tankers had already started its return to base. "We're running low on gas, it's bad weather, night time, and we're in the middle of Afghanistan here behind the time line," said Marzano.

"Fortunately we were able to get them up on the frequency there and my flight lead joked around that there'd be an air medal in it if the pilot of the tanker would come back and get us," he said. The tanker obligingly hooked back around north and they "plugged in with just barely enough gas to divert if we had to do it." Feet wet, they still had to drop a JDAM apiece into a pre-briefed box over the sea to get under the weight required to recover. Free of the unused JDAM, Marzano still was not in the clear as his mission neared the seven-hour point. The "aircraft that was ahead of me got stuck on the wires on the boat, so they had to wave me off for a foul deck," Marzano said. He departed to take on "another 1000 pounds [of fuel] off an S-3 and then come back around" for the landing.

Back on deck he marveled at the twists and turns of the mission. "My wingman wrote a big long point paper on the frustration that he experienced after that one," Marzano finished.[335]

Each of Marzano's no-drop missions illustrated the main features of Operation Anaconda. First, for all its complications, persistence was working. The airwings had months of OEF experience behind them and they knew how to smoothly generate sorties and meet the CAOC's requirements for constant coverage. Hard as it was for the ground controllers to direct the strike aircraft, they were never lacking in airborne firepower. Bombs available outnumbered targets. When one section of aircraft left for fuel, others were ready for tasking. With the carriers providing an average of over 30 sorties per day "I was always excess to need" in terms of sorties available, said Corley at the CAOC.[336]

TRAGEDY AT TAKUR GAR

Still, there were times when controllers used every bomb and bullet available. One of those came a few days into Operation Anaconda during the tragedy at Takur Gar on March 4. Seven Americans were killed in the course of a failed helicopter insertion and aborted rescue missions that stranded 38 on the ground, under intense enemy fire, for over 15 hours.

The ridge at Takur Gar commanded a view of the entire Shahi Kot valley. Below it was Objective Ginger, the southernmost and last of the original blocking positions still not in US hands. Special Forces had been on top the ridge to help with airstrikes and reconnaissance but a team exfiltrated along with part of the 101st Airborne troops' command post when fighting got too hot on the first day. Objective Ginger was still not in US hands and commanders needed a SOF team to return to the area before the next push to take the southern blocking point.

A U.S. Army soldier with 1st Battalion, 187th Infantry Regiment, 101st Airborne Division (Air Assault), mans a .50-caliber machine gun in the Shahi Kot mountain range during a battle in Operation Anaconda. U.S. Army photo by Spc. David Marck Jr., 314th Press Camp Headquarters.

A team tried the reinsertion in the early morning hours of March 4, 2002. But on Takur Gar's shaded side, new snow masked hardened sites where al Qaeda fighters were ready to put up deadly resistance. They hit one helicopter through the hydraulic lines, forcing it to lift off hastily. A Navy SEAL, Petty Officer Neil C. Roberts, fell from the back of the helicopter and later died of a bullet wound while fighting on the ground. The damaged helicopter crash-landed 7 kilometers away, while a second helicopter picked up the team and took them back to save Roberts. The team "dropped much of their equipment to lighten them up" and returned to a landing site just below the ridge "taking just their combat gear and additional ammunition," said the military official who studied the battle for Franks.[337]

An Army Ranger quick reaction unit from Bagram Air Base sent two helicopters with combat search and rescue specialists and rangers to aid the trapped team. One CH-47 landed "about 50 meters from that bunker at the top" as an RPG took off the rear rotor, dropping the Chinook onto the mountain. Another RPG killed the right-side gunner. Four died instantly, and several more were wounded. Surviving aircrew and soldiers set up defensive positions 150 feet from one of the snow-concealed bunkers.

Until the teams were extracted that night at around 2000 hours, all they had to rely on was their own will to survive and a steady stream of close air support to keep al Qaeda pinned. Their ground FAC, codenamed Slick 01, later estimated he controlled about 30 close air support sorties throughout the day.

The experience of a division of F/A-18s that arrived around dusk illustrated it well. The first section of F/A-18s under ground FAC control dropped five GBU-12s on three targets, one as close as 200 meters east of the friendly position on Takur Gar. The other two F/A-18s contacted the ground FAC, then the Predator, then yet another ground controller while holding overhead the crash site, but did not receive any tasking to drop. Persistence and precision gave the team on the ground a life-saving supply of air support.

THE PUSH FOR OBJECTIVE GINGER

Despite the tragedy at Takur Gar, by March 5, the land component was getting ready to take Objective Ginger and seal the Shahi Kot Valley. New estimates on enemy strength now guided planning. As Myers said in the middle of the operation, "before we went in there, we heard everywhere from 200 to several thousand. We think there were hundreds. And what's left, we think, is a small part of that, but it's still going to take some time to figure that out."[338]

Kennedy relieved *Roosevelt* in the North Arabian Gulf on March 6. "It was particularly satisfying for us to report on station," said Tomaszeski.[339] Fitzgerald, Zortman and Tomaszeski made sure their staffs coordinated the turnover and kept up the pace for Operation Anaconda. As *Kennedy*'s air wing entered the fight, Captain Harv Henderson spoke to them over the 1MC. "Our namesake John F. Kennedy wrote that *'a single person can make a difference, and every person should try.'* Tonight, *we* make a difference!"

Kennedy was just in time for some of the most intense sorties. With the final push impending, the land component got serious about coordinating help from the air component. Planners now consulted with the land component daily on a series of pre-planned target coordinates for strike aircraft to use in cases of bad weather or diminishing vul times. For its part, the air component made several changes in procedures to smooth out the flow of aircraft and get more bombs on target.

Marzano, Taylor and other pilots noted the differences right away. Taylor flew one such mission with a 2000-lb. JDAM on March 8. "As soon as we finished our tanking, [we] checked in, proceeded to the airspace and they gave us a target immediately and then we released on that target, tanked and went home," he said. With JSTARS there to pass along the coordinates, the entire strike was completed in one vul period.[340]

The final assault on Objective Ginger marked the peak of concentrated air attack in Operation Anaconda. It began with choreographed airstrikes. A B-52 attack was

An F/A-18C Hornet makes a carrier arrested landing on the USS John F. Kennedy on Apr. 19, 2002 after completing a combat mission over Afghanistan. U.S. Navy photo by Photographer's Mate Airman Joshua Karsten.

followed by eighteen minutes of F/A-18 attacks on preplanned targets with Mk 82s, GBU-12s and JDAM in the vicinity of Objective Ginger. To the west, Marine AH-1 Cobras attacked "the Whale" at the same time.

Taylor and Marzano flew a mission on March 10 that illustrated how the air component had tuned its strikes to the needs of the ground battle. They launched with a mix of two GBU-12s on each aircraft plus two Mk 82s fused for airbursts. Those Mk 82s were targeted at troop concentrations – good for "air-bursting al Qaeda into the next life," as Moseley put it.[341] "This time around," Taylor said, they "were given coordinates up in the hills." His target was an intersection with a small cluster of al Qaeda fighters. From "my FLIR picture I had a big mountain range kind of down to the south, a ravine running down through there and then another kind of ravine that connected in from the north. And they were at the intersection of those two," he said. "One pass dropped two LGBs on that intersection."

Taylor circled back to re-attack the intersection with Mk 82s. As he set up the run, he "could see the B-52s, the contrails coming in overhead the same target area getting ready to release. Everything was timed out pretty well but you knew he was coming and you knew he was going to release something on that run, so it made you a little uneasy coming through there." Taylor released the Mk 82s and got out of the way.

Strikes continued until just before 2000 local time when the troops began their assault. Objective Ginger was taken by mid-morning on March 10, 2002. It was the two heaviest days of bombing during all of Operation Anaconda with 327 total weapons released on March 9 and 340 on March 10.[342]

The al Qaeda cluster was gone. Fresh groups of Afghan forces captured the key points in the Shahi Kot Valley and linked up on the morning of March 12. Weary ground soldiers began to withdraw back to Bagram. Other teams, aided by a contingent from the Canadian Forces Princess Patricia light brigade, started sensitive site exploitation of the area. By March 16, Operation Anaconda was over. "Thank goodness for the bravery of those soldiers that we were able to take the fight to the enemy and be successful here," said Myers.[343]

LEARNING FROM THE FIGHT

With the clearing of the Shahi Kot Valley, Operation Anaconda turned from slippery slope to success. "Operation Anaconda sought to clear the enemy in that valley area and in those hills," Franks said a month later, "and succeeded in doing so where many operations in history had not been able to get that done."[344]

Persistent and precise close air support proved it could handle emergency conditions – and deliver more firepower than ever before. The CAOC came through with a consistent average of 60 strike sorties per day. Leading the way were the F/A-18s and F-14s of *Roosevelt*, *Stennis* and *Kennedy*. They delivered precision LGBs and JDAMs along with significant numbers of airburst Mk 82s around the clock with little difference between the totals of day drops and night drops over the course of the campaign.

Operation Anaconda put the carriers at the center of a remarkable employment of air component firepower. By any measure, the rate of strikes delivered in Operation Anaconda's battlespace, and so close to friendly troops, surpassed that of Operation

As the sun rises, an F-14 Tomcat goes to full afterburner as it is launched from the flight deck of the USS John C. Stennis on Jan. 2, 2002. U.S. Navy photo by Photographer's Mate 3rd Class (AW) Jayme Pastoric.

Desert Storm a decade earlier. On February 25, 1991 (D+1 for the ground war, Day 39 for the air war) coalition aircraft flew 140 strike sorties (both interdiction and CAS) against the armored Republican Guard's Tawakalna Division and 12th Armored Division in Killbox AE6. This was the single highest number of airstrikes against any killbox during the ground war. If each strike sortie delivered 6 weapons, Killbox AE6 took 840 bombs that day—or an average of .93 bombs per square mile. Contrast that with Operation Anaconda where the 64-square mile area took an average of 253 bombs per day—or about 3.9 bombs per square mile—about four times the peak intensity seen in this example from Operation Desert Storm.[345]

For the pilots, it felt good. The intense operation "was a big deal to us," said Marzano. "We actually got to feel like we participated and helped guys out on the ground, like we were actually making a difference for them," he said.[346]

Yet the operational significance of Operation Anaconda came not only from the role of the carriers and its immediate results. The lesson in firepower was all to the good but no one wanted to take on a big fight in Iraq with the poor component coordination of Anaconda. Afterwards, CENTCOM's components redoubled their efforts to improve coordination and build bonds among senior commanders. Top generals in the Air Force and Army got to work to fix close air support procedures from the tactical level on up. It was all for one purpose: to prepare the joint force to perform at an even higher level.

During one of the last days of the operation *Stennis* got a high-level visitor: Vice President Cheney. He delivered a revealing message during his March 15, 2002 visit. "Our next objective is to prevent terrorists, and regimes that sponsor terror, from threatening America or our friends and allies with weapons of mass destruction," Cheney said. "We take this threat with great seriousness," he said, adding: "The United States will not permit the forces of terror to gain the tools of genocide."[347]

CHAPTER 7:
Preparing for Iraq

"It's a fundamental precept with a carrier that whenever we are at sea, we have to be prepared for conflict." – Captain John Miller, CO, *USS Constellation*, January 2003[348]

The end of Operation Anaconda allowed CENTCOM to scale back and leave just one carrier operating in the North Arabian Sea for the first time since OEF began. "As it has been all along, airstrikes have been used as needed and if we find a target, we'll attack by air. But there haven't been any since Anaconda ended," Marine Lieutenant Colonel David LePan at the Pentagon said on April 9, 2002.[349]

The USS Theodore Roosevelt powers through the Mediterranean Sea on March 20, 2003. USN Photo by PHAN Todd M. Flint.

John C. Stennis arrived home in May and *Kennedy* shouldered the OEF tasking alone. They converted back to days – but soon found that they were still on "24 hour ops," said Tomaszeski. It was a scheduling game with the CAOC: "are you going to be available? What planes are going to be available?" he explained. *Kennedy* negotiated via the NALE. They "would work 9 or 10 days in a row and we would request one down day" for maintenance, said Tomaszeski.[350]

Kennedy's aircrews still spent plenty of time over Afghanistan. Occasionally they lamented the lack of activity. "It can get very dull, quite frankly," said CAG Captain Bill Gortney. Show of force missions broke up the boredom. For example, in June, Special Forces requested low, fast passes to dispense flares and disperse crowds. "There was a lull for a long time, but then it started getting exciting again working with these Special Forces teams," said F-14 pilot Lieutenant Bill Mallory.[351]

While the carrier provided air for Operation Enduring Freedom, CENTCOM was deep in plans for Iraq. Dealing with Iraq had been "out of the question" for President Bush until Afghanistan was no longer a safe haven.[352] Now, with the first phases of OEF winding down, attention shifted to Iraq. Bush himself told a television interviewer on April 8, 2002: "I made up my mind that Saddam Hussein needs to go."[353]

IRAQ AND WEAPONS OF MASS DESTRUCTION

The reason, as much as anything else, was that Saddam had ceased to cooperate with the UN inspection process, and that made Iraq a lethal question mark in the debate on terrorism and weapons of mass destruction.

Four years after the last inspectors were thrown out in 1998, the post-9/11 world wondered what sort of arsenal Saddam had left and whether any of the research programs were active. The truth may never be known. What was most relevant by the spring of 2002 was that uncertainty about Iraq was mounting; to President Bush, British Prime Minister Tony Blair and others, the uncertainty was intolerable.

Of one thing, there was no doubt. There was constant concern about weapons of mass destruction and this concern shaped planning for all military operations in the global war on terror. CENTCOM kept an eye out for research sites in Afghanistan, and senior leaders in Washington spoke out about their apprehensions.

For example, on November 11, 2001, Rumsfeld summed up the prevailing view of why weapons of mass destruction remained the ultimate problem in the war on terrorism. "It's not like you could deal with Afghanistan, take a great big sigh and say well that takes care of that, because it just doesn't," he told an interviewer. "The problem of weapons of mass destruction and their availability is just too immediate and too urgent and there's too many countries that have harbored and financed and encouraged and facilitated terrorist networks that have weaponized biological weapons and chemical weapons and actively seeking nuclear material."[354]

Saddam was clueless. He "had not realized the nature of the ground shift in the international community," Charles Duelfer of the CIA Iraq Survey Group, later said in Senate testimony.[355]

As for Bush, he had decided at least as far back as December 2001 that preventing terrorists from attacking with weapons of mass destruction was his personal responsibility

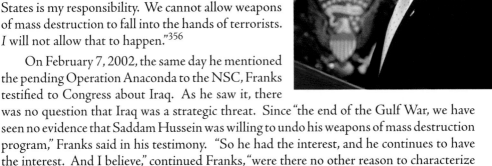

President George W. Bush addresses military and Department of Defense personnel at the Pentagon on Jan. 10, 2002. DoD photo by Helene C. Stikkel.

as President. According to Franks, Bush told a Cabinet-level group assembled by VTC on December 28, 2001: "Protecting the security of the United States is my responsibility. We cannot allow weapons of mass destruction to fall into the hands of terrorists. I will not allow that to happen."[356]

On February 7, 2002, the same day he mentioned the pending Operation Anaconda to the NSC, Franks testified to Congress about Iraq. As he saw it, there was no question that Iraq was a strategic threat. Since "the end of the Gulf War, we have seen no evidence that Saddam Hussein was willing to undo his weapons of mass destruction program," Franks said in his testimony. "So he had the interest, and he continues to have the interest. And I believe," continued Franks, "were there no other reason to characterize Iraq as a strategic risk, I would do so. In my opinion, this pursuit of weapons of mass destruction is a great threat to a great many nations on this planet."[357]

However, the Bush administration was far from ready to commit to an invasion plan and CENTCOM had a long way to go to prepare one. More than a year of exhaustive diplomacy would pass before the US took action against Iraq. During that time, every carrier set to deploy and every airwing completing its training at Fallon did so with the

Pre-dawn flight operations begin aboard the nuclear powered aircraft carrier USS Harry S. Truman on Mar. 24, 2003, as an F/A-18 Hornet strike fighter sits in tension awaiting a catapult launch from the ship's bow. U.S. Navy photo by Photographer's Mate 1st Class Michael W. Pendergrass.

knowledge that they might be part of Gulf War II. "Since 1997, every carrier that has deployed has gone into combat, every carrier deployed has been in combat operations," said Captain Martin J. Erdossy of *George Washington*. Still, as Erdossy acknowledged, "I won't tell you this is the same as the others. These are new and very extraordinary times."[358]

A CONCEPT PLAN

Growing concern about weapons of mass destruction did not translate immediately into a clear plan for action.

Franks first briefed Bush on a concept plan for operations in Iraq in late December 2001. From the beginning, Franks made four things clear. First, he did not want to wage Desert Storm II with a long air war and 400,000 troops marching up from Kuwait. Second, he wanted "simultaneous ground operations from Kuwait, Jordan and Turkey" if possible. Third, he hoped to find ways to truncate the initial airstrike phase or combine it into "a simultaneous joint air-ground operation." Fourth, Franks felt he had to assume that "Iraq possessed and would use weapons of mass destruction, so our forces would likely be fighting in a toxic environment."[359] For now the timing and duration of the operation and its phases was left open-ended.

Nichols saw the planning start off in early 2002 and marked its progress at the end of the year as he prepared to return as Moseley's deputy. "Initially in OIF planning, which would have been as early as January, February, March 2002, when the administration started making noise about going after Iraq, the same old thinking comes in," he said. The thought process was: "what we'll do is we'll build up the force, go back for about a month. And then we will start heading north. Forty-five days later we'll be in Baghdad."

"From this discussion the fundamental shape of the plan was bomb and then maneuver," Nichols said. That combination did not change, but the balance did. Specifically, the questions were: "How long is the bombing piece going to be? What's going to be the characteristic of maneuver? What about apportionment and allocation once the maneuver starts?"

It would all affect how much naval airpower to deploy, and where to position the carriers.

CENTCOM spent most of 2002 engaged in an iterative planning process: debating, testing and gaming options for an attack to depose Saddam Hussein and secure Iraq. Small groups on the CENTCOM staff prepared versions of the plans. Once a month or so, Franks convened conferences of his component commanders and key staff to review them.

General Tommy Franks, Commander, United States Central Command, and members of his staff land at a forward-deployed air base in the Middle East. U.S. Air Force photo by SSGT Derrick C. Goode.

A "component commanders' huddle, he called them," said Keating of the meetings. As the new Maritime Component Commander, Keating had a vital role both in positioning naval forces and planning how best to employ their strike power. At his first "huddle" he saw many faces he knew, and a few he didn't. "The personalities were not insignificant," he said of the gathering, yet from the start he recognized "there wasn't anybody in there who was service first, CENTCOM second," he said. "Franks was adamant that it not be that way. That it be a band of brothers, Shakespearean term. He made us believers. We were inclined to believe anyway. But it's a good thing we were. Because he would not tolerate otherwise. He was not shy to express his occasional dislike of service Title X parochial concerns when measured against, or at the expense of, joint coalition warfare. He was quite serious about our integration. And he would have weeded us out individually had we not been willing disciples."[360]

The huddles gave commanders time to build trust and to debate options. "We spent a lot of time going back and forth," said Keating. "There were differences in opinion, but there weren't emotional differences of opinion. How long should the air war last? How are we going to prosecute the ground campaign? Where do the special operations forces fit in. How are we going to know where they are? How will we sustain the pace that Franks wants us, [and] wants the ground troops to sustain? How will we protect the infrastructure? How will we make sure that Saddam doesn't blow the oil wells? How will we utilize strategic information, operational deception?"

Iraq planning juggled several different options during the spring and summer of 2002. Two chief alternatives, nicknamed Generated Start and Running Start, outlined the options for how the war might begin and illustrated how much this campaign depended on politics, both foreign and domestic.

Generated Start emerged by February as a concept for two months of force build-up above and beyond normal theater operations in the no-fly zones and Afghanistan. It featured a 20-day air campaign followed by 135 days of decisive ground operations.

Running Start, added in March 2002, covered what to do if Iraq triggered war, leaving the Coalition to start the fight using only the forces available in theater at that moment. "We call it the Running Start because the units reaching the theater would not wait for follow-on forces to arrive, but rather would proceed directly toward their objectives," Franks later said.[361] This plan gave the air component 16 days to hit Iraqi ground forces and strategic targets while more forces flowed into theater. Then, G-Day – the start of the ground attack – would follow.

In May, the *Red, White and Blue* plans were added to the slate after discussions at the White House on what to do in case Saddam started the war. The color plans followed response options like Desert Badger – or as Moseley termed them all, "desert small animals."[362]

+ White was a medium-level response on the scale of 1998's Operation Desert Fox.

+ Blue covered a single event and used only forces in place.

+ Red was for a large response to WMD employment, for example. A red response initiated the time-phased deployment of forces and again left a 16-day margin for airstrikes while forces closed in theater.

113

However, in 2002, the Bush administration was not yet ready to upstage ongoing diplomatic efforts with a massive and visible military build-up. There was no formal decision to go to war and alliances – particularly with key nations in the region – were still being tested, negotiated and formed. Added to that was Franks' quest for operational surprise and penchant for security. He "was agonizingly strict about security," said Keating, to the point that "we were very circumspect in even discussing with our staffs, sometimes, the rationale behind an issue."[363]

It made for real uncertainty for the air component. Every plan called for significant air action, with overflight and basing rights. However, the Coalition was not fully formed and CENTCOM still had multiple planning options in the works.

Under these conditions, plans for how to execute various parts of the air campaign went ahead. Out of Franks' huddles "would come planning exercises or in my case the strategic attack for the CAS, conops for the urban CAS, conops for the ISR piece," said Moseley.[364] CAOC planners refined the major concepts.

How to position forces for either a generated or running start was another matter.

The 1991 Gulf War style of deploying and waiting was out of the question. "There was a great unknown on both sides, both Navy and Air Force, in terms of airpower. One was we weren't allowed to bring a lot of airpower into the theater early," Robb said. It would be too revealing. "Fly 500 airplanes over there...and people are going to say, 'well...'"

SUBTLE SCHEDULING

Planners now opted for a technique of subtle scheduling that was the very opposite of 1990s-style fixed-schedule presence. While CENTCOM wanted crisis response forces on station, planners also did not want to let naval force movements signal the start of a war. So planners calculated "when the carrier schedules allowed you to bring a lot of firepower together from the sea" based on the natural turnover point when there would be "four or five carriers at sea. If two of them are turning over then there's double [the] number in the Gulf," explained Robb. "We started tracking and there was a deliberate modification of carrier schedules to try to build windows where there would be large amounts of carrier airpower available. Those windows were overlaid onto the environmental windows that were to the best advantage of the ground force."

Summer was a red area – "no go" for the ground forces due to the heat – so the key was to build carrier strike power around an option to mass force in the timeframe of October/November 2002 or March/April 2003. "Just make it so that you can rally 5 or 6 ships at one time without looking like you're doing it," Robb said of CENTCOM's intentions at the time.[365]

That strategy played out in the work-up and deployment schedules for *Abraham Lincoln, Constellation, Harry S. Truman, Kitty Hawk, Theodore Roosevelt* and the *Nimitz*. All six carriers would find themselves participating in Operation Iraqi Freedom in 2003.

For now, crews, captains, CAGs and battle group commanders had to be ready for an October/November surge or for action in early 2003. First to the line-up was *USS George Washington*. The carrier left Norfolk on June 20, 2002 to relieve *Kennedy*

The USS George Washington sails along side the Military Sealift Command ship USNS Supply while conducting a replenishment at sea on Aug. 19, 2002. U.S. Navy photo by Photographer's Mate 1st Class David C. Lloyd.

off Afghanistan. *Lincoln* sailed from San Diego in July and officially took over OEF duties from *George Washington* on September 11, 2002. "We prepare to be able to go anywhere anytime to perform the missions assigned to us," said Rear Admiral John Kelly, commander of Cruiser-Destroyer Group Three, and of the *Abraham Lincoln* Carrier Battle Group. "We will be ready. The president told us to be ready."[366]

The air wing's role "was one of maintaining tactical aircraft and command and control capability over top of what were at that time very widely distributed small unit forces that the US had," said Kelly. They did not expect to drop a lot of ordnance. However, the requirements for coverage persisted and pushed *Lincoln* to some intense phases of operation. "It was not a 24/7 coverage but it was pretty close because we launched a number of aircraft on demand," Kelly explained.[367]

The hand-off freed *George Washington* to transit the Suez Canal and work for the next three months on exercises in the Mediterranean. With *George Washington* near Iraq's northern flank and *Lincoln* to the south, two carriers were constantly available to serve as a basis for strike operations under a "running" or a "generated" start.

Kelly took over duties as CTF 50, which made him "very aware of what was going on" as plans for Iraq progressed. "We were extremely well briefed and supported by 5th Fleet," he said. As a result, "we had in-depth knowledge of the evolution of planning that was going on. We did not know a timeline. We had no advance knowledge of that. It was obviously prudent to be very prepared."[368]

Responding to President Bush's admonition to "Be Ready," Sailors on the 4-acre flight deck of the USS Abraham Lincoln spell out their response on Sept. 11, 2002. U.S. Navy photo by Photographer's Mate Airman Gabriel Piper.

The challenge was to maintain a base from which to start operations if necessary while keeping up OSW duties. Over time, carrier readiness and training could degrade due to the constraints of a long deployment in a confined station area. But if operations began late in the year, *Lincoln's* air wing and crew could not afford a drop in proficiency. "One of the things that we did was we worked very, very hard at maintaining air crew proficiency," Kelly pointed out. Kelly opted to make training requirements a priority along with mission requirements. "It was a very deliberate choice," he said. "We sacrificed a lot of things to support that. We looked at where we would operate the carrier and we put both requirements on the table, not just one."

Kelly positioned the carrier and the battle group to take advantage of available ranges whenever possible so that the air wing could "drop exercise ordnance to maintain very high levels of individual air crew proficiency," Kelly added. If that meant tacking on a few extra minutes to the long OEF sorties over Afghanistan, so be it. CVW-14 dropped an "extremely high" amount of exercise ordnance, "which turned out to be a real good thing to have done when the tasking evolved" Kelly said after OIF.[369]

Another part of keeping the *Lincoln* battle group on its toes included scrutinizing ingress and egress routes over Iraq and "working hard on how we would take best advantage of joint capabilities. We were sending high quality people into the JFACC trying to build our experience base [and] our lines of communications," to the CAOC, Kelly said.[370]

AIR COMPONENT CHANGES

The CAOC in Saudi Arabia was also refining preparations for war. Moseley, who was still the CFACC, intended to make some changes in the way the air component did business. He wanted a CAOC with better joint service representation, smooth channels for SOF coordination, and a detailed plan for the worst-case scenario: ongoing urban CAS in Baghdad.

Part of the job included expanding the NALE. Nichols left the CAOC in March 2002 with instructions from Moseley to "go put together the Navy piece of the CAOC, which included the NALE and then the Navy folks we embed in purple jobs with the CFACC or in the CAOC," he said. Nichols, who was assigned as Commander of NSAWC, "worked 2nd and 3rd Fleets and others to get the right bunch of people in there" to the CAOC for Iraq.[371]

Navy participation at this critical node increased in two ways. First, the NALE itself was bulked up. Second, Navy O-6s took on key jobs throughout the joint CAOC structure itself. The majority of all senior positions were double-manned due to the requirements of 24-hour operations. Some were triple-manned. Navy captains shared leadership at the A2 intelligence slot and A3 operations staff, as well as the Strategy cell, which reported through the staff at that time. The three CAOC directors, two Air Force brigadiers and an air commodore of the RAF, had two Navy captains as deputies. Combat Operations had one Navy captain in place and Combat Plans had two. The Deputy Chief of ISR was also a Navy captain. All three branches reported to the CAOC directors.

A total of 158 Navy personnel were assigned to the CAOC – including 10 afloat.[372] They included junior officers who checked lines on the ATO as well as the senior officers. It was a world away from Nichols' recollection of being in a room with "about 300 colonels" before Operation Desert Storm in 1990 and feeling the Navy "didn't draw much water in that crowd."[373]

Quiet increases in manning levels throughout the region soon brought the CAOC's key elements to combat status. "Moseley and his crowd had a footprint and it snuck up significantly," said Robb of the CAOC's quiet pre-war preparations.[374]

Other major changes at the CAOC since Afghanistan included reforming the TST process. "We had a TST process where decisions were made in the joint fires coordination center which was really the CAOC. So, none of that ROE stuff, none of that decision-making on time-critical or time-sensitive targets was an issue in OIF," confirmed Nichols.[375] Politically-sensitive TSTs such as leadership targets, terrorist sites and suspected WMD sites got their own category. As a CENTCOM spokesman explained, "the President, Secretary [of Defense] and General Franks have a very good agreement [that] only those key targets have to be elevated" and for other targets, "we allow the battlefield commanders to make those decisions" with pre-established rules.[376]

TIMING

Heading into the summer of 2002 CENTCOM now had two major planning concepts and several trigger response options on the books.

On August 5, Franks gave a briefing to the NSC that put forward a revised timing increment in days of 45-90-90 for the first three phases of the campaign. The 45-day period of shaping the battlespace would combine an air campaign and SOF operations *à la* Afghanistan. Then came 90 days of initial staging and ground operations followed by another 90 days of "decisive offensive operations" and after that, the open-ended Phase IV Stability operations. CENTCOM did not even attempt to put Phase IV on a timetable.

Then came the Hybrid – the plan that served as the springboard for what became Operation Iraqi Freedom. This alternative counted on local access and basing. It featured a two-week air and SOF war for shaping the battlespace and up to 90 days of decisive military operations. All plans assigned the air component the task of attacking Republican Guards forces to prevent a Fortress Baghdad urban warfare siege.[377]

Exhaustive planning exercises did something more than just prepare options. One lasting benefit was an intangible: mental rehearsal. As Franks later put it, for "a period of about a year, a great deal of intense planning and a great deal of what-iffing by all of us has gone into this."[378] Moseley compared it to weapons school instruction. Building, changing and reviewing a series of plans gave commanders and staff alike a crash course in terrain and tactics and made the Iraqi battlespace a familiar one. "After all of that, you have an intellectual construct," Moseley said. "You have thought about this so much that you intuitively and instinctively know how far it is from al Qaim to al Kut to al Amaud back to al Qaim to Mosul to Kirkuk to the southern oilfields."[379]

Robb at CENTCOM saw the benefit of the planning iterations, too. All the adaptive planning "forced the air component guys into a huge library of ATOs that they then could pick from if we changed our mind." Whatever CENTCOM could come up with, chances were the air component had "already gone through that contingency in some way," he said.[380]

Hard and fast planning was not feasible – or needed. Keating observed that the Iraq planning process was different when it came to risk. "Franks was willing to accept risk," said Keating. He coached his commanders with what Keating termed "some fairly melodramatic expressions" about how willing he was to accept risk.[381] Nichols explained that Franks understood "the most risk was in a strategic sense, so he was willing to accept risk at the operational level, in other words not have things exactly like all of us wanted to have them, before we started the fight."[382] To Franks accepting operational risk was worth it to increase the chances of operational surprise – which he saw as a guarantee against giving the Republican Guards time to position for an "attrition slugfest" around Baghdad.[383] Accepting a degree of risk in deployment, timing and other operational matters "in effect mitigates risk at the strategic level," Nichols finished.[384]

The flexibility enjoyed by CENTCOM owed much to the abilities of the air component. With carriers on station (and an air bridge that could beef up deployments swiftly) the air component stood out as a readily-available decisive tool that could go into action on demand, and set the terms for dominance in the air and on the ground.

OPERATION SOUTHERN FOCUS

In fact, the process was already underway. While planners were scrubbing options, aircrews on patrol in the no-fly zones after June 2002 were seeing plenty of action in a controlled but relentless air campaign to pick apart Iraq's air defenses. Kelly described Southern Watch as "very much a live ordnance exchange."[385]

There was calculation behind it. "We took Southern Watch and tuned it to do several things," said Robb. "One of which was to take a lot of imagery of the rest of the country. In other words, we updated all the targets. Aircrews knew southern Iraq very well."[386]

From January to early September, Coalition airmen flew over 4000 sorties in the OSW no-fly zone. The Iraqis were taunting them with brief incursions across the 33rd Parallel, anti-aircraft fire, and SAM posturing. "We want to continue to use response options to degrade the Iraqi Integrated Air Defense System," Franks explained at an NSC meeting in August. "If it ever comes to war, we'll want their IADS as weak as possible."[387]

An F-18 Super Hornet launches from one of four steam catapults on the flight deck of the USS Abraham Lincoln on Oct. 30, 2002. U.S. Navy photo by Photographer's Mate 2nd Class Aaron Ansarov.

It worked brilliantly. Missions in late September showed how the air activity was carving out air dominance in southern Iraq. Two air defense facilities were hit – one at al Kufa, about 80 miles south of Baghdad, and the other in Basra, 245 miles southeast of the capital. "These strikes were in self-defense," said Pace.[388] The strikes were staying within OSW's self-defense rules, but they were also hammering away at a valuable target set.

Late November saw another spike in activity. November 21, 2002, supplied a typical example as Coalition aircraft bombed Iraqi air defense communication facilities near Al Kut and Basra in southern Iraq.

Lincoln's aviators were getting more than a taste of battle in Operation Southern Focus. "If some of you wake up this morning feeling like seasoned warriors there's a reason," said the voice over the PA system on November 25. "Last night more bombs were dropped on target than ever before. Yesterday was a good Navy day."

"I can tell you it certainly feels like someone is trying to wage war on you when you're shot at on every patrol. It's pretty hairy out there," attested one pilot. Aviation ordnanceman Vince Martin said: "All I can say about last night is that there must have been one hell of a lot of shooting going on."

"We've got this country staked out," commented Ken O'Donnell, a veteran pilot aboard *Lincoln*.

At the Pentagon, Joint Staff spokesman Rear Admiral David Gove said that the pilots in the no-fly zone "are essentially flying combat missions. Any opportunity that they have to understand the capabilities and the layout of Iraqi air defense weapons systems is useful for their own experience base. And there has been degradation of the integrated air defense system in Iraq," Gove acknowledged.[389]

By the end of the year 2002 CENTCOM calculated that "Iraq fired at Coalition aircraft nearly 500 times" which led to about 90 retaliation missions.[390] "The air threat had been essentially neutered throughout up to the 33rd, probably higher than that," Robb assessed. "We had a pretty good start on the air part of it."

"Make It Five"

"I came back in January to get ready for OIF," said Nichols of his return to the CAOC. NSAWC would have to get along without him for awhile. Moseley had months before requested that Nichols rotate back to be the Deputy CFACC for Operation Iraqi Freedom.

An F/A-18C Hornet launches from a waist catapult aboard the aircraft carrier USS Constellation on Feb. 1, 2003. U.S. Navy photo by Photographer's Mate 2nd Class Felix Garza Jr.

Two F/A-18 Hornets prepare to launch from the flight deck of the USS Harry S. Truman on Mar. 13, 2003. U.S. Navy photo by Photographer's Mate 1st Class Michael W. Pendergrass.

For the air component, Franks' Phase II, Shaping the Battlespace, was already well underway via Operation Southern Focus. Nichols said that "in Phase II, we expanded the target set in southern Iraq to do all we could do to set the conditions so that when Phase III started we were further down the road in terms of air superiority, air supremacy, enabling SOF and some other things."[391]

CENTCOM had first pick of Navy assets. From the beginning, Admiral Clark had made clear to Keating: "*you let me know what General Franks wants. Don't make a big deal of it. I will see that you get them.*"[392]

Indeed, the Navy and Marine Corps would bring 250 F/A-18s – the biggest single number of strike aircraft – to the fight. Keating "had the capability to bring eight carriers into the AOR" depending on what the air component needed. There were plans to position carriers in the Mediterranean, the Red Sea, and the Arabian Gulf or to "mix and match" as Keating said at any or all of the three locations. Franks still did not want to push force deployments past the tipping point. It was "easier for naval forces to do this than Army boots on the ground and Marine boots on the ground," Keating said. He kept the presence of carriers close to a normal rotation. "We just kind of held them for a little while and then brought the people who would have been normal rotational relief" and "before you knew it, we had five with the 6th coming and one on duty in West Pac."

The January plan called for five carriers for Operation Iraqi Freedom. According to Keating that decision was delivered at one of the commanders' huddles at the end of the month. "General Franks turned to Buzz Moseley...and he said, '*can you get it done with five?*'

"Moseley said '*I can.*'

"So Franks turned to me and said '*make it five.*' That was it," said Keating.[393]

Dividing up the tasking for five carriers was easier said than done due to unpredictable access questions. There was operating room for two or three carriers in the Persian Gulf. Extending *Lincoln* was key to the battle plan. Christmas 2002 found *Lincoln* in port at Perth, Australia, preparing to head home. By New Year's Day, there were new orders to "be available as required to meet national security requirements," as the official Navy announcement phrased it.

It wasn't a complete surprise by any means. "When we headed to Australia, we could see that tensions were high," Kelly recalled. Kelly and his staff kept tabs on maintenance and training tasks in case they were called back to the North Arabian Gulf. They also stayed in touch with 5th Fleet by "reaching back and monitoring the comms, [and] everything else that was going on, so that even while we were down in Australia, we knew the daily blow-by-blow of how things were evolving and developing."

Lincoln used the time in port well. "The one thing we needed was to resurface a significant portion of flight deck," Kelly said. "We had simply worn out the non-skid" due to the high operations tempo. Resurfacing "was undertaken once we arrived in Australia."394

The USS Constellation steams through the ocean with ships in its Battle Group on Nov. 30, 2002. U.S. Navy photo by Photographer's Mate 2nd Class Timothy Smith.

Joining *Lincoln* in the Persian Gulf would be *Constellation*, and *Kitty Hawk*.

Where to place the *Harry Truman* and the in-bound *Roosevelt* was more complicated. With *Harry Truman* on scene, planning for the 6th Fleet's task force fell to Stufflebeem, who was now the battle group commander. "We did not know when or how we would be used," he said. "In the north, in the south, going over Baghdad – so all I really concentrated on was saying, let's take two carriers worth of capability and build what I called the on-ramps, the highway to Baghdad. Whatever the main thrust was going to be in terms of the general war plan, we wanted to have on-ramps to the highways to be able to get in and support that," he said. Planners "figured out the mechanics of flying through the eastern Mediterranean, through Turkey, over Syria, over Israel, and Jordan and then down Egypt into KSA [Saudi Arabia] and then up" if it came to that.395

Once the carriers were assigned positions, it was time to define specific roles for each in the air component's tasking. It was done on a ship-by-ship basis, taking into account location, sortie generation, and CENTCOM's requirements. The key – and a lesson learned from Afghanistan – was to spell out the level of effort in advance and tailor each carrier's operations to a segment of the battlespace.

"We worked hard to have contracts for each carrier," said Nichols. Gortney and his staff at the NALE were "really the centerpiece for working those." The "contracts" were shaped by "where the carrier was, where we needed to go, the characteristics of the airplanes" and so on. Generally, there were "contracts made for a certain number of sorties on a certain number of mission lengths of cycle times. And that worked pretty well because the expectations in the CAOC matched what the ship thought it could do," Nichols said.[396] The individual plans for each carrier combined into reliable striking power available on a twenty-four hour basis. To the CAOC, these were not individual units, but a mass of sea-based striking power.

DIPLOMATIC COUNTDOWN

Even with war preparations underway, the fall of 2002 had brought a flicker of hope that diplomacy and disarmament might prevail. To Franks there was no question about the danger posed by Iraq. He laid his logic bare in October 2002. "Iraq is a state sponsor of terrorism," Franks said. "Iraq has weapons of mass destruction. The linkages between the government of Iraq and other transnational terrorist organizations like al Qaeda is not the issue with me. The issue is the potential of a state with weapons of mass destruction, passing those weapons of mass destruction to proven terrorist capability. And I believe that that risk exists, yes," he said.[397]

On November 8, 2002, the UN Security Council passed Resolution 1441. "The world has now come together to say that the outlaw regime in Iraq will not be permitted to build or possess chemical, biological or nuclear weapons," President Bush said of UN resolution 1441.[398] The latest resolution offered Iraq "a final opportunity to comply with its disarmament obligations." It called for unrestricted access for weapons inspectors and warned that any "false statements" or other non-compliance would put Iraq in material breach not just of 1441, but of the long series of binding UN resolutions dating back to April 1991.

The world watched to see what Iraq would do. By December, the signs were disappointingly mixed. Iraq delivered a 12,000-page document that supposedly detailed its lack of weapons. Meanwhile, force movements continued.

CENTCOM was shielded from direct involvement in the diplomatic dance but the drawn-out decision-making process had its impact. "If you look at our footprint in the region," Franks had said that fall, "we have had, over the last 12 months, 10 or 15 or 20 different footprints."[399]

As 2003 began, the focus remained on war plans and the expectation was that execution was coming soon.

Hans Blix announced to the UN Security Council on January 27 that Iraq was cooperating but might well still have weapons, including anthrax and up to 6,500 aerial bombs to deliver it. "Iraq appears not to have come to a genuine acceptance – not even today – of the disarmament which was demanded of it and which it needs to carry out to win the confidence of world and to live in peace," Blix concluded.[400]

The deployed battle groups got a further sign that war was coming when the decision was made to begin anthrax shots in early February.[401]

An F/A-18C Hornet sits ready on catapult three aboard the aircraft carrier USS Kitty Hawk on Feb. 17, 2003. U.S. Navy photo by Photographer's Mate 3rd Class Todd Frantom.

On February 5, 2003, Powell reported to the Security Council that "Iraq never had any intention of complying with this Council's mandate." Powell cited evidence for Iraqi possession of weapons of mass destruction and referred to Iraq's proven record of willingness to attack its neighbors and to use chemical weapons on its own people.[402] War was now almost certain; the timing still was not.

In the weeks that remained the air component had to show unusual flexibility in order to be ready to pull off whatever execute order came from CENTCOM.

Carrier skippers, battle group commanders, CAGs and their deputies checked in to learn what they could of the latest plans. Dialogue with the CAOC – and each other – was constant.

Kelly, in the Persian Gulf, expected "that General Franks was going to take advantage of the tactical situation anywhere he could." Everything from TLAM strikes to carrier close air support sorties could change on the fly. One step Kelly took in anticipation was to "put in place a series of steps to significantly improve the communications between the three carrier battlegroups." "We sent people to talk to the Army; we sent people to talk to the Marines. We worked through the JFACC. We took every path we could think of to improve awareness, to raise people's appreciation for what we would be doing, the timeline we would be operating on," Kelly finished.[403]

Stufflebeem jumped in to see what the Mediterranean carriers could provide. "I was talking to the guys in Riyadh and I said, we can do this a couple ways, we can mass firepower if that's what you want, we can rush a lot of sorties by having two carriers do it simultaneously. Or we can stagger the carriers, where we can't generate the same level of sorties at one time; we can provide a longer period of coverage."[404]

The CAOC asked for two different inputs: short term surge, and sustained, 24-hour operations. Ultimately "we figured that we could probably push about 30 combat sorties per carrier per swarm," he said. That meant "we could almost generate 40 to 60 combat sorties from the carriers simultaneously, 20 to 30 tactical jets per carrier flight deck as a surge." Surge would be tough on the deck crews and aviation ordnancemen. "Once you got the first group off you were in pretty good shape because then you got a lot of acreage that you could open up," Stufflebeem reasoned.

Sustained operations were more straightforward, and built directly on the lessons of persistence in Afghanistan. The numbers showed Stufflebeem that the two carriers could probably "go up to about 25 to 30 tactical sorties per event, then we just stagger the carriers to provide that coverage over the 24-hour period. That didn't stress us that hard," he said.[405]

In the south, three carriers were on the roster to provide striking power from the Persian Gulf. *Kitty Hawk* with CVW-5 was "the third carrier," as Driscoll described it. Driscoll found "they didn't want the information to get out of theater in terms of what the real plan was – like to keep that close hold. But in order for us to prepare, I had to have some idea what our mission was going to be," said Driscoll. He got in touch with the CAOC en route and with other CAGs. In this case, the CAOC NALE had a very clear plan for *Kitty Hawk*. It was "a hundred strikes sorties a day. All organically tanked," said Driscoll. CVW-5 was going up close to provide support for the Army's V Corps led by 3d Infantry Division.[406]

"Close air support would be key to the operation," as Franks said.[407]

DECISION

Close air support and strikes on counterland targets were certainties – but they were among the few for the air component. "We didn't know how it was going to start because the political situation was still fluctuating," said Robb. The variables were big ones: the UN, a second resolution, Turkey's national referendum, other basing agreements, all influencing "who's on the team. So you didn't necessarily know how big the force was going to be, you didn't know, depending on how quickly it started, [if] you'd have to sort of crank an initial air war and then work over time to build capacity" for ground operations. "The ideas were very just-in-time, very flexible," Robb summarized.[408]

Nichols and Robb both saw the unusual political pressures that shaped the start of the campaign.

Having carriers available was a big asset, even if they, too, needed tanking and overflight arrangements. "Let's face it: we didn't have whole bunch of folks on the ground who wanted to let us use their runways," said Kelly.[409]

Although the plan had been in place since January, diplomacy was slowing down the potential start date for war. From mid-February through early March 2003, Bush tapped the brakes.

An F/A-18C Hornet waits in an alert status aboard the aircraft carrier USS Kitty Hawk on Feb. 22, 2003. U.S. Navy photo by Photographer's Mate Airman Theron J. Godbold.

The main cause was the impact of a February 14 report from Hans Blix indicating that the Iraqis were generally cooperating with the UN inspection teams. Nothing had been found during 300 site inspections. Still, Blix could not be definitive. He pressed Iraq to cooperate more fully and thus shorten the disarmament inspection process.[410] The US opted to seek a second resolution, reconfirming UN Resolution 1441, that would serve as an indisputable basis for going to war.

Then on March 7, UN inspectors published a 173-page report listing 29 areas where Iraq had not provided sufficient information to the inspectors. The report concluded that Iraq could easily still retain weapons such as the nerve gas agent VX.

US and Coalition forces were poised for war and to withdraw them would erase what little power remained in the UN inspections process.

On March 14, Franks held another commanders' huddle, this one at the forward headquarters in Qatar. He picked a short, sharp air war: not weeks or days, but just 96 hours of air and SOF operations with full ground operations to begin on the fourth day.

"There were all kinds of discussions of timing and there were questions as to whether there'd be 14 days between A-Day and G-Day and then six days or three days or no days," recapped Air Force Major General Daniel Leaf, who was at land component headquarters as Moseley's chosen liaison to CFLCC McKiernan. "I think it's important to point out that in reality, there were 12 years between A-Day and G-Day," Leaf said.[411]

Fortunately, in Operation Southern Focus the aircrews had "worked all the air dominance piece before the war started to the point where Moseley was satisfied to collapse the air war section of the [plan] – he had bought into four days," Robb concurred. A four-day air war would leave major Iraqi Republican Guard formations largely intact as ground forces began their advance. But the gains of Operation Southern Focus meant the air component could operate in most of Iraq. Four days was enough to start ground force attrition, and kick off other major target categories for the multi-faceted air war. Counter-Scud targets were a big part of that initial target set, along with some key military communications and other strategic targets.[412]

The last huddle left no doubts about Franks' commitment to simultaneous operations. "The decision was made," said Nichols. Franks told them that "on D-Day and D+1 we're going to expand the no-fly zone essentially into northwestern Iraq." That would start the counter-Scud fight out west with SOF supporting the air component. Two days later, at D+2, would be A-day, with a major schedule of strategic targets to be struck by aircraft and TLAMs. Twelve hours later the ground war would start.

By now, Bush was resolved to go to war. The hoped-for second UN resolution never came up for a vote. Canvassing indicated that the US did not have the votes it needed in the UN Security Council. On March 16, Bush, Blair, and Spanish Prime Minister Aznar met in the Azores and decided that UN Resolution 1441's threat of "serious consequences" for non-compliance and lack of full cooperation created a sufficient legal basis to justify war with Iraq.[413]

On March 17, 2003, Bush was back in Washington meeting with Congressional leaders and stressing Saddam's defiance. That evening, he issued his ultimatum. "Saddam Hussein and his sons must leave Iraq within 48 hours," he said. "Their refusal to do so will result in military conflict, commenced at a time of our choosing."[414]

In London, Blair faced a confidence vote within Parliament to test the strength of his government. On March 18, with British forces preparing for battle, Blair explained why he was committing Britain to Resolution 1441 as the legal basis for action in Iraq. Saddam had been "for years" in material breach of UN resolutions and in his lack of compliance had squandered this last opportunity, Blair told the House of Commons. To Blair, there was evidence that Iraq held weapons of mass destruction. Inaction now would cost dearly – well beyond the confrontation with Iraq. Blair's reasons for leading Britain to war centered on Iraq but looked also to the future world order. "What would any tyrannical regime possessing WMD think viewing the history of the world's diplomatic dance with Saddam?" Blair asked in his speech to Parliament. "That our capacity to pass firm resolutions is only matched by our feebleness in implementing them." One day, he warned, regimes "will mistake our innate revulsion against war for permanent incapacity."[415]

Blair won his vote. The "coalition of the willing" was ready to take on Iraq.

CHAPTER 8:
Operation Iraqi Freedom Begins

"We have a serious task before us and it is to remove that regime and find the weapons of mass destruction, and replace it with a government that does not want those weapons and will not threaten its neighbor and will maintain a single country." – Secretary Rumsfeld, March 20, 2003

O n March 19, 2003, at 0900 Eastern time, President Bush in Washington issued the execute order for Operation Iraqi Freedom. It was D-Day. Night was coming soon for the Persian Gulf region, and within a few hours, over 30 SOF teams inserted into Iraq.

An F-14B Tomcat launches from one of four steam driven catapults on the flight deck of USS Harry S. Truman on Mar. 22, 2003. U.S. Navy photo by Photographer's Mate 1st Class Michael W. Pendergrass.

CENTCOM's plan called for a phased timetable:

- D+0, March 19: Insert SOF and destroy observation posts in Western Iraq
- D+1, March 20: additional reconnaissance and SOF
- D+2, March 21, 0600: G-Day to begin just after dawn in Iraq
- D+2, March 21, 2100: The main strategic attack piece of A-Day[416]

The plan changed when CENTCOM saw satellite imagery of six burning oil wells on March 19. Now, the fear was that Saddam might give orders to torch the Rumailyah oilfields.

This was a chance Franks did not want to take. "It's really very diabolical any time you're thinking about Saddam and what he's going to pull out of his hat," said Robb.[417] Saddam was a master trickster. In 1991, he fired Scuds at Israel and Saudi Arabia, opened Kuwait's oil valves into the Gulf, evacuated MiG-29s and other fighters to archenemy Iran, and launched the ill-fated ground attack at Khafji – all during the air campaign's first two weeks. No one wanted the oilfields to go. "You don't want them pumping stuff out into the water," said Moseley. Given a two or three week air effort, "he [Saddam] would have done all of that."[418]

Franks figured if they moved fast the Coalition had a chance to "get the oil fields" before the Iraqis torched them. "We saw an opportunity to achieve one of our operational objectives, which was to prevent the destruction of a big chunk of the Iraqi people's future wealth," he explained.[419]

Franks ordered the main Coalition ground advance to start eight hours sooner. The air component's strategic attacks for A-Day remained on schedule for the evening of March 21.[420]

ALREADY AT WAR

But that did not mean the air component was sitting idly by as CENTCOM reshuffled the opening attacks. Far from it.

To all intents and purposes, the air component was already at war by March 19. Aircrews had been flying hundreds of sorties per day since the first week of March. Robb at CENTCOM was struggling for more base access and overflight clearances to keep up with the CAOC's accelerating air war. After March 7, sorties soared to 1311 and averaged over 1300 sorties per day through the beginning of the war on March 19.[421] It was a "Herculean effort to plan and manage execution of this many sorties as we were headed into the war," said Nichols.[422]

With the execute order signed by Bush, the CAOC expanded "the no-fly zone essentially into northwestern Iraq," according to

Coalition troops track an ongoing OIF mission at this Combined Air Operation Center. U.S. Air Force photo by SSGT Derrick C. Goode.

Nichols.[423] The coverage made it possible to insert SOF teams in the north, west and south and carry out other shaping actions. "Early battlefield preparations" on March 19 included airstrikes on radars in western Iraq and near Basra in southern Iraq. "Attacks also neutralized artillery in the Al Faw peninsula northeast of Kuwait," said Myers.[424]

For most aircrews March 19 was relatively straightforward. On *Kitty Hawk*, CAG Driscoll said of the first night: "The targets were just like always, there on the ATO, you got a DMPI, you went out, you bombed, you came back."[425] Total ATO sorties surged to 2184 on D-Day.[426]

Commander Jeff Rocha described his March 19 mission. "You could argue whether it was Southern Watch or Iraqi Freedom at that point in time," he said, although in the cockpit it scarcely mattered. Rocha's division was "directed to take out surface-to-surface launchers that were just across the border into Iraq. There was a fear they were going to throw chem at the marshalling areas where the ground troops were. So we were given our JDAM assignments and we were given the execute order once airborne."

Two sorties that night were not routine. At 0534 Baghdad time a pair of F-117s hit the Dora Farms compound, where the CIA believed Saddam might be hiding. A few minutes later, 40 TLAMs launched from warships also hit other downtown Baghdad targets such as an intelligence service headquarters and a Republican Guards installation.

Later intelligence revealed Saddam had not been there. "I'm pretty much convinced there was nothing there, not a bunker, not Saddam. Bad gauge from the CIA like we had all the time through OEF and OIF," Nichols commented later.[427]

G-DAY SURPRISE

March 20 saw air planners – and aircrews – responding to new priorities caused by Franks' sudden moves. Carriers had to make several adjustments to their strike plans.

But the first surprise came from the Iraqis. Shortly after noon local time on March 20, Patriots downed two Ababil-100 surface-to-surface missiles fired at the CFLCC headquarters in Camp Doha, Kuwait. *USS Higgins* detected the launch within seconds and alerted the Camp Doha air defenders. Business was brisk. Four more Iraqi missiles flew that afternoon. One hit within 600 yards of I MEF headquarters.[428]

The Iraqi missile shots caused no real damage but they were a vivid reminder that Coalition forces were bunched up in well-known cantonment areas that easily translated to pre-surveyed missile coordinates. Franks had intelligence reports of Iraqi missile batteries moving unpredictably, and Republican Guard units moving south, possibly with mustard gas or other toxic weapons. Already he was concerned about "a strong possibility of gas attacks into our crowded staging areas in Kuwait."[429]

What if the next salvos had chemical or biological toxins? It had a galvanizing effect. "He shoots missiles at CFLCC forces who were on the berm down in Kuwait," recounted Nichols, and "the CINC says '*holy smokes I can't wait for this.*'" The plan still called for A-Day on March 21 and the main mass of maneuver on March 22 but after the missile shots the reaction was "'*we've got to do this right now.*'"[430]

Moseley at the air component agreed. The "land component was concerned about having itself in those cantonment areas just parking and just receiving fire. I agreed. I told David, [McKiernan] *'Let's get you out of there.'*"[431]

V Corps, I MEF and British forces bound for Basra moved steadily across the Line of Departure and into Iraq just before midnight local time on March 20, 2003. The I MEF under the command of Lieutenant General James Conway began its attack around 6:30 PM local time. Regimental combat teams moved in to help SOF forces secure the southern oilfields and take the city of Umm Qasar. SOF forces capture H-2 airfield in western Iraq and SEALS led the seizure of two Iraqi oil and gas terminals in the Persian Gulf. Then, the Third Infantry Division crossed from Kuwait into southern Iraq in the early morning hours of March 21, 2003.[432]

PULLING TARGETS

Ground war timing nibbled away at the air war plans again.

On the evening of March 20, F/A-18 pilot Commander Kevin F. Greene, from *Constellation*, was flying a typical mission "circling the border of Kuwait," he said. They had no idea they'd be flying into Iraq that night. A radio call informed them the ground assault had started pushing from the Kuwait border up to Basra. The ground forces wanted suppressing fires. A Marine controller relayed instructions for Greene to launch a JDAM – not at precise mensurated coordinates, as would have been required for an OSW mission, but on grid coordinates for an area where Iraqi artillery was firing at US ground forces.[433]

Moving up the ground force attack had a ripple effect on another piece of the air war, strategic attack, by taking some of the southernmost targets off the table. Nichols said, "all the strategic A-day targets that were inside CFLCC battlespace we had to pull because we can't attack those in the CFLCC battlespace. Technically we could have, but we didn't have time," he said. "There was too much uncertainty. We pulled 301 DMPIs including 124 TLAM missions, all the *Kitty Hawk* targets went away. We re-rolled those missions."[434]

"It happened so quickly that a lot of pre-planned targets went away, because the Army and Marines went past them," said Moffit.[435]

U.S. Marines from the 2nd Battalion, 1st Marine Regiment escort captured enemy prisoners of war to a holding area in the desert of Iraq on March 21, 2003, during Operation Iraqi Freedom. DoD photo by Lance Cpl. Brian L. Wickliffe, U.S. Marine Corps.

"All of our targets that were scripted that night were overrun," said Driscoll. "So now we can't bomb there." Instead, "that day we got word, *'now you're doing close air support.'*"[436]

In a taste of things to come, the sheer volume of sorties available proved overwhelming. Re-rolling to CAS did not work out for Driscoll's pilots from *Kitty Hawk*. "The ASOC, with our one E-2 controller, was inundated with more sorties than the ASOC could handle. And so all of our aircraft came back that evening with bombs. Not one of them dropped a bomb."[437]

The inability to reschedule *Kitty Hawk's* assets was the first hint of weaknesses in the system for tasking air support to the soldiers of V Corps. More problems would come as the land component forces pushed ahead.

THE FIVE AIR WARS

Despite the juggling at the start, the air component was off to a strong start. Aircrews flew 2339 sorties on March 20.[438]

The OIF air war was simultaneous – doing everything at once. "We essentially had five concurrent fights for CFACC," Nichols explained. They were:

+ Air dominance – "air superiority with SEAD, DEAD and DCA"
+ Strategic attack – "A-Day played out all over the country"
+ The West fight – counter-Scud efforts, a "presidential tasking"
+ The North fight – helping SOF teams engage Iraqi forces north of Baghdad
+ The South fight – support for the CFLCC's V Corps and I MEF. The south fight ultimately came to dominate sortie allocation and it drove requirements for carriers in the Persian Gulf.

"Of course there were multiple subsets of each of these," he added.[439]

Air dominance had begun with Operation Southern Focus, but the first several days still required strikes on air defense targets such as Iraq's major airfields. Aircrews on early missions saw plenty of anti-aircraft artillery fire.

The West fight involved a dedicated force of fighters and bombers – including a shore detachment of four F-14s from *Kitty Hawk* assigned to work with SOF forces, who wanted their two-man crews and advanced reconnaissance capabilities.

Still to come was the main thrust of the strategic attacks. Scrubbing some southern targets impacted timing but did not alter the overall importance of the air component's strategic attack. Operation Iraqi Freedom centered on regime change and only the air component could strike the first direct blows. Franks' guidance to Moseley was clear: You will strike regime command and control. You will strike regime security. You will strike headquarters elements, personalities, high-priority targets. Strategic attacks on targets like these would put the Iraqi leadership behind the power curve in assessing and reacting to the war.[440]

Nichols described strategic attack as "a great continuum of targets" that "made sense" as part of the larger joint plan. It wasn't an air war unto itself.

Nor was it the 'shock and awe' campaign much-anticipated by the media. Prior to OIF, "OSD folks had a sort of shock and awe doctrine that they were trying to push, and this was early in the planning," said Robb. Those closest to the war disavowed the term. "We weren't going to shock and awe Saddam out of his house," Robb said. "It was all kind of really meaningless."[441] Moseley bluntly said: "The term shock and awe has never been a term that I've used. I'm not sure where that came from."[442]

However, Robb acknowledged that due to the hype "the press sure expected that there was going to be some sort of a giant fireworks show."[443]

"A-Day" delivered just that with air and missile attack on March 21, at about 9 PM local time in Iraq. It blended elements of all five air wars, concentrating on strategic attack and air superiority, but with many other significant targets included.

"This is the night we've been talking about," Rear Admiral Barry Costello, battle group commander aboard *Constellation*, told the crews. "As a result of the mission you're doing tonight, the world is going to be a better place tomorrow. Godspeed," he said.[444]

Strikes assigned to the *Constellation's* aircrews that night included targets in and around Baghdad. Around the capital, air defenses were up and running in a zone called the Super Missile Engagement Zone or Super MEZ, marked out on the planning charts as an ink-splat of overlapping circles of SAM rings. "This was varsity stuff," said Nichols.[445]

Keating quizzed him on the plan. Carrier aircraft were chopped to the CFACC for operational control, but administratively, Keating owned those in the 5th Fleet AOR, and the status of the Super MEZ was enough to make any combat aviator feel the responsibility keenly.

"I've got his airplanes fragged into these darker and darker blue circles," said Nichols. "He looked at them and said 'Nickel, are you sure about this?'

"I said, 'Timbo, we got every possible defense suppression thing we can do. We're going to lose airplanes. But the CINC said losing airplanes is okay. This is war.'"[446]

In fact, the CAOC painstakingly worked to deflate the effectiveness of the Super MEZ. "We were allowed to use the defense suppression techniques that we wanted to use," Nichols said. The first couple of nights featured plenty of pre-emptive HARM shots, then the "pre-briefed HARM dropped off pretty quick."[447]

Still, the Super MEZ did not disappoint. On the approach to Baghdad, intense anti-aircaft fire reflected off a cloud layer. "It was like being in a stadium with a million camera flashes going off," said CAG Captain Mark Fox.[448]

A-Day's combined attacks surged to over 2500 total sorties. The results were excellent. "Their ability to see what is happening on the battlefield, to communicate with their forces and to control their country is slipping away," Rumsfeld proclaimed as the attacks got underway.[449]

Top of the list were counter-air strikes that accounted for 40 percent of air targets over the first two days but tapered to 28 percent from March 21-24 and down to 15 percent by March 25, an average that held for the rest of OIF. Opening attacks also struck at 59 separate national headquarters, command and control centers, and VIP residences. Regime security and support was another major target category. It included 104 targets such as intelligence services, security facilities, Special Republican Guards facilities, Ba'ath Party Headquarters, and known Fedayeen facilities. The air component also attacked 112 communications targets consisting of cable and fiber optic relays, repeater stations, exchanges, microwave sites, some television and radio transmitters, antennae, and more.[450]

WAR IN THE NORTH

Of all the five air wars, the north fight had perhaps the most twists and turns at the start. *Truman* and *Roosevelt* were on station in the Mediterranean to lend major support to the "north fight" – however it might evolve.

"In any case, there will be a northern option, with or without Turkey," Myers stated on March 5.[451] On March 10 the decision was made to swing the TLAM shooters through the Suez Canal and into the Persian Gulf since overflight clearances for their missiles were in jeopardy. Two weeks later, chances for a conventional second front plummeted from slim to none, given the Turkish political situation. Still, Franks was not yet ready to relinquish the deception effect by publicly taking the option of employing the 4th ID off the table. But the division was not going ashore – even if ships carrying its equipment lingered in the Med.

An F/A-18C Hornet awaits launch from the flight deck aboard the USS Theodore Roosevelt on Apr. 13, 2003. U.S. Navy photo by Photographer's Mate Airman Aaron Burden.

"That left us with about a thousand SOF troops in the north to fix 11 Iraqi divisions, supported by two carrier air wings," said Nichols.[452] The north fight would look much like Afghanistan, with US and Coalition SOF teams on the ground directing airstrikes and teaming with the Kurdish Peshmerga forces, diehard opponents of Saddam's Ba'athist regime.

Access constraints regulated the pace of the north fight by affecting overflight clearances and tanker distribution. "I'd say the day before the war I'm still wrangling with the Egyptians, the Jordanians, and the Turks over trying to get carrier air over Iraq," Robb said. "And the tankers to support them."[453] Without Turkish overflight routes and tanker basing there was no efficient way to bring the two airwings into the fight. One possibility was to put *Truman* and *Roosevelt* on hold for a few days to smooth out overflight and tankers. However, on March 20, "we were directed to include the Med carriers in A-day strikes even if they had to go across the Sinai," Nichols said.[454]

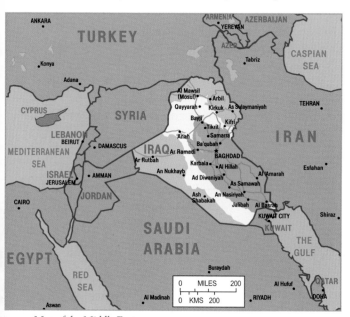

Map of the Middle East.

The CAOC knew it was a suboptimal use of the carrier air wings but they opted for a back-up plan to route strikes around from the west. Even so, it was touch and go as to whether all the pieces would fall into place for the complex routing. CENTCOM now had overflight clearance for Saudi Arabia and that opened up the Sinai routing plan. "I had to get a bump-up of over flights over the Sinai, which we got from Egypt, from 100 to 400 a day," said Robb. Then "we flew the carrier air south across the Sinai and then over to Saudi Arabia then up into Iraq."[455]

"There was lots of hate and discontent over the tankers," Nichols said. But it was not confined to the carriers. Host nation access problems left the whole air component scrambling. Nichols contrasted the tanker situation to Operation Desert Storm, where the air component had 350 tankers at five principal bases, each with "big old pipes running to them with fuel." In March 2003, the fight started with 210 tankers at *fifteen* bases which got their fuel stocks from miles-long delivery lines of tanker trucks stretching out the gates.[456]

Navy, Air Force and Coalition aircraft were all affected and griped about sorties they couldn't fly due to lack of available tankers. "This was a combined air force, so if it was bad news, it was bad news for everybody," said Nichols.[457] Complaints quickly hit the press but as Keating said later, "it didn't affect the overall campaign." The air component was "able to move gas around tactically and operationally, if you will, near

136

real-time, and then make some accommodations in the air tasking order."[458] In the end, the units "that complained most about not getting tankers were the A-10 guys and the F-15E guys," pointed out Moseley.[459]

Logistics aside, the north fight got underway, beginning with pre-assigned targets that were part of the strategic attacks of A-Day and beyond. Stufflebeem, on *Truman*, was told to "be ready on a moment's notice to be sucked through the Suez and reestablished in the Red Sea." That would be a better solution than continuing to fly the long Sinai route. Then, "Turkey came through with their air coordination permission and we raced up and then just used the highway we already planned for and built the on-ramp up north," said Stufflebeem. Now *Truman* and *Roosevelt* became airpower mainstays of the north fight. In the end "we only did about 5 days worth of servicing the master attack plan and just hitting targets and very quickly shifted to supporting these teams on the ground." He termed it "directed fires more than traditional close air support."[460]

Several pilots were Afghanistan veterans and one such was Lynch, who again found herself on the night carrier, this time, the *Roosevelt*. She found the combat missions "more intense than Afghanistan missions just because the threat in Iraq was real."[461]

Lynch described a typical mission. After launching and taking on fuel from an S-3, strike aircraft headed toward Iraq along the pre-planned route. "The driveway took about an hour and a half. Once we got at the end of the driveway into northern Iraq, they had big wing tankers up there on different stations and then we would go in to

Over the Middle East, an F/A-18 Hornet assigned to the USS Harry S. Truman conducts refueling operations with a U.S. Air Force KC-135R Stratotanker on Apr. 16, 2003. U.S. Air Force photo by Tech Sgt. Robert J. Horstman.

our assigned tanker and get our gas. Generally, after we got our gas, we'd be talking with AWACS or whoever to give us our airborne targets and we'd go to our station, and then we basically wait for them to tell us alright, go on in and contact a ground FAC on this frequency, and then we would start talking with the ground FAC. And we would do coordination with them and they'd tell us when we could come on in and drop."[462]

WAR IN THE SOUTH

While air and SOF held the north, the main movement of Coalition forces was in the south.

CTF 50 in the Persian Gulf under Kelly's tactical command became "the strike commander for the three carriers," Kelly said of the tasking. That meant assuming duties for area air defense over the Red Sea as well as the Persian Gulf, and positioning and deconflicting the TLAM shooters. Another task was "to integrate three air wings" operating in a busy and confined sea space that was "roughly half the space that the carriers operated in during Gulf War I."

"We had to decide on a scheme of maneuver that would enable the carriers to operate in enough water so we didn't scrape paint off the bottoms," Kelly said. Typically two carriers were about 15 to 20 miles apart, with the third 60 to 70 miles away.[463]

Sometimes there just didn't seem to be enough room in the Gulf. *Kitty Hawk* was on the eastern side at the north end of the Gulf to cut the range for the F/A-18s. Moffit recalled the ship "plowing towards an oil platform at a high rate of speed and we're waiting for this guy to get aboard and it's that typical naval aviation situation where you're trying to judge your closure with the aircraft's arrest and it got pretty close," he said.[464]

"But we worked very hard to compress the distance," Kelly said, because "every mile we moved further in greatly improved the flexibility and in the end bought you more time on station." Delivering what the CAOC called counter-land support was all about persistence. "Time on station equated to resolving the fog of war. Time on station equated to a higher percentage of ordnance delivered against a valid target," Kelly knew.[465]

On the ground, the land component's objective was to move ahead on the main highways with the Army on the left and the Marines on the right. Lead elements of the 3rd Infantry Division penetrated 100 miles into Iraq by March 21. Their advance had "already moved the distance of the longest maneuver of the 1991 Gulf war in one quarter of the time," a CENTCOM spokesman announced.[466] The 101st Airborne Division also crossed into Iraq behind the spearhead of the 3rd Infantry Division. As the supporting effort, I MEF set its course for Baghdad, swinging in from the east to link up with V Corps' advance.

Lieutenant Commander Zeno Rausa from *Constellation* saw an "encouraging" sight on a night sortie on March 22: "A wall of lights going north, about 10 miles long," Rausa said. "It was our troops advancing forward toward Baghdad."[467]

The objective was for V Corps to reach the Karbala area as quickly as possible. From there, the Army and Marines could then move forward, encircle the southern approaches to Baghdad, and drive into its heart to topple the regime. They planned to bypass cities in southern and central Iraq and maneuver around Iraqi regular army units.

The fast pace multiplied demands for air support, and the carriers prepared to meet it. "The ground war as it developed presented the opportunity to General Franks to accelerate the fight, to rapidly move forces forward, across a very broad front," said Kelly. It was not maneuver "in the traditional way of a line of forces moving, having cleared out everything and having safe territory behind, but instead [it was] like a patchwork quilt... which often left a substantial amount of the enemy behind them," he explained. The ground forces were "trading [the] higher order effect of the rapid movement on winning the conflict, for increased risk associated with not having sanitized what would then be behind all these units."

"Let me clarify, it was as much killbox activity as it was CAS," said Moffit of this period. He noted the value of strike coordination and reconnaissance where qualified airborne FACs positioned over a group of killboxes to direct inbound strike aircraft to targets. "They would go to the killbox and identify targets," Moffit said of the airborne FACs, "and then the bomb trucks – the F/A-18s – would come in and the FAC would place them on targets and eliminate those targets."[468]

It was up to the air component to reduce that risk with deep attack ahead of the land component and on-call airpower anywhere it was requested. Together these killbox interdiction/close air support taskings would consume 79% of the air component's strikes during OIF. "KI/CAS" – gleefully pronounced *kick-ass* – was the top commodity provided by carrier strike across a complex battlefield. The maneuvering pincers of V Corps and I MEF created what Kelly termed "this checkerboard, a checkerboard times a thousand in its complexity." *Lincoln, Constellation* and *Kitty Hawk* were now "launching massive numbers of sorties because all of those individual units now have increased risk associated with them. They all need close air support in a much smaller and much

USS Harry S. Truman Deputy Carrier Air Wing Commander discusses strategic flight coordinates with an Intelligence Officer on Mar. 19, 2003 in the ship's Carrier Intelligence Center. U.S. Navy photo by Photographer's Mate 1st Class Michael W. Pendergrass.

more dynamic environment than we have flown close air support [in] before." As Kelly noted, the "communications requirements to sustain that massive complexity provided very high stress on the overall battle management system."[469]

COORDINATION

The air component now had three major challenges in the south fight: rear area security, forward battlefield assessment, and most of all, keeping up the pressure on Iraq's military forces.

The land component met its first serious resistance at An Nasiriyah. Army forces took the city's key highway junction then drove on north toward Karbala while the Marines moved in from the right to surround and secure the city. However, Special Republican Guards forces had "infiltrated forward in an effort to conduct these types of raids as our troops come through the area," CENTCOM Deputy Commander Lieutenant General John Abizaid later said.[470] They were not enough of an army to defend Nasiriyah but they could and did take a toll on Coalition soldiers and marines.

The carriers wanted to push their strikes forward and deliver as many bombs as possible. "After the initial surge of air operations, we are increasingly transitioning to support those ground operations," said Kelly on March 24.[471] But the switch from pre-assigned targets to counterland support tasking and emerging targets did not go smoothly at first.

For *Kitty Hawk*, pledged to land component support, early glitches with the Air Support Operations Center (ASOC) directing support for V Corps now mushroomed. Until OIF, the ASOC was a mythical beast for most naval aviators. "I'd never worked with an ASOC," Moffit recalled. "I'd never worked with their entire organization."[472]

V Corps, moving fast, needed the air component to shape the battlefield ahead. Unfortunately, the lack of familiarity surrounding the ASOC had now gone beyond growing pains and turned into real discrepancies that affected operations. The ASOC (an Air Force unit technically part of 9th Air Force but attached to V Corps headquarters for operations) was still in Kuwait. Driscoll and other CAGs had been ashore to meet with the ASOC. The command and control just wasn't working. "They didn't have enough awareness on the ATO; they weren't getting the ATO at first," Driscoll recalled. "They had no idea what was coming to them. They had a hard time getting the demand from the field. They just had not exercised and trained at that volume of warfare," he assessed.[473]

Problems at the ASOC were vexing because it was the ASOC's job to direct in-bound strike packages to airborne forward air controllers, ground forward air controllers, or open killboxes where pilots could release ordnance at will under the ROE. Lack of coordination was wasting time, bombs and sorties. The ASOC "couldn't keep up with the speed of advance of the ground force," said Nichols. "So frequently they'd be 40, 50 miles behind the FSCL. And they didn't know what was going on on the other side of the FSCL, so they couldn't get our guys handed off to a FAC."[474]

Fixes soon came from the CAOC and from the carriers. Driscoll, with Moffit's approval, sent another Navy liaison from the *Kitty Hawk* air wing to the ASOC and brought an Army major out to the ship.

Then, the E-2s stepped into the fray, and they made all the difference.

Driscoll initially tasked an E-2 for a local mission "to go up there and talk to the ASOC, talk to the AWACS, talk to everybody, get all of our clearances, find out where all the tankers are, and get all the frequencies all the way to the forward controller and then when the Hornets check in, you tell them everything they need to know and get them cleared so we don't waste all of our gas and all of our time trying to get the C2 part of it squared away."

The experiment "worked like a champ," said Driscoll. The next day, "we tried the same thing, but we did it for all of our flights, and it worked." Instead of relying completely on the ASOC – and having to turn back with ordnance unexpended – "the E-2s took over that role as airborne command and control."[475]

"They did a really wonderful job of coordinating the movement of the ordnance to where it needed to be," said Moffit.[476] The E-2s worked the tasking line-up for both the V Corps sector and the I MEF Sector. They made every aspect of the mission from tanking to command and control more efficient. CVW-5 also "spent a lot of time working for the Marines," Driscoll added. If communications with the ASOC failed or controllers there had no targets "the E-2 would roll over and check with Marines if they needed CAS and we'd support them as well. We called it 'shopping for dropping,'" Driscoll said.[477]

Ultimately, the ASOC released 625 of 2117 – almost 30% – of its assigned strike sorties to "other controlling agencies," V Corps reported later.[478]

An E-2C Hawkeye launches from one of four steam powered catapults aboard the USS Harry S. Truman on May 22, 2003. U.S. Navy photo by Photographer's Mate 2nd Class Danny Ewing Jr.

Higher headquarters shared the opinion of the operators. "We found that given anywhere from 300 to 600 close air support sorties, we needed somebody in the air to manage those. And it turned out to be the United States Navy E-2s," Nichols said.[479]

Deep Attack

Getting strike aircraft to their targets was critical because it was up to the air component to shape the battle ahead of the land component forces. Franks' speed plan depended on short, sharp, successful engagements. The soldiers and Marines of the Coalition were more than a match for their Iraqi counterparts in close fighting. However, on paper the Iraqis outnumbered the Coalition by three to one. They also had the advantage of being on the defensive. Breaking regular Iraqi Army and Republican Guards units apart was essential.

Just as the carrier airstrikes were intensifying, a failed Apache attack on the Medina division proved just how much the Coalition was relying on the air component.

On March 23-24, as V Corps lead elements pressed on toward Najaf and the Karbala gap, Wallace wanted to bring firepower to bear on the Medina division sitting astride the approaches to Baghdad. Although air attacks were continuous, Army commanders worried that the Medina was so dispersed that they could not be spotted from the air, so it would take low-flying Apache helicopters to root out and attack its equipment.[480] V Corps hastily established a forward arming and refueling point and arranged a preparatory ATACMS strike to blast a corridor for the low-flying Apaches. CFLCC headquarters pushed V Corps' FSCL far ahead to keep the air component attacks out of the way.

Thirty Apaches took off to fly 50 miles ahead to attack the Medina division. But the Iraqis knew they were coming. Farm lights blinked signals of their approach. Small arms fire, the traditional foe of the helicopter, came at them in waves. The Army's official after action report remarked: "no one really understood that small-arms and light ADA cannon could be showstoppers."[481]

Unfortunately, extending the fire support coordination line restricted the air component's fixed-wing attacks by closing off killboxes over the Medina division. It was a rare but regrettable example of discord between the components. The CAOC realized it would happen. Nichols explained that the land component wanted to "push the FSCL out as far as they can so they can use Apaches or ATCMs or whatever to engage targets between them and the FSCL. And I was the guy who agreed to all those FSCL movements," he said. He "thought it was too early to move the FSCL, but I didn't think it was going to be worth the fight we were going to get in over it." Nichols argued for making provisions to bomb inside the FSCL but "it didn't happen."[482]

While strike fighters were kept out of the action, the Apache deep attack failed. "Virtually every helicopter came back with bullet holes in it and no effect with their weapons," said Nichols.

"As our attack aviation approached the attack positions, they came under intense enemy fire," Army V Corps Commander Lieutenant General William Scott Wallace later said. One Apache was shot down and the 29 others had to break off the attack after suffering battle damage. "The attack of the 11th Aviation on the Medina Division did not meet the objectives that I had set for that attack," Wallace acknowledged.[483] The Apaches averaged 15-20 bullet holes apiece.[484] "Not a single tank or artillery piece of the Medina division was damaged in the attack," Franks confirmed.[485]

"On the one hand it was a cheap lesson, because I believe we only lost one helicopter," Nichols later said. "On the other hand, it induced a little bit of doubt in these guys who'd been running hard for a couple of days."[486]

Strike fighters and other fixed wing air were the appropriate tools for taking apart the Republican Guard. Flowing air into the "checkerboard" as Kelly termed it became even more imperative. Concern about the location and status of the Republican Guards had been a big part of the CFLCC's reason for launching the Apache attack. Its failure threw the matter back to the air component. Questions abounded. Were Coalition lines of communication secure? Could the Republican Guard divisions that lay ahead mount a counterattack or fall back and put up a defense of Baghdad?

TROUBLE BREWING

"Then the weather went crappy," said Nichols.[487] Weather experts preparing the five-day forecast for the joint components were tracking a powerful storm belt gathered over the Mediterranean. Sophisticated computer modeling of the storm's atmospherics made for an unwelcome forecast. This front would travel over Saudi Arabia's flat deserts and stir up fine dust and blowing sand. Once it hit Iraq and Kuwait the storm would morph into a vicious *shamal* or sandstorm. Forecasters at the CAOC started to color in "red" status for certain airbases in its path. Dust would also degrade electro-optical and infrared sensors.

Franks realized that in 24 hours "we would have no helicopters and no Predators in the air."[488]

"And that's when CFLCC turned to CFACC and said *'ok, what's out in front of me dead?'"* Nichols recalled.[489]

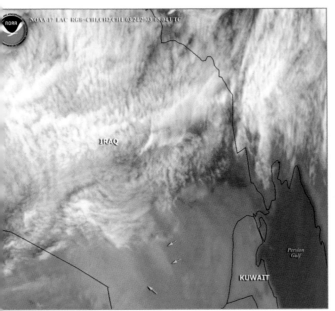

Assessing the level of attrition on the Republican Guards units was imperative. Rear areas were becoming a source of concern, too. Ahead and behind them the land forces faced uncertainty as the weather closed in.

A NOAA polar-orbiting satellite captures images of large sand storms spread over a wide area of southern Iraq on March 24, 2003, at 3:04 a.m. EST. Photo courtesy of NOAA.

The fast forward drive of OIF had left major pockets of resistance in its wake and CFLCC forces were starting to feel the persistent weight of irregular forces attacks. "This was a symmetric battlefield, conventional force *vs.* conventional force," Nichols said. "But there were a whole bunch of potential asymmetric threats that we had to be ready for," he added.

One came from Saddam's irregular forces. Most of the units had been formed in the 1990s, after the Gulf war. They included Al Quds Ba'ath party militia, the Saddam Fedayeen, and Special Republican Guards forces. In 2003, CENTCOM put the total numbers of irregular forces at about 40,000. Little was known about their command and control structure. The focus on the regular Army and Republican Guards put the Fedayeen in the shadows during the year of planning. Franks said that prior to OIF, "at no point had I thought these forces would be moved into the south to fight as guerillas."[490]

Soldiers and Marines at Nasiriyah and along the roads to Baghdad quickly learned otherwise. Fanatic Fedayeen, apparently under local Ba'ath party control, were conducting attacks on Coalition forces wherever they could. The attacks were not coordinated offensives but they posed a serious problem in rear area security.

It was like Saddam's reaction to Operation Desert Fox in 1998 when he strengthened internal control measures and conducted "minor movements" of irregular forces for counterinsurgency operations. There were "units dedicated to this," Zinni had said at the time, and they kept up brutal counterinsurgency operations against the Shi'ites in the south during the four days of Operation Desert Fox.[491]

"Thousands of fedayeen fighters, who wear black uniforms or civilian clothes, are now in the southern zone, according to American estimates, and have produced the largest American casualties so far," noted a *New York Times* reporter accompanying McKiernan on March 24.[492]

Wallace later spoke of his surprise at the Iraqi tactics in the initial contact at An Nasiriyah. "He was willing to attack out of those towns toward our formations, when my expectation was that they would be defending those towns and not be as aggressive," Wallace said of the Iraqis.[493]

Rear areas were the most vulnerable to *fedayeen* attacks. From Basra to the front of the spearhead near Karbala, every city held a threat of *fedayeen* attack. "The irregular element has been greater than we predicted, and their resolve has been greater than expected," commented a colonel with Britain's 7th Armored Regiment, which was fighting near Basra. More than two hundred miles ahead, leading Army elements were finding the same level of resistance in sporadic but fierce firefights. "Their tactic is to put those trucks right in your face," said Lieutenant Colonel Terry Ferrell of the 3-7 CAV, at the front of the V Corps spearhead. "They're not afraid to die. They're not afraid to fight.[494]

Attacks from these unconventional forces created a major test for Coalition airpower during the sandstorm of March 25-26, 2003. Only the air component had the flexibility to cover rear area support and keep up the deep attacks at the same time.

"I Could Taste the Dust..."

The storm front made landfall moving west to east and fetched up sand from the Saudi desert, holding it in layers up to 15,000 feet. A gritty orange haze reduced visibility and wind gusts, rain and thunderstorms followed. "It was biblical," said Colonel Rick Gibbs, 101st Airborne. "There's a movie – *Scorpion King* – that shows this same kind of sandstorm. That's the only other place I've seen it like that, and I grew up in Texas, where we had plenty of this," Gibbs attested.[495]

"I could taste the dust on the rim of my coffee cup," said Franks of the afternoon of March 25, 2003.[496]

At sea, sand blew in the open bridge wing doors of the *USS Shiloh*, part of the *Abraham Lincoln* battle group. The dusty haze made normal flight operations impossible at times. Aboard *Kitty Hawk*, "we shut down flight operations and lost about two or three cycles so we probably lost 20 sorties," said Rocha.[497]

"You have to remember it isn't all about the airplanes," said Kelly of the sandstorm. On land, airbases could close and ground forces could hunker down. At sea, they had to keep moving.

"You've got a ship's command team that is running a hundred thousand ton ship around through sandstorms at 30 knots in a extremely dense contact [environment]. The logistics ships that are doing the same thing. The degree of professionalism shown by the Navy team in sustaining those operations despite that extremely adverse weather was amazing," Kelly continued. When "one carrier was enveloped and just not able to fly, the other carrier was picking up the slack increasing sorties, literally real time."[498]

An E-2C Hawkeye prepares to launch from the flight deck aboard the aircraft carrier USS Kitty Hawk on Mar. 27, 2003 while a sandstorm blows across the Arabian Gulf region. U.S. Navy photo by Photographer's Mate 3rd Class Todd Frantom.

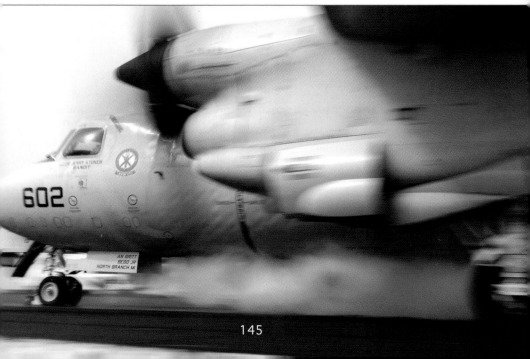

Nekamoto was returning from a mission when the sandstorm shut down *Constellation's* flight operations. "We had a tanker that was going home that had 30 or 40 thousand pounds of opportunity gas," he said. With full tanks they took up position near the ship to try to recover. But the sandstorm continued. One F/A-18 with plenty of gas tried an approach but the pilot never saw the ship. After that, with the sun coming up, Nekamoto and others diverted to Shaik Isa airfield, where the weather was not much better. They decided to land right away before the full force of the sandstorm hit there, too.

It was just in time. "Literally 15 minutes after we landed – we're still in the jets taxiing to the little transient ramp, [when] the sandstorm comes blowing through there," he said. Hornets, Prowlers, an E-2 and some S-3s also diverted. "You could barely see the other jet that was parked next to you. They made makeshift covers and put duct tape over the pitot tubes to keep the sand out. "Before we started up the next day, we had to sweep out the intakes. There was literally probably a quarter inch of sand in the intakes."

Then *Constellation* got a call that "some of our Marines were about to get chemical attacked down near al Kut," recalled Greene, who was standing current ops watch at the time. No one was flying. But *Constellation* launched a few airplanes with JSOW "knowing full well the weather back at the ship was not conducive to landing," said Greene. The package mixed senior and junior pilots so it was "a pretty proud day for *Con* and for naval aviation." All recovered aboard ship.[499]

Due to plenty of advance notice the air component turned the sandstorm period into a "JDAM-fest," as one planner called it. GBU-12 expenditures dipped while JDAM strikes soared. Some sorties were cancelled due to weather – but the switch to SAR for ISR platforms and to JDAM weapons loads ensured the overall intensity did not diminish. The level of effort graph for the air component was still on the upswing.

Even more important, the air component provided an indispensable source of firepower for ground forces facing regular Iraqi army or Fedayeen counterattacks.

Lieutenant Michael Rovenholt later said his most satisfying mission was one he flew from *Kitty Hawk* during the sandstorm. "We dropped a couple of JDAM for some guys in V Corps," Rovenholt said. "They were taking fire and they had their coordinates and they wanted the JDAM on these coordinates." Following a special briefed procedure, the pilots "read back those coordinates" then called "*thunder*" for the JDAM release.[500]

Kelly saw nothing but increased determination in the faces of his aircrews. The ground war was growing more intense and complex and "despite extremely adverse weather, the air crews were determined to be over top" the engaged ground forces. "That manifested itself in coming back to the ship with ever-decreasing fuel reserves, and accepting more and more risk on the part of each and every air crew in order to turn around, in order to get back in the air over top of those guys on the ground and to be there when they needed," he noticed.

He had to counsel them not to let their willingness to take personal risks make them forget that creeping incremental acceptance of risk had to be kept under control for the good of the squadron, the air wing and the campaign as a whole. It took a direct stab at a very emotional point to convince them. "You lose the airplane, forget about the risk to yourself, you lose that airplane, I've lost 200 sorties," Kelly told his aircrews. "If your goal is to be there when they need you, then you can't allow yourself to accept

Waiting on deck on Apr. 15, 2003, an F-14 Tomcat displays the bombs and missiles, below the canopy, that this Tomcat has dropped in support of Operation Iraqi Freedom. U.S. Navy photo by Photographer's Mate 2nd Class Felix Garza Jr.

inordinate risk on any particular missions. You need to fly in a way and preserve your safety margins sufficient that you are going to bring that airplane back and be able to turn it around and use it again."[501]

Momentum was everything. Said Keating: "we did not dramatically decrease the total airborne sortie rate during the bad sandstorm in late March. We had sensors to which weather is irrelevant and weapons that don't care about the weather."[502]

Ahead, the air component employed SAR sensors to keep targeting the Republican Guards. "The sandstorm was a blessing in disguise because the Iraqis believed that they could hide. And they believed that they could mask movement. Global Hawk didn't care about that. Nor did JSTARS. Nor did JDAM," summed up Moseley.[503]

Closer in, airstrikes delivered support across all the southern and western killboxes where soldiers and Marines were protecting the LOCs.

One unit that appreciated it was the 3-7 CAV, which began its mission to isolate An Najaf from the south on the morning of March 25 and fought continuously for 60 hours in the "negative illumination" of the mud storm, as one soldier called it. The 3-7 CAV had artillery support but later recorded that "CAS had provided the lion's share of support with 182 sorties" during their battle.[504]

"The bombardment that lasted from the night of March 25 through the morning of March 27 was one of the fiercest, and most effective, in the history of warfare," Franks praised.[505]

CHAPTER 9:

Decisive Combat Operations

"This was a different war.... It was joint war fighting at the highest form of the art I've ever seen." – Admiral Timothy Keating, June 2003[506]

Juggling the opening blows and coping with the sandstorm saw Operation Iraqi Freedom off to a strong start after just one week. Ahead lay the main tests for carrier striking power. Decisive combat operations depended on fixing Iraqi forces in the north, defeating the Republican Guard and taking Baghdad itself.

An F/A-18 Hornet catches the wire during an arrested landing on the flight deck during night flight operations in support of Operation Iraqi Freedom. U.S. Navy photo by Photographer's Mate Airman Justin McGarry.

THE PAUSE

First the land component had to conduct an operational pause and concentrate for the attacks toward Karbala and on to Baghdad.

V Corps "all but ceased moving north from 25 to 29 March," the Army's official report later attested. Combat "had by no means stopped or even slowed during the refit operations" but during this time the focus was on resupply and "cleaning up the roads and key chokepoints between the Kuwaiti border and Objective RAMS, in the vicinity of An Najaf."[507] Meanwhile, the air component kept up attacks on the Republican Guard and other targets in the west, south and north of Iraq. As Franks explained it, the fighting forces passed the ball so that "sometimes air, sometimes ground, sometimes Special Forces, sometimes a combination of two of the above, sometimes all three" were engaged.[508]

The air component did not experience a pause, but a steady increase in strikes.

Air strikes after the sandstorm "ramped up to about 1000 sorties a day against those formations. They got no pause," said Moseley. "What we see in many formations of the Republican Guards is some effort to try to reposition internally within their defenses," Brooks at CENTCOM said on March 28.[509] Lieutenant General James Conway at I MEF confirmed that "while we were stationary, we were, in fact, attacking with our air, taking maximum advantage of intelligence, surveillance and reconnaissance capabilities to determine what the enemy was that we faced."[510]

The pending restart of the V Corps drive redoubled the importance of hard-hitting air component attacks. Strike sorties for KI/CAS reached peak levels in late March and early April.

Carrier strike aircraft continued to deal with fixed targets and an upward swing in rapid tasking to killbox and CAS targets, coming from different sources.

Over the Middle East, F/A-18C Hornets are ready to return to their mission in support of Operation Iraqi Freedom after refueling from an Air Force KC-135R Stratotanker on Apr. 16, 2003. U.S. Air Force photo by Tech. Sgt Robert J. Horstman.

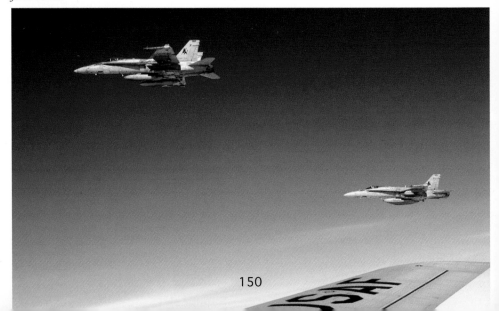

It still took persistence and skill. That began in the cockpit, as when a pair of F/A-18s also helped Apache helicopters get back into the fight with a more successful attack on the 14th Brigade of the Medina on the night of March 28. Lead Apaches spotted targets southeast of Karbala and after trying to work through channels to the ASOC, gave up and broadcast on emergency frequency. Gospel 01, a division of F/A-18s, picked up the call, contacted the lead Apaches, and continued the engagement.[511]

Gospel 01's ingenuity pointed out the on going problem with getting target tasking in the V Corps sector. In contrast, the DASC "was much better ready to manage a whole bunch of close air support sorties," said Nichols. "Those Marines rehearse and train in the combined arms fight with their DASC."[512] It helped that the DASC was focused on the division-level fight – in contrast to the ASOC, focused on a wider span of the Corps-level fight. The DASC was not set up for an organic deep fight across the theater with multiple assets but it was an efficient air control system to open the spigot for organic and Coalition aircraft into I MEF's hottest sectors. The DASC also put in place a supplementary Battlefield Coordination Line or BCL about 30 kilometers beyond the front to facilitate tasking; beyond the BCL, most killboxes were automatically open.

Correspondingly, the DASC had a bred-in-the-bone preference for organic Marine assets – in this case, those based ashore, not the Marine squadrons integrated into the afloat carrier airwings. But as I MEF pushed toward Baghdad, they needed, wanted and got much more than organic air. "Not very long into it, we started to get a whole lot of stuff coming in from CFACC in real-time or near real-time

Coalition troops track an ongoing Operation Iraqi Freedom mission at this Combined Air Operation Center. U.S. Air Force photo by SSGT Derrick C. Goode.

and shifted over to support our efforts," said Major Rich Hilberer of the DASC. The "amount we ended up getting from CFACC was way more than we ever expected."[513]

Then there was the CAOC, which generated pop-up tasking from lists of special targets for CENTCOM and used its ISR and operations cells to develop other dynamic targets. Pre-war procedure changes paid off in better handling of retaskings for TSTs by CENTCOM and the CAOC. For TSTs, additional ROE smoothed timely execution. First, TSTs were grouped in three categories as leadership, terrorist sites or potential WMD targets. Second, instead of constantly calling up the CAOC in the middle of heavy operations and demanding they hit what Predator had on video, CENTCOM generated a list of special targets and passed them to the CAOC. "We called them CINC critical targets," said Nichols. "They were equivalent of bombing the guy on the street corner. But they came out every day; they were put in front of our TST planners and executors. So if we had shot opportunities against these targets we went after them." It was also a good way to soak up "excess capacity off the battlefield" by routing aircraft that hadn't dropped ordnance for CAS to work the list. All told, 156 true TSTs were struck by the air component through mid-April 2003.

The CAOC had a second category termed dynamic targets: those of military importance, but not in the CENTCOM TST criteria. The air component hit 686 dynamic targets.

THE NORTHERN FRONT

As forces in the south regrouped at Karbala, the 4th Infantry Division with its 62,000 soldiers was at last on its way to the docks in Kuwait.

From the land component's perspective, the absence of the 4th Infantry Division even as a feint left open the question of how to deal with Ba'athist enclaves and Iraq's northern divisions, which could deepen the fight with the Republican Guard south of Baghdad and make it harder to take the city itself. Franks also wanted to secure the oilfields near Kirkuk and ensure no problems cropped up in the city of Mosul. Finally, Coalition forces would have to gain control of Saddam's native city and powerbase, Tikrit.

The north fight now depended entirely on carrier air, SOF forces, Kurdish Peshmerga and paratroopers from the 173rd Brigade.

Already on scene were the SOF forces who were in contact with Kurdish opposition forces. Like Afghanistan, the task was to keep striking power on call at the right times and get it to the right places. And like Afghanistan, the battle in the north ebbed and flowed. "There were only 56 ODA teams at the extreme in the north," explained Stufflebeem, and "then not every one of them was engaged in combat ops; they would still be crawling on their bellies developing reconnaissance and didn't need our services. They just needed to know we were there on call if they got into trouble."[514]

Truman and *Roosevelt* pumped sorties into the battlespace night and day. Aircrews were contending with several challenges. "The big issue for us was weather," said Stufflebeem. Big-wing tanking – as in Afghanistan – was a sporting challenge.

"We had young pilots who had to go fly to these tankers," said Stufflebeem. "Two things happened. One was that the tankers had started to convert to war configuration with the wing tip aerial refueling pods. On big-wing tankers, those big long hoses have much more movement than what we're used to," he said. Factor two was weather. There "were a lot of storms," he said. Sandstorms and thunderstorms bedeviled the aircrews. "So here are the tankers up at 40 thousand feet with these baskets flailing about out there on the wingtips in bad weather. And the guys having a long run to get there and then trying to safely get tanked and then into the fight and then back to tanking. That was a huge challenge for them," he noted.[515]

"Tanking in Iraq. Whew," Lynch recalled. "That was much more difficult than Afghanistan, and the reason was that the weather up there in northern Iraq was horrible." Lynch, like others, had at least one mission where post-strike refueling became critical. Two tankers went sour on her that night and "I was getting to the point where I was thinking I was going to have to divert into Turkey," she said. Diverting was unappealing. As Lynch put it, "you didn't want to go into a strange country, especially a country that really wasn't happy that you were there." In the end, tanker number three was available, and "I got gas, got to make it home," she finished.[516]

On the plus side, "I personally never had it happen to me and I don't know of anyone in the entire air wing who ever had a tanker not show up for them," said Lieutenant Geoffrey Bowman, an F/A-18 pilot on *Truman*. "So the Air Force was great in that respect." For the most part, "they would move the tanker track for us and try to get a bit of clear air space.[517]

Yet tanking and the weather were by no means the biggest challenges of the north fight. That honor, predictably, went to the task of coordinating with the teams on the ground.

BEYOND THE GREEN LINE

Early in the war most of the sorties flown by the Med carrier aircrews were preplanned targets. That changed as the carriers moved east and airwings started using the "highways" over Turkey and into Northern Iraq. "Once we moved to the north I'd say 100% CAS for me," Bowman said of the missions. "Every once in a while there'd be a preplanned target, but typically that would change. It was pretty much on-call stuff the entire time we were there in the north." Usually they "never had a pre-planned target assigned" but got coordinates over the radios.

"Originally we were going to support the whole northern invasion front," Bowman said. As it turned out, "we were up there supporting 1200 or so guys that were just dropped in."[518]

They were paratroopers from the Army's 173rd Brigade. On March 26, fifteen Air Force C-17s departing from Aviano AB, Italy dropped the paratroopers and their equipment on a soggy, 7,000 foot runway at Bashur in Kurdish-held Northern Iraq. The formation of airlifters spread out over a hundred miles long to space out each aircraft's time over the drop zone. Protection for the mission came from *Truman's* EA-6Bs, F-14s

U.S. Army paratroopers prepare to board a C-17 Globemaster III. U.S. Air Force photo by Tech. Sgt. Stephen Faulisi.

and F/A-18s. The airdrop was the largest since Panama in 1989 and it was intended "to provide additional combat power to the special operating forces that had already inserted themselves into Kurdish-held territory," said Air Force Major General Gene Renuart, at CENTCOM.[519] The next day, more C-17s started ferrying in additional members of the 2000-man brigade along with Bradley fighting vehicles, ammunition and other equipment and supplies.

With the 173rd on the ground the way was clear for a series of attacks beyond the Kurdish-controlled "Green Line" and into Iraq. Carrier airstrikes under SOF direction had already made an impression. As early as March 28, Kurds on the ground reported that some of the Republican Guard units from Kirkuk were drawing back to Tikrit, while others farther south were being siphoned off to reinforce Iraqi lines around Baghdad.[520] JSOTF-North, the 173rd Brigade and the Kurds attacked four different Iraqi divisions from March 30 to April 2. On April 2, the battalion-size Task Force Red Devil from the 173rd moved ahead 40 miles to Harir airfield near Irbil. Now Iraq's regular army 1st corps forces were less than 15 miles away.[521]

Additional combat power generated additional CAS taskings. Bowman said "those guys were dropped in with usually one qualified FAC per platoon, then they'd split the platoon up." As a result "it wasn't uncommon to get in contact with somebody who really didn't have [a] trained FAC, you know, they're trained in it, but you could tell in their comm that they weren't as smooth [and] they didn't exactly know all the comm to get your bombs on targets." The solution was to "be a little more careful with those guys, make sure you knew exactly what they were talking about, exactly where they were, before you start dropping."

Challenge number one was directing strike aircraft to the right locations. "We didn't have the link that would give us the blue force tracker or any of that sort of stuff. So guys just didn't have good situational awareness when they went into the north," said Stufflebeem.[522] Strike aircraft checked in with AWACS or E-2s for assignment to FACs waiting ahead in a particular killbox.

An E-2C Hawkeye launches from flight deck aboard the aircraft carrier USS Harry S. Truman during the beginning of daily flight operations on Mar. 27, 2003. U.S. Navy photo by Photographer's Mate Airman Dustin Gates.

Once strike aircraft were in contact with the right controllers the challenges continued. "The teams carried small handheld radios that are relatively low-powered so you had to go down pretty low to find these guys on the radio," said Stufflebeem. Many of the pilots were "neophytes in this business of JCAS. It was rough."[523] As Lynch said, "actually doing the missions and coordinating the ground FACs presented a challenge in that you wanted to do it right, you didn't want to screw it up, you didn't want to hurt any friendlies."[524]

There was no JACE to coordinate the SOF requests. "I don't know why," said Stufflebeem, "but it never got into theater." As with the south fight, there was no dedicated "airborne command and control platform that could fill in the space" as ABCCC once did, he added.[525]

Once again, it was the E-2s to the rescue. "They kind of knew more what we needed and they knew our gas constraints and so forth and they seemed to work a little bit harder for us to get us targets right away," said Bowman.[526] The E-2s from *Truman* and *Roosevelt* were able to get into Iraq about 50% of the time, according to Stufflebeem. They set up satellite communications links via the CAOC, and got in touch with SOF forces on the ground. Then the E-2s used basic voice communications "to transmit initial directions to fighters, either divisions or sections, coming off tankers, to go to certain kill boxes," Stufflebeem explained. When the crews launched, they did so "never knowing what [the] mission was going to be."[527]

Bowman and others worked a wide variety of targets under control of the 173rd and SOF and Coalition FACs. He described them as "anything from troops in the open to vehicles to even some buildings, and what they called command and control centers" which often turned out to be not much more elaborate than "a building with an antenna on top," according to Bowman.

The air war in the north demanded a variety of munitions. "We very much expected to go over and drop JDAM the whole war," Bowman recalled, and work-up training had emphasized it. Unless targets were pre-planned, JDAM rules mandated precise coordinates, which the ground controllers rarely supplied, in his experience. Controllers did

This F/A-18 Hornet is carrying a Joint Direct Attack Munition (JDAM) on its left wing pylon and a laser guided bomb (LGB) on its right wing pylon while conducting missions in support of Operation Iraqi Freedom. U.S. Navy photo by Lt. Perry Solomon.

not always have "the equipment necessary to give you very precise coordinates," he said. Types of targets affected the munitions used, too. The end result was that LGBs, dumb bombs and even the guns got frequent use as SOF teams and Army forces spread out their attacks across the Green Line.

Stufflebeem was determined not to run low on weapons – as he had seen happen in Afghanistan. Hornets with loads too heavy for recovery at the ship diverted to the RAF base at Akrotiri on Cyprus. "They landed, and they downloaded the big weapons, and then they just came back to the ship," explained Stufflebeem. "And we used CH-53s to lug those bombs back to the ship" to be used again.[528]

The 1000-lb. GBU-16 became a weapon of choice "because you could drop it and lase or you could drop it like a dumb bomb if you needed to roll in on something." They also carried "quite a bit of dumb ordnance," both the Mk 83s and Mk 82s. Also, "our Hornet squadrons up there used the gun quite a bit. Probably 70% or so of my flights, I came back without bullets," Bowman said.[529]

If troops wanted strafing they gave it to them. "It's a great CAS weapon," Bowman said of the gun. Typically FACs called for bombs first and "you would go in and expend your bombs. That would kind of shake up the nest." Bombs flushed out Iraqi troops in the open and that was "usually when the FACs would request 20 mm." Often that meant going below the 10,000 foot hard deck so pilots stayed on the alert for anti-aircraft fire or man-portable SAMs. On average, they gave the FACs two strafing passes expending all rounds. By then, it was time to go home, because "you'd probably already been in the area for about 10 or 15 minutes working the bombs, and now you're pretty predictable."[530]

The north fight quickly found its rhythm. Lynch remembered "little things, like talking with the ground FACs, just hearing their excitement level, when they would say stuff like 'awesome hit' and they would just be so excited," she said. That "was really fantastic to hear and it really felt good to know that you were helping them out or assisting them or taking out troops whenever they were under attack."[531]

In this fight, unlike the south, "we rarely used our Tomcats as FAC-As," recalled Bowman. "They certainly had the capability but with the guys we were supporting on the ground, it didn't seem necessary. They could usually talk our eyes on to it. And they didn't have the threat down there that typically took 5 sections to get rid of, usually when you're working FAC-A, they'll stack up 5 sections out there. He'll become familiar with the target set and start bringing them in 2 by 2, whereas we could usually go in with one section [and] take care of everything that particular group needed."[532]

DANGERS

There were still dangers. Lynch and her flight lead were on CAP over Tikrit when a SAM "launched up in our vicinity," she said. Clearly this missile "was for us. But it was not guided, we never got any indications, but we could see it." It was close enough "it really caught my attention. But not so close that we had to do any sort of evasive maneuvers."[533]

Supporting troops on the ground carried other risks. Bowman's most memorable mission started with a JDAM pass. He had JDAM, AMRAAM and the gun plus a wingman "with a full CAS-type load-out." They checked in with a FAC north of Mosul who was taking mortar fire from "one of those so-called command and control buildings." Fortunately this Coalition SOF FAC was well-equipped with a laser designator and the ability to pass precise JDAM coordinates. "He lased the LGB from my wingman's jet and hit one of the bunkers." Then Bowman's JDAM hit the command and control building. "At that point I guess about 30 or 40 troops came out and started moving the mortars, and started engaging the SOF unit again with mortars, and they requested 20mm."

Bowman and his wingman set up a strafe pattern overhead. "Strafed once. Good results out of each of us." Then on the second pass Bowman saw "a giant yellow flash in my face." A round had jammed halfway down and exploded in the barrel. "Then I realize I'm still holding the trigger, nothing's happening. So I let off the trigger and realize I'm still pointed at the ground." He pulled up, and headed immediately for the tanker. His lower canopy was "covered in gun soot" and the "radar had obviously frozen because it exploded the whole nose of the airplane." Fortunately, the fuel probe was undamaged, so Bowman made it to the tanker for gas. Back at the ship the LSO helped him as he "flew the airspeed instead of the AOA" for the night landing. The jet "looked like somebody just kind of stuck their fingers through the metal and peeled it back."[534]

Among the targets for the north fight were also fixed sites, including the known terrorist camps used by the Jordanian terrorist Zarqawi and Ansar Al Islam on the Iranian border.

Lynch got a chance to hit a terrorist site – while leading a junior wingman, at night. "One of my first targets was on the Iraq-Iran border on the northern edge and it was an al Qaeda camp," Lynch said. "I particularly remember that because, that's the whole root of September 11th and so I was pretty pumped up to go and take out an al Qaeda target."[535]

An F/A-18C Hornet pilot prepares to launch from the flight deck aboard the USS George Washington on Apr. 30, 2004. U.S. Navy photo by Photographer's Mate Airman Joan Kretschmer.

Airstrikes and TLAMS put it out of business. After reviewing BDA, Myers described it as "the former terrorist training camp." "The camp, in and around the villages of Gulp and Sargat, was being used by an estimated 300 to 500 Ansar al-Islam terrorists, with elements of the al Qaeda network in there with them. We believe they were developing poisons for use against civilians in Europe and the United States," Myers stated.[536]

By the first week of April the northern front was picking away at a network of bunkers and Iraqi forces near Irbil. Then on April 6 came a pitched battle at Debecka Ridge. A platoon of Iraqi T-55 tanks, backed with two platoons of mechanized infantry and more troops in trucks, attacked straight up the road in daylight toward a concentration of SOF and Kurdish Peshmerga. SOF forces aimed Javelin anti-tank missiles at the T-55s. They "destroyed the Iraqi supporting weapons either with their own mortars or by calling in CAS," according to an official report.[537] One tragic incident occurred when F-14s under SOF direction released bombs accidentally killing 18 Kurds plus several SOF forces.

Truman and *Roosevelt* provided a significant share of the air support for the north fight. "Every once in a while we'd hear an A-10, kind of straggling all the way up there," Bowman said. F-16CJs also began a mini-SEAD campaign, trolling for real-time targets. However, for the most part, "it was just the two carriers, so when we were flying during the day it was pretty much all us, and then they were flying at night, it was pretty much all the *Roosevelt*, so yeah it was pretty satisfying to run the whole northern air campaign from one spot," Bowman summed up.[538]

LAST DAYS OF THE REPUBLICAN GUARDS

In the south fight, the focus was on the Republican Guards. Saddam's best chance to stop the drive to Baghdad depended on them. These elite forces had spearheaded the invasion of Kuwait and some had escaped in retreat screens after Operation Desert Storm. In 1998, Operation Desert Fox targeted Republican Guard equipment, infrastructure and command and control. "Understand the role of the Republican Guard," Zinni said at the time. "They are the most significant, most loyal, most ruthless of his forces."[539] In 2003, military analyst Anthony Cordesman credited the Republican Guards with as many as 600 T-72s and 300 T-62s, for a total of about 900 top-of-the line tanks. Other Soviet-export equipment such as T-55s remained on their table of equipment, too.[540]

Airstrikes had destroyed and degraded most Republican Guards forces south of Baghdad – but there might be remnants, and there had been attempts to reposition.

Even more worrying, CENTCOM believed the Republican Guards might be linked to WMD. CENTCOM's leadership had seen enough intelligence reports and battlefield evidence to keep that worry alive – such as the border posts where Iraqi soldiers had chemical gear, gas masks and atropine dosages. "All source intelligence indicated that Republican Guard and SSO troops arrayed around Baghdad were holding WMD, and we could expect them to use those weapons as we closed the noose on the capital – unless we got there before the Iraqis were ready," Franks later said.[541]

Of all the potential opportunities for Saddam to order the use of WMD, Nichols thought the most likely was that "he was going to save it until regime collapse," he said. "That's when we thought he might use it. Down south of Karbala, in there, we thought when we get here, it could get ugly."[542]

"Everybody had their gear with them. This was not something they were taking lightly," said Robb. As Coalition forces neared Baghdad "there was some sensitive intel that came in," he added, suggesting a "red ring or tripwire" where with the right code words, Iraqi forces could unleash a chemical or biological attack.[543]

The land component was ready to move beyond the Karbala gap but they needed to know how much damage had been done by the Coalition's airstrikes during and after the sandstorm. Franks gave a hint of how important the combat assessment was when he said on March 30: "what I pay very close attention to is the amount of force in aggregate in any particular piece of geography inside Iraq."[544]

Confirming how much the air component had degraded the Republican Guards was essential. But as Nichols caveated, "there's more art than science in this operational level of maneuver." Formal responsibility for BDA rested with CENTCOM J2, not the components. The problem was that the land component needed an operational assessment they could count on as they planned to move forward.

A pre-strike and post-strike photograph of Baghdad state and regime-controlled TV Studio and broadcasting facility was shown in a press conference with embedded media on Mar. 29, 2003. DoD photo.

BAGHDAD STATE AND REGIME CONTROLLED TV STUDIO AND BROADCAST FACILITY, IRAQ

PRE STRIKE

POST STRIKE

"CENTCOM had no idea what was really killed. We brought in Global Hawk to work through the weather, primarily various imaging radars" and deployed it to "target fielded force Iraqi army and Republican Guard." The high-altitude, long-endurance platform "had some pretty good effects there over about a 48-hour period," providing a SAR data stream used in real time to adjust targeting. Still, "nobody could tell us what the assessment of our effects was so CFLCC could pick up and go north again," said Nichols.[545]

At CENTCOM, analysts struggled to match reports of airstrike damage with the equipment of specific Republican Guards units. "Is it the Adnan division? Is it the Nebuchadnezzar division? Is it the Medina division? Is it a mix of all of them?" wondered Moseley.[546]

The land component "wanted to ensure that specific units that were key to the Iraqi forces were properly prioritized and then were rendered ineffective or at least reduced in their effectiveness," Leaf, the CFACC liaison, explained. "That was pretty difficult to do in the fog and speed of war and the hodge-podge of Iraqi forces" since they "weren't operating in a templated manner."[547] Leaf monitored mission reports from returning aircrews and his staff kept a running count of locations of the most recent bomb hits as mission reports filtered in 12 to 24 hours after the day's airstrikes.[548]

Finally it came down to "windage," Nichols said. "We dropped this many bombs, we're pretty sure about this," he added. "And they took off. Worked out okay."[549]

The air component had done its job well. V Corps forces advancing out of Karbala did indeed find that airstrikes had "destroyed or severely degraded" most of the Republican Guards forces.[550] In some areas, advancing land forces found "a tremendous amount of destroyed equipment and a significant number of enemy casualties as they moved toward Baghdad," Leaf noted. They also "found areas where there was a great deal more equipment than there were attendant casualties." Debriefs of the Iraqi POWs showed that it "became pretty clear to them there wasn't much future in sticking with your T-72 tank, Leaf concluded.[551]

CUMULATIVE EFFECT

The five air wars were now closing in on Saddam's regime. Moseley credited the strategic attacks with giving the Coalition forces an edge over the Iraqis on many levels. Operationally, it constrained their command and control options. "I believe the strategic attack piece and the [strikes on] command and control got us 48 to 72 hours ahead of anything they could do," he said. "I believe their intel was CNN and Al Jazeera," he added.[552]

From start to finish this strategic air war was very different from air campaigns of the past. First, it stayed away from canonical targets like the electricity grid. "There are other ways of taking down the integrated air defenses rather than just pulling the plug on the electricity," explained Keating.[553] Destroying industrial sites and oil production was not necessary to support a high-speed ground attack and quick occupation of Iraq. Besides, anything the Coalition blew up they would probably end up repairing after the war.

Second, it was precisely calibrated for maximum effect and minimal collateral damage. "The pounding that Baghdad has taken has been extraordinarily precise in

Aviation Structural Mechanic Airman Frank Wendt signals the pilot of a P-3 Orion to start engine number two in preparation of flight operations in support of Operation Iraqi Freedom on Apr. 11, 2003. U.S. Navy photo by Photographer's Mate Airman Chris Otsen.

its nature," said Joint Staff spokesman Major General Stanley A. McChrystal, US Army, in early April. "It has been nothing like what some people visualize as the destruction."

Steady reconnaissance was also essential, and here the P-3 again played a big role, especially for I MEF. "Mattis will tell you that he had P-3s overhead his Marines at all times as they were going from Basra to Baghdad, and he regarded that as essential to his ability to prosecute his campaign," said Keating. "And P-3s in other parts of the country were helping special operations forces."[554]

As the land component resumed its drive forward, XCAS and SCAR dominated the tasking.

Nekamoto recalled "the battlefield was moving so quickly it was really difficult to get designated targets. Things were moving around, pods of Republican Guards were either getting dispersed or wiped out or surrendered or whatever they were doing. It was really hard to get specific missions nailed down."[555]

The Republican Guards command and control was degraded and with their battlefield positions under attack, none of the divisions were able to launch a coherent counterattack. However, they did move in smaller units.

Near al Kut, Navy SEALs spotted a column of tanks. Nekamoto and his wingman attacked with GBU-12s and JDAM. "We tried to stop the column, which we were semi-successful in doing. We stopped them for a little while," he said. "Fortunately, a section of [F-15E Strike] Eagles came in right after us and cleaned up the rest, which was nice."[556]

Persistence over the battlespace counted more than ever as the volume of counterland support increased. To stay in the game, carrier strike sorties in the south depended on "strat gas" from Air Force and Coalition tankers to increase times on station. After the end of March, the CAOC moved some tanker tracks into Iraqi airspace to be available to strikers closer to Baghdad. Even *Kitty Hawk*, which depended most heavily on its S-3s, saw the benefits when the air component moved tankers closer to the scene of the action. *Kitty Hawk's* S-3s were already driving the strikers north to Basra. "The real assist there for us was when the strat gas started moving their refueling tracks farther north," said Commander Jay Bynum, XO of a *Kitty Hawk*-based F/A-18 squadron.

Kelly had pushed *Kitty Hawk* as far north as he could to get the carrier close to the battlespace. "We took them out of the tanking loop. We said you're going to fly in, you got to extremely quickly engage with the tactical situation up there, deliver your ordnance and come back. And that was a unique challenge that the *Kitty Hawk* took on and did extremely well," he said.

That was due in no small part to the continued efforts of the E-2s and S-3s. Close combat placed continual demands on battlespace management and the E-2s "injected themselves into that process and started taking over the role of the ABCCC that wasn't there." JSTARS supplied the overall ground picture of SAR and moving targets, while AWACS was tasked with managing the airspace and airborne battle management.

But pilots were still finding that AWACS put them in long queues. Said Bynum: "The initial thing, if you checked in with AWACS, they would just send you to la la land. Okay, you're going to be airplane 16 and 17 in the stack way down in the southern killboxes," he recalled. "We were looking for something a little more meaningful that would allow us to play."[557]

An S-3B prepares to make an arrested landing on the flight deck aboard the USS George Washington on May 4, 2004. U.S. Navy photo by Photographer's Mate Airman Joan Kretschmer.

F/A-18F Super Hornets conduct in-flight refueling exercises over Iraq on May 19, 2003. U.S. Navy photo.

As in the north, the E-2s worked as agents for the strike fighters, "coordinating the movement of ordnance where it needed to be," as Moffit phrased it.[558]

"The connection node between all those command and control assets was really Navy E-2s," Bynum said. It worked so well that "regardless of what battlegroup or strike group you came up with, you just get the call sign and those guys would do the job."[559]

Throughout it all S-3s were providing fuel right after launch, waiting as recovery tankers, and dragging strike fighters as close to the battle as they could. Day 14 of the air war was typical. The Navy flew 298 strike sorties, assisted by no less than 109 organic tanking sorties: 83 for the south fight, 26 for the north fight.[560]

"I would go down to the S-3 ready room and thank them profusely for being there when they were needed," Moffit said. "Shoot, they were flying two, three missions a day making this thing happen and actually hot-turning on the deck, not even shutting down, just going back up and launching."[561]

"Navy organic tanking made a big, big difference," Nichols said of the effort. In the "NAG, it helped us get some airplanes there without strategic tanking, in the Med it created options when airplanes were low on fuel."[562]

SUPER HORNET

Operation Iraqi Freedom also marked the combat debut of the F/A-18EF Super Hornet – both as a strike platform, and as a combat tanker.

The first operational squadron of Super Hornets, embarked with the *Lincoln,* was already in action. Another was on its way aboard the *Nimitz.*

Lieutenant Commander James Haigler was one of the pilots taking the Super Hornet to war for the first time. Initially, the squadron did combat missions, including making use of the F/A-18EF's ability to carry four 2000-lb. JDAM – though as Haigler said, that heavy load made the airplane "perform a little bit more like a pig." More typical loads were two of the JDAM plus air-to-air ordnance.

Soon the Super Hornets added refueling to their list of accomplishments. For these missions, they launched with drop tanks and air-to-air missiles. "We would take two Super Hornets a cycle," said Haigler, "and fuel four Charlies [F/A-18Cs]." The Super Hornet pilots tanked them once right away, then dragged them up to Basra before a final top-off. In total "we'd give them 12,000 pounds of gas, 6,000 pounds each, which was enough for them to get to Baghdad, hang out for about 45 minutes, then come back."[563]

Kelly found the Super Hornets so useful he decided to bring a detachment of them forward from *Nimitz* to join combat operations with *Abraham Lincoln*. "First of all," he explained, "the Es have tremendous tanking capacity – real transformation in the capacity of aircraft to get gas in the air, and to be able to reach out and provide that gas in support of tactical missions." By the same token the F/A-18Fs came ahead "because I wanted the FAC-A two seat capability, again to help compensate for this incredibly dynamic ground war," said Kelly.[564]

Nimitz launched them; *Lincoln* recovered them and put them to work.

Later, when *Nimitz* replaced *Lincoln*, the squadron gave Lieutenant Michael Garcia – a Super Hornet pilot who had never flown a Navy strike fighter other than the F/A-18EF – a chance to log over forty combat missions. He complimented the exceptional maintenance reliability of his new jet. By that point, a lot of the missions were on-call CAS or as he said, "a lot of hanging out over a point and waiting to be called on," he said, although early missions featured some JDAM drops.[565]

"I think the F/A-18EF proved their operational suitability and effectiveness – what we're buying them for," Nichols concluded.[566]

"I would have given my eyeteeth to have a squadron of Super Hornets on board," said Moffit. "Because they truly stayed in the game," he noted, adding that "the internal range of each and every aircraft was far more than what I could generate off the *Kitty Hawk*."[567]

IMMINENT DEFEAT

Even under the weight of air attack, Republican Guards forces did try to reinforce divisions under attack in the south. Central Command confirmed that elements from the Nebuchadnezzar Division were moving south. Pace told media the Nebuchadnezzar Division was being "badly damaged" in the process. Elements of the Adnan Division, stationed in Tikrit, were also on the move.[568]

Tuesday, April 1, was the beginning of the end. Airstrikes pounded the last known locations of the Medina division and other units between the land component and Baghdad. Myers said "what we're trying to do with both ground and air forces there is to decrease the combat capability of the divisions that have been arrayed south of Baghdad to stop the 1st Marine Division and the 3rd Infantry Division and the 101st [Airborne Division] from making progress towards Baghdad."[569]

Rumsfeld doubted that the Republican Guards were having any luck with their attempts to reinforce. "It's hard to tell," he said. "The Republican Guard has been taking a pounding for some days now. And some of the Republican Guard units from up north have been brought down south to try and reinforce Republican Guard units in the South that have been badly weakened. That process goes on. They're being attacked from the air. They're being pressured from the ground. And in good time, they won't be there."[570]

Land forces moved out with a two-pronged attack later that night. The 3rd Infantry engaged the Medina and Nebuchadnezzar divisions. On April 2, they passed Karbala and moved north. I MEF also began to move.

"We're now engaging the Republican Guard divisions defending the outskirts of Baghdad, and irregular forces throughout the south supporting the Iraqi regime. We've moved to within 30 miles of Baghdad, but there remains tough fighting ahead," said McChrystal on April 2.[571]

That pushed the carrier airstrikes of the south fight up to the outskirts of Baghdad, and sometimes to Tikrit and beyond. Reaching that far required a three cycle mission. Sometimes it also required heavy ordnance. The F-14D was dropping 2000-lb. JDAM for the first time in OIF, after NAVAIR specialists had put in supreme effort to certify it earlier in the year. The F-14s carried up to four of the 2000-lb. weapons.

The Super Hornet picked up a heavy ordnance load, too. On one occasion, a division from *Abraham Lincoln* was assigned, but just before the strike, one aircraft dropped out. Haigler had a fourth JDAM loaded onto his Super Hornet while the wingmen carried two, and they executed the attack on a Republican Guards barracks as a three-ship.

Haigler recounted a mission that found him taking on a group of four tanks in a field just outside Baghdad, this time, in the V Corps' sector. He spotted the stationary tanks east of the city then "spent the next ten minutes making sure that they weren't friendly tanks, [talking] to the Army and to another convoy that was rolling" before he and his wingman positively identified and committed to the target. The ground controllers wanted them to roll in for Type I CAS identification, which was not an optimal attack profile for the LGBs. (In retrospect, "what I should have done was set it up to buddy lase," Haigler said later.) Their first pass with four GBU-16s hit one of the four tanks. "But then I got to roll in with the gun, and I strafed two of the tanks and one of them blew up. It was pretty cool to see."[572]

F/A-18 Hornet (top) and an F-14 Tomcat prepare to launch from the flight deck aboard the USS Harry S. Truman on Apr. 8, 2003. U.S. Navy photo by Seaman Jose L. Barrientos Jr.

April 2 saw the last major WMD scare. Intelligence intercepted a signal from the Medina division. It repeated the codeword: *blood, blood, blood.* McKiernan told Franks he had ordered all units within indirect fire range of the Republican Guards to keep their MOPP gear nearby.[573]

In fact, the Republican Guards never took the chance – and may never have had it. By early April they were melting away. The impact of airstrikes was undeniable. "Their Republican Guard forces are being defeated by coalition airstrikes and by effective ground engagements. The Baghdad and Medina Divisions have suffered serious blows," Rumsfeld said on April 3.[574]

Based on what he saw, Myers added that the Republican Guards were "trying to reinforce those rings of defense and not abandon them. That's the primary push we see right now." Republican Guard activity was mixed. Myers said "some forces have in fact retreated into cities, others have just left and gone home, still others have surrendered, still others are still there fighting and have been reinforced both with remnants of other Republican Guard units and also regular army forces."[575]

On the approaches to Baghdad about the only things moving were "much smaller combat formations that have been cut off from their central command and control," Moseley stated on April 5. "As far as large fighting formations, we haven't seen any of that lately because again, we've been attacking steady for about six or seven days now."[576]

"It's tough to speculate what their intent is. Clearly they are arrayed for a defense on the southern side of Baghdad at this point and on the flanks as well. Whether they intend to defend in place, or delay, is just not clear," said McChrystal.[577]

The carrier aircrews had spent considerable time striking targets under the heading of counterland support. Flexibility and persistence were key. Sometimes targets were pre-assigned or coordinates came from the ASOC or DASC. Sometimes ground controllers had targets ahead for Type I, II or III CAS. Often, FAC-As guided strike fighters to open killboxes and placed them on targets. According to Moffit on nearly every flight "the pilots were either speaking to a FAC-A or a ground FAC" and that made the strikes "much more effective. I mean, we were hitting targets that actually had value whereas I think Desert Storm was more of a volume issue, instead of a quality issue."[578]

Quality was beyond dispute. An Army report later credited the air component as a whole with some impressive statistics in V Corps' operating area: destruction, by air alone, of:

+ 424 of 843 artillery pieces (50%)
+ 421 of 660 tanks (64%)
+ 107 of 859 other armored vehicles (12%)
+ 76 of 159 air defense artillery systems (48%)
+ 1144 of 2000+ other Iraqi military vehicles

This was the sustained, precise and lethal air power that brought the Coalition to the gates of Baghdad.

An F-14 Tomcat embarked aboard the USS Harry S. Truman flies a combat mission in direct support of Operation Iraqi Freedom on Apr. 11, 2003. U.S. Navy photo by Paul Farley.

CLOSE AIR SUPPORT OVER BAGHDAD

Now, inside that city, true CAS might become a life or death matter. Lead elements of the 3rd Infantry moved beyond Karbala to within 30 miles of Baghdad on April 3. The right pincer of the I MEF was about 60 miles south of city, bridging the Saddam Canal. With US forces set to enter Baghdad, a remarkable plan for urban CAS kicked in.

The CAOC was ready to prove its ability to generate sustained, tailored and plentiful close air support. Smith, who had flown in OEF, was now assigned to the CAOC for OIF. He noticed that "a lot of the close air support procedures had really been nailed down." The air component's strategy for urban CAS in Baghdad began with one simple requirement: plenty of bombs available. The CAOC's plan called for "airborne forward air controllers over the city 24 hours a day, and multiple sets of fighters with multiple munitions options stacked up 24 hours a day to be able to respond to the land component requirements inside the city if we have to," Moseley said.[579] Munitions options – from guns to Mavericks to 500-lb. LGBs – would let operators "truly select the right weapon for the right situation."[580]

The CAOC mapped the city and divided it up into detailed grid coordinates. "The whole city had common reference points," said Nichols. Whatever happened, "I was pretty comfortable we were going to be able to hit what we were aiming at," he said.[581]

Flights checked in 40 miles out from the Baghdad Restricted Operations Zone or B-ROZ and were directed to FACs. Altitude and heading separations kept inbound aircraft apart from egressing aircraft. Incoming flights then joined one of four CAS stacks on different radials over the city. Ten strike aircraft and four airborne Forward Air Controllers filled each stack, and bombers were on station, too.

To increase time on station, the air component pushed the tankers close to Baghdad. That "took some missionary work," Nichols commented. Moseley "went up and hopped in a tanker [and] flew a mission 50 miles south of Baghdad to demonstrate that it could be done without dying," he said. After that plenty of "strat gas" was on hand for the CAS stacks.[582]

Special Instructions (or SPINS) to aircrews included guidance on compensating for smoke and debris, and how to fly the safest attack angles. Baghdad's airspace was still dangerous, even with the Super MEZ largely out of business after March 30. There was no way to eliminate all of the mobile, short-range SAMs and anti-aircraft guns. "Eventually you will kill the Rolands, the SA-8s, the SA-6s and all that stuff that can be hidden in the town," said Moseley, but "you're never going to be able to walk away from the MANPAD threat and the small arms threat. And you have to accept the notion that you're going to live in a very, very threatened world of SA-7s and MANPADs," he said.[583]

An F-14D Tomcat makes a hard landing after returning from a mission in support of Operation Iraqi Freedom on Apr. 15, 2003. U.S. Navy photo by Photographer's Mate 2nd Class Felix Garza Jr.

Moseley anticipated that not every sortie would drop – and that was fine with him. Effectiveness, not efficiency, was the main goal for the air component. To that end, the CAOC figured half of the aircraft in the CAS stacks would bring their ordnance back unexpended during the first two weeks, and perhaps as many as two-thirds would return to base with full bomb-loads after that. If the battle went beyond a month planners had detailed tables of munitions to be positioned in theater.

The guiding principles of the urban CAS plan were passed on to the air wings. Greene, on *Constellation*, described it as "having plenty of airplanes, plenty of ordnance airborne." When a few pilots expressed frustration after their missions, Greene reminded them that "the mission was close air support and your number one requirement is to be there." Getting there on time and with the full amount of gas for a long loiter was the main thing. "If we're there, we got bombs, we're doing our job. If they need us and we're not there, we didn't do our job. It's not all about you getting your bomb off and putting a tick mark on the board of how many bombs you dropped," he said to them. "It's a bigger picture than that. And it's a lot more complicated than you can ever imagine. So just having an airplane on hand is a big part of the battle."[584]

Precision – and the discipline that went with it – were still top priorities. Ground controllers and pilots alike worked to minimize collateral damage. "A lot of our restrictions were for collateral damage purposes, wanted to make sure we didn't have anything that would burst above ground," said Bynum. Delayed fusing was a top tactic. Sometimes, ground controllers asked the carrier strike aircraft what fusing they had on their bombs and on occasion, "if you didn't have the right fusing, that was a show-stopper for the guy on the ground. So he'd say yep sorry, can't take you, wrong, you got an instantaneous fuse."[585]

The aircrews "had to do an enormous amount of integration in the air, in their heads, in the cockpit," said Kelly, "and they did that with extraordinary skill. The percentages of making the right call by those aircrews in the air was absolutely amazing."[586]

TAKING BAGHDAD

Air attacks helped V Corps blast through the Republican Guard screen. "If you really want shock and awe, it was the effects outside of Baghdad that were decisive in that regard," Robb said, turning the slogan on its head.[587]

In just one more week of fighting, the Army and Marines would link up in downtown Baghdad.

Elements of the 3-7 CAV – the same soldiers who'd stood fast against Fedayeen attacks during the sandstorm – started probing toward the international airport in Baghdad amidst light resistance on April 4. The next day, just before 9 AM Baghdad time, the 2 BCT of the 3rd Infantry made a "thunder run" with armored vehicles into the center of Baghdad itself. "Truthfully, everyone's nerves were on edge for this mission," said one soldier of the unit. Iraqi military and paramilitary forces hit them at every turn but "a steady stream" of direct fires from the US forces chewed them up.[588]

The show of force demonstrated beyond doubt that Baghdad could be taken, and swiftly. "The last couple of days we have demonstrated...we can drive anywhere in Baghdad we'd like. But we do not yet have forces throughout the city."[589] Two days after the thunder run, the I MEF was making its way through the eastern outskirts of Baghdad and V Corps was in position to close the pincer. The 3rd Infantry captured two presidential palaces in Baghdad and began its "inside out" operations in the western part of the city, seeking and destroying pockets of resistance.

"Of the six Republican Guard divisions, which are their main fighting force, two are assessed to be totally destroyed. The remaining four are assessed that about one half of their tanks, artillery, armored personnel carriers have been destroyed," said Pace on April 6.[590]

"Republican Guard divisions have only been able to conduct sporadic attacks on our forces," Myers recapped the next day. "Of the 800-plus tanks they began with, all but a couple of dozen have been destroyed or abandoned."[591]

Special Operations Forces move through west Baghdad on April 12. Special Operations Forces are patrolling the outer perimeter to provide security for a local hospital in support of Operation Iraqi Freedom. U.S. Air Force photo by Staff Sgt. Jeremy T. Lock.

Linking up V Corps and the I MEF was the culminating task. The pincers closed from left and right. First, soldiers penetrated into the center of Baghdad from the west while Marines moved in from the east. "So far we have been dividing the area into zones of responsibility for each of our battalions, and then clearing them one by one," said Major Dan Healey, commander of Baker Company in the 1st Battalion, 7th Marine Regiment. "Today was about enabling further passage into Baghdad."[592]

At the same time, other soldiers and Marines broke off and moved along the outskirts of Baghdad to capture major road intersections and encircle the city to the north. At the Tigris River on April 8, the battle came to a climax. Army soldiers fought off a counterattack on the bridges. Marines crossed the Diyala river and headed for the east bank of the Tigris.

In the north, SOF forces were quieting resistance around Kirkuk. "We have been targeting them aggressively, both from the air and then with the Special Operations Forces, for the last several days," said JCS spokesman McChrystal. "And we judge their capability to have dropped significantly, both from casualties and also from people just simply leaving the battlefield." According to Myers, those forces had been "subjected to bombing by air power and will continue to be dealt with in that way for some time."[593]

"We'd go halfway into Iraq and tank and then fly right over Baghdad like it was LA," said Nekamoto of a mission to Tikrit. "The rest of the 150 miles or so of Iraq were just administrative," he added. "Here we were initially shooting into Baghdad from 40 miles away, and the last day of the war, now we're just transiting straight over Baghdad towards other missions."[594]

On April 9, V Corps and I MEF linked up. Marines passing by with an M88 tank recovery vehicle helped Iraqis pull down a notorious statue of Saddam Hussein.[595] Iraq's capital was in Coalition hands.

Achievements of Carrier Strike

Operation Iraqi Freedom marked new tactical directions for carrier strike. "The whole idea of the application of air war is going in two different directions," reflected Robb. "And one of them is the support for the ground guy. Which means maybe a lot more CAS, lot more precision disabling of mechanized forces. A lot more precision against interdiction points and where the capacity is either being built or put together and mobilized." The other aspect "is trying to get down to the smallest number of targets possible to have the strategic effect," Robb concluded.[596]

OIF also saw a compressed timeline. As Kelly saw it, for carrier aviation the fundamental change between the late 1990s and Operation Iraqi Freedom hinged on "the time period of the fight." As seen first in OIF, "we are going to a much more compressed much more violent, much more demanding command and control combat systems environment in order to provide overwhelming force in a very short period of time," Kelly said.[597]

The foundation for the success of carrier strike was massing five together, for full participation in the joint air component's five fights. OIF required steady, disciplined work in what added up to a 2200-sortie per day effort. Carrier aircraft made their mark with smooth integration, effective tasking, and flexibility.

"We had the capacity to surge and sustain and then the capability to do what made a difference to the joint commander in the fight," said Nichols.[598]

Total sorties from the five carriers mirrored the strike effort of the joint air component as a whole. Sorties gradually ramped up after March 24, passing through a combined total of about 250 strike sorties at the end of March, then accelerating to a peak in the first week of April.

In fact, the carrier strike capacity was not pushed to the limit even by OIF. Planners calculated that the sustained sortie rate was about 350 sorties per day, with a surge rate near 428 sorties per day. It was only during the most intense period of destruction of the Republican Guards in early April that the carriers' combined strike totals got near the projected sustained sortie rate, topping off with a one-day total of 326.

The record reflected overall air component requirements, which were to be excess to need. "We only got to what our maxed sustained rate is for a little period," Nichols said of the carriers' sortie generation. "We never got near what our surge rate was." It "didn't have anything to do with our ability to generate sorties. It was about other limiting factors," said Nichols. In effect, the carriers turned in an outstanding performance – and still had something in reserve.

An F/A-18F Super Hornet prepares to launch from the flight deck of the USS Nimitz on Apr. 19, 2003. U.S. Navy photo by Photographer's Mate 3rd Class Elizabeth Thompson.

An EA-6B Prowler lowers its tail hook in preparation for landing aboard the nuclear powered aircraft carrier USS Nimitz after returning from a mission in support of Operation Iraqi Freedom on Apr. 17, 2002. U.S. Navy photo by Photographer's Mate 2nd Class Michael J. Pusnik, Jr.

The main Iraqi military resistance collapsed much faster than CENTCOM expected in its January 2003 plan allotting 135 days for decisive combat operations. "Frankly, in one sense we overestimated their capability," Nichols later said of the Iraqi military. "On the other hand, it wasn't imprudent to kind of give them the capability they had to shape the things that we had to do."[599]

The five carriers had more than fulfilled their contracts. They had demonstrated the ability to wage five different air wars, calling for everything from JDAM strikes in the sandstorm to multiple low strafing passes with troops-in-contact. They helped the air component keep the joint campaign on the offensive during needed pauses for logistics support or unexpected ones due to weather. It protected those same supply lines by making it all but impossible for the Iraqis to mass their forces. The air component drained the combat effectiveness out of the Republican Guards and set the conditions for the final assault on Baghdad. Disciplined close air support backed up the soldiers and Marines who repulsed fierce Iraqi counterattacks on the ground.

THE END OF THE BEGINNING

Carrier air was still providing support to Marines moving through Tikrit and Mosul. On April 11, "we launched near 200 power projection sorties," said Keating.[600]

The overall total for OIF was impressive. "Since the 20th of March, aircraft flying from our carriers have flown over 7,000 sorties in support of Operation Iraqi Freedom as part of the air component command power projection mission," briefed Keating on April 12, 2003.[601]

It was part of a powerful and tailored air war. "The effects were incredible," said Robb. "Drive around Iraq and you'll find building after building after building with a single hole in the roof." This campaign was done "with absolute minimal collateral damage, so that part of it really couldn't have been any better," he said.[602]

In the key category of counterland support, the air component got high marks. The official Army report on Operation Iraqi Freedom, Phase III said: "Time and again during OIF, airmen intervened at critical points on the battlefield." This report also concluded "evidence suggests that the high rate of desertion among Iraqi units can be directly attributed to strikes by fixed-and rotary-winged aircraft."[603]

Decisive combat operations in Iraq tapered off in mid-April. With *Nimitz* on station, and sorties diminishing, it was time to send most of the carrier strike force home. Keating described the decision. "I called Buzz Moseley and said, 'It looks to me like the requirement for all these power projection assets is gone as the war is in its final hours and minutes.'

"He said, 'I agree.'

"So I called General Franks, after checking with the CNO, and said, 'I believe we can let these carrier battle groups go home.'"[604]

"Here's the good news: D+27 we sent everybody but two carriers home," said Nichols. "Put one in the Med, one in the NAG. This was a three-week fight. D+30 we flew our last flights from the Med carrier. D+31, one month from A-day, back to a single carrier. That's pretty good news," he finished.[605]

On May 1, 2003, President George W. Bush stood on the deck of *Abraham Lincoln* off San Diego and told America's armed forces: "Because of you, the tyrant has fallen, and Iraq is free."[606]

The end of Phase III's decisive combat operations did not mean conflict in Iraq was over. The next challenges would be difficult ones as OIF transitioned to Phase IV, Stability Operations. Rumsfeld was reminded of Churchill's quote, made in another time of hope and peril: "'This is not the end, it is not even the beginning of the end, but it is perhaps the end of the beginning.'"[607]

President George W. Bush passes through the "side boys" on May 1, 2003 after a successful trap aboard the USS Abraham Lincoln in a S-3B Viking designated NAVY 1. U.S. Navy photo by Photographer's Mate 3rd Class Tyler J. Clements.

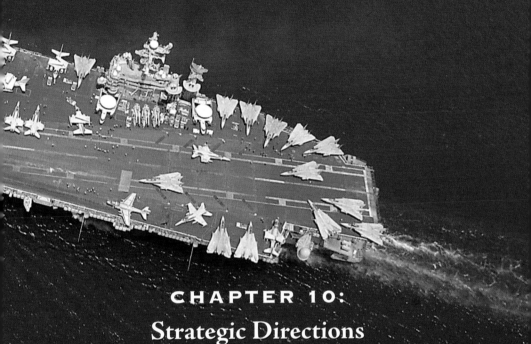

CHAPTER 10:
Strategic Directions

"I would rather muster two battle groups for three months and do something really significant internationally, and cooperate with partners in training and so forth, than to just go over and hang out for six months without a purpose and just kind of mark time." – CNO Admiral Vern Clark, August 2003[608]

Afghanistan and Iraq changed the concept of operations for carrier striking power for the 21st Century. From the rapid beginning of Operation Enduring Freedom to the ongoing role of carrier striking power in stability and counterinsurgency operations in Operation Iraqi Freedom, the test of battle forged fresh carrier tactics, and a new role for carrier strike in the joint air component, in Seapower 21 strategy, and in future national security.

An F-14B Tomcat launches from the #3 catapult of the USS George Washington in support of Operation Iraqi Freedom as an EA-6B Prowler is readied on the #1 catapult and a second Tomcat moves toward #3. U.S. Navy

Afghanistan's first lesson was that carriers proved they could be a core warfighting force when it was most needed. Massing *Enterprise, Carl Vinson, Theodore Roosevelt* and *Kitty Hawk* for the opening days of OEF was an achievement that would have done Mitscher or Spruance proud.

Basing the bulk of airpower at sea was not the first choice of CENTCOM planners, but it quickly became their only option. "There is great irony here," Nathman commented later. Countries in the region that could have provided "counter-offensive leverage for US forces rolled up their sidewalks,"[609] but fortunately, not their airspace or divert bases. However, the main source of air superiority, defense suppression, and on-call striking power was the carrier force.

This achievement cannot be overstressed. The month of October 2001 would have looked very different indeed without these four carriers going into action – and as a result, the global war on terrorism probably would not have had its first successes in Afghanistan until sometime well after the fall of 2001. What other consequences there might have been in that case will never be known. One thing is clear beyond doubt: carrier aviation helped take away al Qaeda's number one "safe harbor" as rapidly as possible.

OIF brought the lesson of adaptability in carrier deployments home again in a different way, as CENTCOM used subtle scheduling methods to keep carriers in place for either a "rapid" or a "generated" start to the war with Iraq. During 2002, that flexibility kept one carrier in the north (the Med) and one carrier in the south (Persian or Arabian Gulf) and served, in fact, as one of the steadiest points in CENTCOM's continually pivoting war plans. Five carriers massed in mid-March 2003 for OIF, and according to Keating, eight could have been provided if necessary.

Carrier striking power proved its value again in the irregular warfare and stability operations that picked up in Iraq in late 2003 and 2004. The air component remained heavily tasked to provide intelligence, surveillance and reconnaissance, plus readily-available, tailored striking power to forces in Iraq engaged in stability operations. Carrier air wings rotating through the area conducted operations over Fallujah, Najaf and other hotspots. Their aviators learned the freshest lessons of persistence, deconfliction in the crowded urban ops airspace, liaison with ground controllers, the pressures for exact weapons drops, and the ever-changing hunt for high value targets. From the start, the air component was able to provide major advantages scarcely seen before in urban warfare, such as expanded situation awareness to the tactical level, rapid precision strikes, and airlift and support.

Operations such as the second battle in Fallujah in November 2004 called for concentrated strike power. "Right now we are flying the exact same levels that the guys did during the Operation Iraqi Freedom [start] in '03," Captain Mark D. Guadagnini, commander of Air Wing 17, aboard *Kennedy*, said on November 10, a few days into the battle.[610] Evolution in carrier strike power – both technologies, and tactics – changed the calculus for insurgency operations in the urban environment.

GRADING THE TEST OF BATTLE

The "battle-tested" lessons of Afghanistan and Iraq form a unique and strong basis for future requirements.

Persistence. Persistence has become the watchword for air operations from "persistent ISR" to the clear preference of JTACs to have a section of strike fighters

A U.S. Navy plane captain signals the pilots of an E-2C Hawkeye to start their engines during evening flight operations on the flight deck of the aircraft carrier USS Harry S. Truman operating in the Persian Gulf on Dec. 26, 2004. DoD photo by Airman Ryan O'Connor, U.S. Navy.

remain on station for longer periods, so their situational awareness can be built and they can execute strike tasking before having to hand off to others. Carriers proved their ability to achieve persistence over Afghanistan and Iraq. Of Afghanistan, Zortman said "the value of persistence brought on either by the characteristics of the airplane or enhanced by refueling from tankers is a big deal. We knew that, and we re-proved it."[611] Urban operations and stability operations proved to be no less demanding than major theater combat in terms of the requirements for persistence.

Sea-basing sets up a trade-off matrix between access and time on station. In the future, even low-intensity conflict scenarios in the littoral will benefit from maximum persistence over the battlespace. Future carrier strike commanders may well be called upon to provide ever-longer periods of availability – and to do so in varied threat environments, from greater distances. In any event, carrier strike will have to continue to come through with persistence – under any set of conditions – to deliver maximum value to the joint force commander.

Weapons Mix. Along with persistence the key to providing air support in the global war on terrorism and in future conflicts is a mix of air-to-ground ordnance tailored to the fight of the day. Afghanistan and Iraq showed there was utility for every weapon, from the 2000-lb. JDAM down to the 20mm gun. In fact, strafing became common in OIF and has remained so in stability operations.

Aviation Ordnanceman Jeffrey W. Brannon loads a laser guided bomb onto an F-14 Tomcat aboard USS Enterprise Jan. 5, 2004. U.S. Navy photo by Photographer's Mate Airman Milosz Reterski.

There was also a definite trend toward smaller weapons because of their increased suitability in areas with a potential for collateral damage. The GBU-12 was the most commonly expended weapon – until, perhaps, the 500-lb. JDAM made its combat debut in the fall of 2004. The munitions lessons point to variety and quantity, and to keeping the lessons of history in mind. "After every war, we throw away the lightest bomb," cautioned Rear Admiral Charles Johnston, Deputy Commander, Naval Air Systems Command.[612] To Johnston, it brought to mind the 250-lb. Mk 81 that was a 1960s and 1970s inventory staple.

For the future, it will also be important to build up stocks of the best new munitions fast – a case in point being the Small Diameter Bomb. Carrying the right weapons is essential because the air component is expected to produce an ever-wider range of tailored effects. A clutch of Small Diameter Bombs meets that requirement, and provides "a real advantage for stealthy aircraft" with internal bomb bays, like JSF, said Johnston.[613]

Evolving weapons requirements also focus on "not just suppression, but the death of enemy air defenses," as Johnston said. Improvements to HARM and new research programs will yield advanced capabilities in this arena.

Fusing. A corollary to the need to have a variety of weapons in stock is the need for a full range of fusing. Again, collateral damage is a main driver, but the lesson is that fusing options are increasingly essential to air component operations. They can make a larger bomb act like a smaller one and vice versa and that is the kind of flexibility essential for air operations in the "bugsplat" environment.

Airman Eric Overstreet observes as an S-3B Viking launch from one of four catapults aboard the nuclear-powered aircraft carrier USS Enterprise on Jan. 5, 2004. U.S. Navy photo by Photographer's Mate Airman Milosz Reterski.

An F/A 18 Hornet patrols airspace near the North Arabian Sea in support of Operation Enduring Freedom on Nov. 14, 2003. U.S. Navy photo by Lt. j.g. Perry Solomon.

Organic tanking. The value of the S-3 in organic mission tanking was proven beyond a doubt in both Afghanistan and Iraq. Having S-3s available with each airwing simply made it easier to keep to deck cycle times and there was no doubt that strike pilots appreciated everything about the S-3. While the F/A-18EF will pick up some of their role, the retirement of the S-3 is a good opportunity to rethink the role of organic tanking in future carrier operations. However, organic tanking suits the carrier more than it does the air component as a whole, and should not be pursued to the point that it becomes a limiting factor in persistence. Forward thinkers in the naval aviation community may have a good opportunity to conceptualize how joint tanking conops can be built to work in service of multiple deployed carriers.

Shore detachments. Assisting the SOF fight was a major task for naval aviation in OIF's "west fight" and in fact, in engagements across Iraq. Two very different shore detachments made major contributions. One was the detachment of F-14s from *Kitty Hawk*, valued in part for their FAC-A and unique reconnaissance capabilities. The other was the deployment of HCS-4 and HCS-5. HCS-5 did just about everything that could be demanded of aircraft: from leaflet drops to photo reconnaissance to armed reconnaissance, not to mention the usual slate of insertions, extractions and resupply of SOF forces during OIF phases III and IV. "The squadron did whatever was needed, where and whenever needed," said Fitzgerald, and logged over 180 missions for CENTCOM.[614]

From strike fighters to helicopters there may be times in the future when detachments of naval aircraft are deployed ashore. The prime ingredients in making that work are mission planning, and maintenance away from the ship. Those and other considerations deserve plenty of war-gaming study so that detachments can go ashore in the future "where and whenever needed" on short notice. The questions, said Kelly, are "can I flow aircraft from a carrier deck, sustain them with a minimum amount of support ashore and lily pad them. Does that make more sense? And what are the lessons to learn on that?"[615]

"Not so well." In addition to the successes, there were "some things that did not quite go so well," said Keating. First on his list was fratricide in OIF. "We lost a Hornet, late in the war. Inexcusable. We have to find ways to not just reduce [fratricide] because we've gotten better...but to eliminate the potential for blue on blue. Air-to-air air-to-ground, ground-to-ground, all of them," said Keating. "We must do better as a department on that. Folks are working it."[616]

Also, he cited other areas for improvement such as narrowing "differences in how we execute some fairly fundamental tactics, [such as] close air support. The Army and Marine Corps have different doctrine. We are getting better. We know that there is a difference. We are addressing those differences. JFCOM is integral to that effort. We need to do it faster and better," Keating concluded.[617]

Net-centric Operations. Finally, net-centric operations hold the key to success in the future battlespace due to increasing requirements – and abilities – to collect, distribute and share data. Already, in Afghanistan and Iraq, the reach-back for time-sensitive targeting stood as an example of net-centric operations. For the future, net-centric air operations will blend strike and ISR roles and enhance cooperation for finer coverage of larger target areas. This will become a core competency for carrier strike groups. Digitization and datalinks form an essential part of combat capability. Enhancing the role of all platforms in net-centric operations will be a mark of future utility.

CARRIER STRIKE IN THE
JOINT AIR COMPONENT PERSPECTIVE

Battle-tested experience pointed toward future requirements, but the true impact of carrier striking power in Afghanistan and Iraq echoed across the joint force. The operational level of war is the arena for joint integration. It lies between and connects the tactical to the strategic level of national goals, and it was here that carriers made their mark.

The role of carrier strike in joint operations was completely different from Operation Desert Storm.

"It is hard to overstate the leap that the joint services in general, and the Navy carrier aviation wing in particular made in that 12 year period of time," said Keating of the period from Operation Desert Storm to Afghanistan. "Huge. Quantum. Transformational change. Every airplane off of the Navy carrier deck can deliver precision weaponry now," said Keating in 2004.

The level of integration of sea-based air forces and land-based air forces was like nothing ever seen before. While most strikes worked to provide direct support to SOF or land component forces, execution

An F-14B launches off the flight deck of the USS George Washington during evening flight operations in support of Operation Iraqi Freedom. U.S. Navy photo by Photographer's Mate 1st Class Brien Aho.

responsibility rested directly with the air component (which played both a supported and a supporting role in both campaigns). It took the perspective of the joint air campaigns to gauge the real contributions of naval aviation.

Praise came fast. Moseley, the air component commander from November 2001 through August 2003, remarked on the high number of sorties generated in Afghanistan. Of OIF, he said simply, "I've had five joint assignments and this is the best joint cooperation that I have seen."[618] The Army called the air component "central to decisive joint operations."[619]

That praise was based on operational performance. The role of carriers for the joint force stood out in two ways: weight of effort, and impact on the joint campaign. Both are at the core of future carrier strike concepts.

Weight of effort in the air component. Beginning with Afghanistan, carrier strike forces took on a significant total weight of effort and many unique responsibilities essential to the air component's tasks in the overall campaign. From the perspective of the joint air component, Afghanistan was nothing short of a revolution in sea strike.

In Iraq, the total air component force was larger, but the five "contracts" for sorties from the carriers added up to a substantial piece of the joint air component's striking power. For example, the 250 F/A-18s deployed were the dominant strike fighter by number and top workhorses of the campaign, second only to the F-15Es in total munitions employment.[620]

Impact on the joint campaign. The Army's post-OIF compliments on the "efficacy" of airpower stood as a reminder that much of the work of the joint air component was judged by results on the ground. Every OEF aircrew which spent hours pursuing TSTs or targets for SOF controllers knew this. Every OIF pilot who dropped LGBs or JDAMs, then made multiple strafing passes over the same target, north or south of Baghdad, knew it too.

Results depended on battlespace management as well as lethal strikes. This was why the ability of the E-2s to step in and untangle air tasking, making carrier sorties more efficient, was so important to the larger picture. Fast-moving operations proved that operators could also make a big difference by taking the initiative to make improvements on the fly.

One further marker of integration was the robust manning of naval personnel at the CAOC: not only in the NALE, but in other positions. Keeping up the manning is imperative because an active CAOC is the top battle lab for joint air warfare and a major node of operational innovation in net-centric warfare. However, Nichols warned, the "Navy's always been underrepresented in the CAOC, which is sub-optimizing employment of the combined air force." Keeping in step with developments in joint airpower application is vital to carrier aviation for the future. "Fill seams between components, and represent Navy equities. Fill purple positions of responsibility and authority. Build operational-level command and control of joint airpower as a Navy core competency," said Nichols.[621]

From O-3 to O-8, naval aviators bring value to the CAOC mission and they can take away insights on joint operations that cannot be learned anywhere else. Duty at one of the worldwide CAOCs is preparation for higher command of carrier strike in future joint force operations.

Capitalizing on the combat momentum of Afghanistan and Iraq, the Navy reversed the post-Cold War operating concepts of the 1990s, and positioned carrier strike forces for a full spectrum of challenges in a new century. Senior leaders turned battle-tested lessons into several significant changes in operational concepts that unfolded from 2002 to 2003.

First, in 2002, the Navy issued *Sea Power 21*, a roadmap for ongoing transformation. The Sea Power 21 framework took lessons from Afghanistan and applied them to all aspects of the evolution of naval power. Carrier battle groups became carrier strike groups. The Sea Strike, Sea Basing and Sea Shield concepts reflected recent experience, and guided future technologies and "action steps."

The changes built on the 1990s Revolution in Strike Warfare, and on the tactical record of carrier strike in Afghanistan and Iraq. Added to the striking power of the carriers were the over 800 TLAMs fired during OIF, for example. It all pointed in a new direction: toward Sea Strike as an integrated commodity, linked by net-centric command and control, and available to the joint force.

"Sea Strike operations are how the 21st Century Navy will exert direct, decisive, and sustained influence in joint campaigns," explained Admiral Clark. "They will involve the dynamic application of persistent intelligence, surveillance, and reconnaissance; time-sensitive strike; ship-to-objective maneuver; information operations; and covert strike to deliver devastating power and accuracy in future campaigns."[622]

Second, the Navy and Marine Corps also agreed to a landmark deal in August 2002. The Tactical Aviation Integration Plan called for more Marine squadrons to deploy with carrier air wings. It built on the positive experiences of Afghanistan. "I never

A U.S. Marine Corps AV-8B Harrier launches from the flight deck of USS Peleliu in support of Operation Iraqi Freedom on Jan. 5, 2004. U.S. Navy photo by Photographer's Mate Airman Jeffrey J. Klemm.

doubted that the admiral would have the airplanes over my head when I needed them," said Marine Major General Jim Mattis of the deployment of Marines in Afghanistan, referring to the support provided by Zelibor on *Carl Vinson* and the other carriers.[623] The deep air support for Operation Anaconda added to the evidence that Navy and Marine squadrons operating from carrier decks could provide support to ground forces no matter how difficult the conditions. Integration reflected the new reality of joint force objectives, and sea-based strengths.

Third, after carrier strike power engaged in the main combat operations phase in Iraq, the summer of 2003 brought another major change. The Fleet Response Plan realigned carriers (and other forces, such as expeditionary strike groups) so that they could surge to fight whenever necessary.

During the 1990s, "we had fallen into a model of keeping a relatively small amount of the force at a pretty high level of readiness," Zortman said. Afghanistan and Iraq shattered that mold. "One of the things that we learned first in OEF and then in OIF was that we had to be able to generate a significant portion of the force pretty quickly," Zortman continued.[624]

No longer would fixed deployment schedules and single carrier presence take precedence over joint force warfighting objectives. The fleet response plan suited steady state operations, too.

Operational experience demonstrated that by working together carriers could supply combat power for highly integrated joint operations. "We trained and thought about single strike group operations for a long time," acknowledged Zortman. But Afghanistan and Iraq proved that "a battle force isn't necessarily just a carrier plus a carrier plus a carrier."[625]

Fourth, the Navy injected a new philosophy into its future requirements, research and development. It reflected both the first few years of the global war on terrorism, and the technological goals which were logical successors to the 1990s Revolution in Strike Warfare.

An U.S. Navy F/A-18C Hornet heads for a mission over Afghanistan in support of Operation Enduring Freedom on Nov. 5, 2003. U.S. Navy photo by Lt.j.g. Larry R. Smith.

"The platform is no longer the revolution," summed up Johnston at NAVAIR. "It's the systems that go on it." With Super Hornet, the approach has been to take an evolutionary step "and continue the revolution with the sensors that are on it."[626] Later, with JSF, investment will once again pair a revolutionary platform with component networks, sensors and weapons.

FUTURE NATIONAL SECURITY

Finally, Afghanistan and Iraq were tests that confirmed a new role for carriers in future national security. That role rested squarely on the combat achievements of the carriers in the joint force – from weight of effort to the value of counterland support and urban operations.

Still, the role of carriers comes in for questioning on the banks of the Potomac. "The way modern warfare is evolving, carriers are less and less significant, other than for showing the flag," said Charles Pena, senior defense analyst at Washington's Cato Institute, in April 2003. "Since we no longer have to battle the Soviet Union for air superiority, long-range bombers with precision-guided munitions can provide close air support more effectively than carriers and at a fraction the cost."[627]

This criticism ignored many things, among them the fact that bombers cannot seize and hold air superiority. Most of all, it overlooked the fact that naval aviation's combat record and realignments form a strong position for linking up to any new metrics of defense planning guidance and force sizing.

Afghanistan and Iraq and ongoing global operations outlined the most valuable elements of carrier strike for the rest of this decade and beyond.

Multiple carriers. Response, not just presence, is key to carrier strategy for the 21st Century. Captain John Miller of *Constellation* put it well when he said, "the beauty of carriers is that they can respond so quickly. After the September 11 attacks we had a carrier off Afghanistan the next day and two carriers off the East and West coast of the United States. A month later we had four carriers off Afghanistan."[628]

Multiple carriers working together to provide striking power will be just as important in future operations as they were in Afghanistan and Iraq. To Kelly, one overriding lesson was "the carrier deck with its capacity to mass firepower by bringing in multiple carriers and creating the strategic imbalance in our favor where we need it, where we want it, in a timeline that's measured in days, not measured in pouring concrete for runways. These are enormously powerful things that we need to be able to take advantage of in the future," he said.[629]

Federated and Networked Battlespace. To Zortman, the change in operating concepts included "a different way of thinking about how you plan and ultimately, execute" operations. For example, "I think you can federate a lot more of the targeting data than we did," Zortman said. The same held true for fleet air defense, for supporting logistics, for some intermediate maintenance functions. "I think we can put some of those together," Zortman projected. "We did some of it by necessity, but there's a lot more work to be done." The end result? Thinking beyond the strike group level – and up to "the strike force, the battle-force level" as an entering concept for new missions.[630]

Flight deck crewmen duck as an F/A-18 Hornet launches from one of the four steam powered catapults aboard the aircraft carrier USS Harry S. Truman on Dec. 27, 2004. DoD photo by Airman Apprentice Ricardo J. Reyes, U.S. Navy.

Going it alone. The other huge lesson of Afghanistan was that naval aviation must be trained, equipped and ready to deploy as the main striking force of the joint air component when necessary. This is the reverse of the presence and crisis response doctrine, which assumed a larger joint force would quickly roll into theater for the peak effort. That was not what happened in Afghanistan in the fall of 2001 and there may well be other times when access, politics, or both put the principal burden on the carriers, perhaps for months at a time.

Unforeseen scenarios in tough locations such as Africa may call on multiple carriers to take the lead in sustained operations in the littoral or the interior.

As Zortman put it: "One of the things that we learned both in OEF and OIF is that freedom of action comes from being able to operate a significant strike fighter force from a sea base." With a battle force, "we don't have to get too many carriers in the same portion of an ocean and you quickly establish the most capable air force in the region," Zortman continued. That force brought with it inherent operational flexibility. "It's bed-down; it's maintenance support; it's your ordnance; and it's the ability to repair on site," he said.[631]

Deck Mixes. Afghanistan and Iraq also showed that multiple carrier strike groups can be cast in different roles depending on the needs of the joint force.

Rearranging a deck or two to increase ISR assets or assist SOF forces may become even more common. To Driscoll, that will be part of the continued evolution. By the end of the 1990s "the air wing's capability had shifted dramatically to power projection over the beach," Driscoll said. After OIF, "it's starting to transition from that old metric" to another concept where "the flight deck is a piece of real estate that can be used in any way that we need to use it," he commented.

Future operations may center on a tailored mix. "I think eventually we will tailor what's on the flight deck based on what the joint requirement is," Driscoll continued. "So the first carrier is going to be there already. It's going to be a deployer. It's going to be in the AOR because we have a presence mission that we fulfill. That 2nd or 3rd or 4th carrier is going to go over with what the joint commander needs to have on it. So it may be half SOF, half TACAIR. It may be all helos. It may be all strike fighters. Or have a mix of jammers or whatever the requirement is."

But, he warned, "we as the Navy, we need to practice that. We need to train to it. We need to buy the right stuff."[632]

Manned aircraft. War without Predator and other UAVs has become nearly unthinkable. While there is strong commitment to finding the right operational blend of unmanned and manned platforms, it is most likely that manned strike fighters will have unique and important roles to play in future Sea Strike operations.

The complex battlespace of urban, counterinsurgency and littoral operations is shaping that requirement. Many situations in Afghanistan and Iraq demanded that pilots be "eyes-

on" for positive identification of time-sensitive targets, for laser-guided bomb employment, for strafing, and for certain types of close air support. Granted, Predator and Global Hawk operators achieve their own type of "eyes-on" even from another continent.

But there is something more. Virtually every mission in today's complex battlespace demands a level of situation awareness that transcends "eyes-on." One way to describe it is that aircrews must be "brain-on" to deliver real battlespace flexibility. Networks, sensors and weapons function best in a multi-mission role when a highly trained male or female pilot brain is in the loop.

After an early morning round of flight operations, an F-14 Tomcat is readied by maintenance personnel for the next launch from the flight deck of the USS John C. Stennis in support of Operation Enduring Freedom. U.S. Navy photo by Photographer's Mate 3rd Class Jayme Pastoric.

Kelly, for one, concluded that the complex "checkerboard" of operations in OIF was a baseline for future operations, in which warfare would become more chaotic. He judged that future battles would still take manned aircraft to carry out the mission. "Our increasing ability to rapidly take advantage of the developing tactical situation on the ground and our capacity to put aircraft where they need to be tied to a very dynamic ground picture – that is the great strength of manned aircraft," concluded Kelly. Thinking about that future battlespace "demonstrates the power of the aircraft carrier's effect in this conflict and in the future," he said.[633]

Access and survivability. Finally, there is a lesson that emerges only by considering what did *not* happen in Afghanistan and Iraq. Neither featured a drawn-out campaign against air defenses, a lethal littoral, or a tough air superiority battle. Yet survivability and access to the battlespace could become major issues with potential future opponents. "I want them to make sure they're ready for an air-to-air threat that we haven't been confronted with for about 15 years, however basic or advanced that threat is" said Moffit.[634] He also stressed improving urban operations – for both combat and stability operations – and keeping an eye on training for evolving sea control challenges.

SUMMING UP

"Having commanders think in a more integrated way about how they employ the force — that's been our goal," Myers said in mid-April 2003.[635]

In Afghanistan and Iraq, the battle-tested power of carrier striking forces more than proved his point.

Across eight decades, the record of the aircraft carrier in war and peace has been dominated by outstanding operational performance and by debates on operating concepts. The "Navy high command in my opinion shows no proper conception of handling carriers. We have yet to have a permanent two or more carrier task force trained to operate together," complained Admiral Frederick C. Sherman in his diary in April 1943.[636] In contrast, after Afghanistan and Iraq, battle-tested concepts came to the fore right away.

Combat experience continues to create the basis for future tactics, operating concepts and requirements. Carriers are tackling the challenges of these earliest years of the 21st Century based on a proven and innovative combat record.

"The flexibility, and the reach required to project power in the emerging joint battlespace both today and tomorrow, is increasingly dependent on the mobile bases that our carriers provide," Kelly summed up.[637]

The carrier striking group may have its historical roots in mid-20th Century warfare but in Afghanistan and Iraq these splendid forces proved they were not only relevant, but central to the joint force. Their performance was the product of concentrated effort to improve lethality and striking power, and of tactical ingenuity that reshaped operations under combat conditions.

Most of all credit goes to those who fought. As Nathman said of the carriers after Afghanistan:

"They are a battle-tested force."

Endnotes

INTRODUCTION

1   Samuel Eliot Morison, *The Two-Ocean War*, (New York: Atlantic-Little, Brown, 1963), p. 586.
2   VADM John B. Nathman, Change of Command, Commander, Naval Air Forces, August 2, 2002.
3   Morison, *The Two-Ocean War*, p. 181.
4   Clark G. Reynolds, *The Fast Carriers: The Forging of an Air Navy* (Annapolis, MD: Naval Institute Press, 1968), p. 34.
5   Reynolds, *The Fast Carriers*, p. 35.
6   Morison, *The Two-Ocean War*, p. 343.

CHAPTER 1:
REVOLUTION

7   Admiral William A. Owens, *High Seas: The Naval Passage to an Uncharted World* (Annapolis, MD: Naval Institute Press, 1995), p. 4.
8   Interview by Rebecca Grant with Rear Admiral John Stufflebeem, August 4, 2004, Washington, DC.
9   Interview by Rebecca Grant with Rear Admiral James Robb, August 30, 2004, Tampa, FL.
10   William W. Kaufmann, *A Thoroughly Efficient Navy* (Washington, DC: Brookings Institution, 1987), pp. 14-15.
11   Interview with Stufflebeem, August 4, 2004.
12   Interview with Robb, August 30, 2004.
13   Interview by Rebecca Grant with Rear Admiral Matthew Moffit, September 17, 2004, Fallon, NV.
14   Interview by Rebecca Grant with Vice Admiral Mark Fitzgerald, July 1, 2004, Washington, DC.
15   Interview with Moffit, September 17, 2004.
16   Interview by Rebecca Grant with Admiral Timothy J. Keating, October 14, 2004, Washington, DC.
17   Interview with Fitzgerald, July 1, 2004.
18   Interview with Moffit, September 17, 2004.
19   Interview with Moffit, September 17, 2004.
20   David Perin, "Some observations on the sortie rates of land-based and sea-based tactical aircraft," Center for Naval Analyses, January 28, 1995.
21   Interview by Rebecca Grant with Commander Daniel Hinson, July 22, 2004, Lemoore, CA.
22   David Perin, "Some observations on the sortie rates of land-based and sea-based tactical aircraft," Center for Naval Analyses, January 28, 1995.
23   Owens, *High Seas*, p. 4.
24   Interview with Robb, August 30, 2004.
25   Quoted from Federation of American Scientists, "US Navy Ships," fas.org, November 16, 2004.
26   Naval Doctrine Publication 1, *Naval Warfare*, 1994, p. 20.
27   William J. Clinton, *My Life* (New York: Alfred A. Knopf, 2004), p. 827.
28   DoD Press Conference, November 10, 1998.
29   *USS Enterprise* suffered an accident in Atlantic waters on November 8 when an EA-6B Prowler clipped an S-3 that had just landed. There were only two survivors.
30   Interview by Rebecca Grant with Vice Admiral David Nichols, October 13, 2004, Washington, DC.
31   Interview with Fitzgerald, July 1, 2004.
32   President Clinton, Radio Address to the Nation, December 19, 1998.
33   DoD News Briefing, December 21, 1998.
34   Interview with Lieutenant Commander Todd Marzano, July 23, 2004, Lemoore, CA.
35   DoD News Briefing, December 21, 1998.
36   Marco R. della Cava, "Alaskan is First Female Pilot in Combat," *USA Today*, December 21, 1998.
37   Raytheon, News Release, January 28, 1999.

38 Quoted on Navy Website, *"Why the Carrier?"* January 1999.
39 Interview by Rebecca Grant with Rear Admiral John Cryer, September 2, 2004, Dahlgren, VA.
40 Interview with Cryer, September 2, 2004.
41 Interview with Cryer, September 2, 2004.
42 VADM Timothy Keating, "The Aircraft Carrier: A Cornerstone of Our Nation's Defense," *The Hook*, Summer 2001.

CHAPTER 2:
THE RISE OF TERROR

43 DoD Press Conference, August 20, 1998.
44 DoD Press Conference, August 20, 1998.
45 DoD Press Conference, August 20, 1998.
46 Interview with Fitzgerald, July 1, 2004.
47 Bob Woodward, *Bush at War* (New York: Simon and Schuster, 2002), pp. 6-7.
48 Clinton, *My Life*, pp. 865, 873, 900.
49 Interview with Nichols, October 13, 2004.
50 Clinton, *My Life*, p. 891.
51 Interview with Nichols, October 13, 2004.
52 Interview with Nichols, October 13, 2004.
53 Anthony H. Cordesman, "If We Fight: Iraq's Military Forces and Weapons of Mass Destruction," Center for Strategic and International Studies, 2003, p. 22.
54 USCENTCOM, "Interview with David Kay," in *Desert Shield, Desert Storm, Tenth Anniversary Book*, January 2001, p. 208.
55 Bob Drogin and Mark Mazzetti, "Only Hussein Had Full Picture," *Los Angeles Times*, October 7, 2004.
56 Interview with Fitzgerald, July 1, 2004.
57 Tommy Franks, *American Soldier* (New York: Henry Holt, 2004), p. 224.
58 Interview with Fitzgerald, July 1, 2004.
59 Franks, *American Soldier*, p. 218.
60 Interview with Fitzgerald, July 1, 2004.
61 Clinton, *My Life*, p. 925.
62 Clinton, *My Life*, p. 935.
63 L. Paul Bremer, "PBS Newshour with Jim Lehrer," February 5, 2001.
64 Linda de France, "Enterprise Battle Group Counters Terrorism Threat with Training, Technology," *Aerospace Daily*, March 26, 2001.
65 Greg Kakesako, "Life Aboard the USS Constellation," *Honolulu Star-Bulletin*, September 6, 2001.
66 Interview with Cryer, September 2, 2004.
67 Interview with Cryer, September 2, 2004.
68 Interview with Cryer, September 2, 2004.
69 Interview with Cryer, September 2, 2004.
70 Interview by Rebecca Grant with Lieutenant Melanie Lynch, July 22, 2004, Lemoore, CA.
71 Interview with Cryer, September 2, 2004.
72 Interview with Keating, October 14, 2004.
73 Interview with Keating, October 14, 2004.
74 Interview by Rebecca Grant with Vice Admiral James M. Zortman, December 20, 2004, San Diego, CA.
75 Interview with Keating, October 14, 2004.
76 Interview with Keating, October 14, 2004.
77 Eric Hehs, "Interview: Homeland Defense – Conversation with First Air Force Commander Major General Larry Arnold," *Code One Magazine*, First Quarter 2002, p. 5.
78 "NORAD's Response Times," NORAD News Release, September 18, 2001.
79 Interview by Rebecca Grant with Rear Admiral Steven Tomaszeski, August 4, 2004, Arlington, VA.

80 Interview with Tomaszeski, August 4, 2004.

81 Interview with Tomaszeski, August 4, 2004.

82 Interview with Tomaszeski, August 4, 2004.

83 Task Force Enduring Look, HAF/CVA, Interview with Major General Larry K. Arnold, November 17, 2001.

84 Interview with Robb, August 30, 2004.

85 Interview with Robb, August 30, 2004.

86 DoD Press Conference, September 13, 2001.

87 Interview with Tomaszeski, August 4, 2004.

88 DoD Transcript, Shelton interview with Larry King, October 1, 2001.

89 Cesar G. Soriano, "Pilots Continue Mission to Destroy Taliban Targets," *USA Today*, October 15, 2001.

90 Interview with Lynch, July 22, 2004.

91 Bush statement at Offutt AFB, NE, 1:04 PM September 11, 2001.

92 Briefing by Secretary of State Colin Powell, September 12, 2001.

CHAPTER 3:
AFGHANISTAN BEGINS

93 Douglas Jehl, "Tense and Secretive Mood as Jets and Missiles Roar Off Warships," *New York Times*, October 8, 2001.

94 DoD Press Conference, September 18, 2001.

95 Franks, *American Soldier*, pp. 250-251.

96 Interview with Robb, August 30, 2004.

97 Interview with Stufflebeem, August 4, 2004.

98 Woodward, *Bush at War*, p. 44.

99 Interview with Stufflebeem, August 4, 2004.

100 International Institute for Strategic Studies, *The Military Balance: 2000-2001* (Oxford: Oxford University Press, 2000), pp. 159-160.

101 DoD Background Briefing on Afghanistan, October 14, 2001.

102 Franks, *American Soldier*, p. 211.

103 *Military Balance 2001*, p. 160. For Northern Alliance strength, see also DoD Background Briefing, October 14, 2001.

104 Catherine Davis, "Afghans Remember Slain Resistance Hero," *BBCi*, September 9, 2002.

105 Secretary Rumsfeld interview with NBC "Meet the Press" Host Tim Russert, September 30, 2001.

106 Rumsfeld, "Meet the Press," October 1, 2001.

107 Interview with Cryer, September 2, 2004.

108 Interview with Stufflebeem, August 4, 2004.

109 Interview with Stufflebeem, August 4, 2004.

110 Interview with Stufflebeem, August 4, 2004.

111 First Resolution of the 56th UN General Assembly, September 12, 2001.

112 Interview with Cryer, September 2, 2004.

113 General Tommy Franks, Commander in Chief, USCENTCOM, Testimony to Senate Armed Services Committee, February 7, 2002.

114 Interview with Stufflebeem, August 4, 2004.

115 Franks, *American Soldier*, p. 281.

116 Interview by Rebecca Grant with Lieutenant General T. Michael Moseley, Shaw AFB, July 24, 2003.

117 Franks, Testimony to SASC, February 7, 2002.

118 Interview with Stufflebeem, August 4, 2004.

119 Chairman of the Joint Chiefs of Staff General Richard Myers, USAF, DoD Press Conference, October 7, 2001.

120 Rumsfeld, DoD Press Conference, October 7, 2001.

121 Interview by Rebecca Grant with Lieutenant Chris Gasko, July 22, 2004, Lemoore, CA.

122 Steve Vogel, "Many US Pilots See Combat for First Time," *Washington Post*, October 11, 2001.

123 Interview with Stufflebeem, August 4, 2004.
124 Franks, Testimony to SASC, February 7, 2002.
125 Franks, *American Soldier*, pp. 280-281.
126 Cesar G. Soriano, "Pilots Continue Mission to Destroy Taliban Targets," *USA Today*, October 15, 2001.
127 Interview with Cryer, September 2, 2004.
128 Steve Vogel, "Carrier Pauses to Reload for the Next Phase," *Washington Post*, October 12, 2001.
129 Steve Vogel, "Smooth Operations Over Afghanistan," *Washington Post*, October 9, 2001.
130 DoD Background Briefing, October 14, 2001.
131 Interview with Lynch, July 22, 2004.
132 Interview with Lynch, July 22, 2004.
133 Interview with Lynch, July 22, 2004.
134 Franks, *American Soldier*, p. 265.
135 Interview by Rebecca Grant with Lieutenant Scott Smith, July 22, 2004, Lemoore, CA.
136 Interview by Rebecca Grant with Captain Patrick Driscoll, August 4, 2004, Washington, DC.
137 Steve Vogel, "Navy Pilots Under Orders to Visually Verify Targets," *Washington Post*, October 10, 2001.
138 Interview with Cryer, September 2, 2004.
139 Interview with Cryer, September 2, 2004.
140 Interview with Lynch, July 22, 2004.
141 Interview with Cryer, September 2, 2004.
142 Franks, *American Soldier*, pp. 290-294.
143 Interview with Cryer, September 2, 2004.
144 Interview with Cryer, September 2, 2004.
145 Interview with Cryer, September 2, 2004.
146 Interview with Cryer, September 2, 2004.
147 DoD Press Conference, October 8, 2001.
148 Remarks by VADM Nathman and RADM Mike Mullen reported in Lisa Troshinsky, "Navy Pilots Set Flying and Target Records in Afghanistan," *Navy News and Undersea Technology*, January 22, 2002.
149 Interview with Driscoll, August 4, 2004.
150 Interview with Driscoll, August 4, 2004.
151 Interview with Smith, July 22, 2004.
152 DoD Press Conference, October 15, 2001.
153 Interview with Fitzgerald, July 1, 2004.
154 Interview with Fitzgerald, July 1, 2004.
155 David Rohde, "For the Moment, All Quiet on the Northern Front," *New York Times*, October 14, 2001.
156 DoD Press Conference, October 15, 2001.
157 DoD Press Conference, October 15, 2001.

CHAPTER 4:
"BATTLE WAS JOINED"

158 VADM John B. Nathman, "Naval Aviation on Top in Afghanistan," *The Hook*, Spring 2002.
159 Franks, *American Soldier*, p. 289.
160 Jumper interview, July 23, 2003.
161 The Washington Post, "We Were Not Bogged Down," Washington Post Interview with Secretary of State Colin Powell, *Washington Post*, November 25, 2001, p. B01.
162 Franks, *American Soldier*, pp. 296-301.
163 Interview with Cryer, September 2, 2004.
164 Interview with Lynch, July 22, 2004.
165 Interview with Fitzgerald, July 1, 2004.
166 Interview with Cryer, September 2, 2004.

167 Interview with Fitzgerald, July 1, 2004.

168 Steve Vogel, "Pilots Adapt as Emphasis Shifts," *Washington Post*, October 25, 2001.

169 Interview with Fitzgerald, July 1, 2004.

170 Interview with Fitzgerald, July 1, 2004.

171 Interview with Cryer, September 2, 2004.

172 Interview with Smith, July 22, 2004.

173 DoD Press Conference, October 29, 2001.

174 Interview with Smith, July 22, 2004.

175 Franks, Testimony to SASC, February 7, 2002.

176 TFEL Interview with Lt. Gen Maxwell Bailey, January 18, 2002.

177 Franks, *American Soldier*, p. 302.

178 Interview with Cryer, September 2, 2004.

179 Franks, *American Soldier*, p. 303.

180 Secretary of State Colin Powell quoted in Michael R. Gorden, "A Nation Challenged: The Bombing; U.S Bombs Taliban's Forces On Front Lines Near Kabul; Powell Sees Rebel Advance," *The New York Times*, October 22, 2001.

181 Gerry J. Gilmore, "Afghanistan Will Be A Long, Long Campaign; Food Rumor False, Official Says," *American Forces Press Service*, October 24, 2001.

182 Woodward, *Bush at War*, p. 261.

183 "Secretary Rumsfeld Interview with TIME Magazine," December 14, 2001, DoD Transcript.

184 Steve Vogel, "Pilots Adapt as Emphasis Shifts," *Washington Post*, October 25, 2001.

185 Kendra Helmer, "Gen Franks, in Uzbekistan, Says Fight Against Terrorism Has not Stalled," *Stars and Stripes*, October 31, 2001.

186 Myers, Interview with Al Jazeera, DoD Transcript, October 31, 2001.

187 DoD Press Conference, October 24, 2001.

188 Rumsfeld interview with Cokie Roberts, October 28, 2001.

189 DoD Press Conference, October 29, 2001.

190 Franks, *American Soldier*, p. 308.

191 Franks, *American Soldier*, p. 313.

192 Franks, *American Soldier*, pp. 310-311.

193 Interview with Driscoll, August 4, 2004.

194 DoD Press Conference, October 29, 2001.

195 TFEL Interview with Lieutenant Colonel Kenneth Rozelsky, May 20, 2002.

196 TFEL Interview with Rozelsky, May 20, 2002.

197 TFEL Interview with Colonel Michael Longoria, May 9, 2002.

198 Woodward, *Bush at War*, p. 268.

199 Stufflebeem, DoD Press Conference, November 2, 2001.

200 Stufflebeem, DoD Press Conference, November 2, 2001.

201 RADM John Stufflebeem, DoD Press Conference, November 2, 2001.

202 Interview with Fitzgerald, July 1, 2004.

203 Rumsfeld, Speech at Center for Security Policy "Keeper of the Flame" Award Dinner, November 6, 2001.

204 Stufflebeem, DoD Press Conference, November 6, 2001.

205 Woodward, *Bush at War*, p. 297.

206 Deputy Secretary of State Richard Armitage, Testimony to SASC, June 26, 2002. Armitage cited a dispatch he received from a SOF team in Afghanistan in November 2001.

207 Deputy Secretary of State Richard Armitage, Testimony to SASC, June 26, 2002. Armitage cited a dispatch he received from a SOF team in Afghanistan in November 2001.

208 Interview with Stufflebeem, August 4, 2004.

209 Interview with Stufflebeem, August 4, 2004.

210 Interview with Fitzgerald, July 1, 2004.

211 President Pervez Musharraf, *Meet the Press*, November 11, 2001.

212 Hampton Stephens, "Prowler Praised for Tactical Jamming Role in Afghanistan," Defense Information

and Electronics Report, November 8, 2002.

213 Interview by Rebecca Grant with Rear Admiral Anthony Winns, August 20, 2004, Washington, DC.

214 Interview with Stufflebeem, August 4, 2004.

215 TFEL Interview, Lt. Gen. T. Michael Moseley, January 18, 2002.

216 DoD News Conference, November 9, 2001.

217 DoD Press Conference, Novemeber 9, 2001.

218 Interview with Driscoll, August 4, 2004.

219 DoD News Conference, November 13, 2001.

220 DoD News Conference, November 13, 2001.

221 DoD Press Conference, November 13, 2001.

222 DoD Press Conference, November 14, 2001.

223 DoD Press Conference, November 15, 2001.

224 Kim Burger, "Interview with General Keane," *Jane's Defence Weekly*, January 30, 2002.

225 Interview with Cryer, September 2, 2004.

226 Interview with Stufflebeem, August 4, 2004.

CHAPTER 5:
OEF Continues

227 DoD Press Conference, November 15, 2001.

228 Fighter Jets Fly On, But Targets Harder to Identify," *Reuters*, November 15, 2001.

229 DoD Press Conference, November 15, 2001.

230 DoD Press Conference, November 20, 2001.

231 DoD Press Conference, November 20, 2001.

232 Franks, DoD Press Conference in Tampa, November 27, 2001.

233 Stufflebeem, DoD Press conference, 14 Nov 01.

234 Rumsfeld and Franks in Tampa, DoD Press Conference, November 27, 2001.

235 Rumsfeld and Franks in Tampa, DoD Press Conference, November 27, 2001.

236 DoD Background Briefing, October 14, 2001.

237 DoD Press Conference, November 27, 2001.

238 Interview with Nichols, October 13, 2004.

239 Interview with Robb, August 30, 2004.

240 Interview with Nichols, October 13, 2004.

241 Interview with Fitzgerald, July 1, 2004.

242 DoD Press Conference, November 26, 2001.

243 Interview with Nichols, October 13, 2004.

244 Interview with Nichols, October 13, 2004.

245 Interview with Fitzgerald, July 1, 2004.

246 Interview with Fitzgerald, July 1, 2004.

247 Interview with Cryer, September 2, 2004.

248 Interview with Robb, August 30, 2004.

249 Interview with Robb, August 30, 2004.

250 DoD Background Briefing, October 14, 2001.

251 Franks, *American Soldier*, p. 311.

252 Sgt 1st Class Kathleen T. Rhem, "Marines In Afghanistan to Set Up Forward Operating Base," *American Forces Press Service*, November 26, 2001.

253 Secretary Rumsfeld Interview with Dan Rather, CBS, December 4, 2001.

254 Interview with Winns, August 20, 2004.

255 Peter Finn, "...And His U.S. Partners: Wounded Army Captain Details Offensive Against Taliban," *Washington Post Foreign Service*, December 11, 2001.

256 DoD Press Conference, December 2, 2001.

257 DoD Press Conference, December 2, 2001.

258 Edward Gargan, "Desperate Trek to Escape Remnants of Kandahar," *Long Island Newsday*, December 5, 2001.

259 Stufflebeem, DoD Press Conference December 17, 2001.

260 Interview with Zortman, December 20, 2004.

261 Interview with Zortman, December 20, 2004.

262 James W. Crawley, "Stennis Pilots Eager to Join In," *San Diego Union-Tribune*, November 14, 2001.

263 James W. Crawley, "Aircraft Carrier Stennis, Battlegroup Leave for Persian Gulf," *San Diego Union Tribune*, November 12, 2001.

264 Interview with Marzano, July 23, 2004.

265 David Brown, "Workin' on Stennis Time," *Navy Times*, March 18, 2002.

266 David Brown, "Workin' on Stennis Time," *Navy Times*, March 18, 2002.

267 Interview with Robb, August 30, 2004.

268 Franks and Rumsfeld, USCENTCOM News Briefing, November 27, 2001.

269 Franks and Rumsfeld, USCENTCOM News Briefing, November 27, 2001.

270 Franks, Testimony to Senate Armed Services Committee, July 31, 2002.

271 DoD Press Conference, December 3, 2001

272 DoD Press Conference, December 17, 2001.

273 Franks, Testimony to SASC, July 31, 2002.

274 Rebecca Grant, *The Rise of Global Hawk*, (Washington, DC: IRIS Press, 2003) pp. 44-45.

275 TFEL, Intermediate Report Two.

276 General Peter Pace, USMC, Vice Chairman, Joint Chiefs of Staff, DoD Press Conference, December 11, 2001.

277 DoD News Conference, December 12, 2001.

278 DoD News Conference, December 17, 2001.

279 Franks, Testimony to SASC, July 31, 2002.

280 DoD Press Conference, April 17, 2002.

281 DoD News Conference, December 17, 2001.

282 Franks, Testimony to SASC, July 31, 2002.

283 DoD Press Conference, December 19, 2001.

284 Tony Perry, "Fighter Pilots Seek Opponents for an Endgame," *Los Angeles Times*, December 24, 2001.

285 Interview with Zortman, December 20, 2004.

286 Interview by Rebecca Grant with Lieutenant Eric Taylor, July 23, 2004, Lemoore, CA.

287 Interview with Marzano, July 23, 2004.

288 Interview with Taylor, July 23, 2004.

289 Interview with Fitzgerald, July 1, 2004.

290 Rachel Davis, "Kennedy Prepares for Final Training," *Florida Times-Union*, February 6, 2002.

291 Matthew Dolan, "Carrier John F. Kennedy Greets New Skipper," *Norfolk Virginian-Pilot*, February 13, 2002.

292 Interview with Cryer, September 2, 2004.

293 Interview with Cryer, September 2, 2004.

294 Interview with Cryer, September 2, 2004.

295 Tony Perry, "Navy, Army Cooperate in Afghanistan Strikes," *Los Angeles Times*, December 19, 2001.

296 Interview with Robb, August 30, 2004.

297 Interview with Marzano, July 23, 2004.

CHAPTER 6:
AIRPOWER FOR ANACONDA

298 Franks, *American Soldier*, p. 369.

299 Two US Air Force, one US Navy, and five US Army personnel lost their lives during Operation Anaconda. See, Eric Bradley and David Kelly, "8 Men From 3 Services Unite in Fight That was Their Last," *Los Angeles Times*, March 6, 2002.

300 Interview with Zortman, December 20, 2004.

301 Thomas Ricks, "Battle Sends Broader Message of US Resolve," *Washington Post*, March 5, 2002.

302 Thomas Ricks, "Battle Sends Broader Message of US Resolve," *Washington Post*, March 5, 2002.

303 Interview with Robb, August 30, 2004.

304 TFEL Interview with Major Pete Donnelly, May 20, 2002.

305 Interview with Zortman, December 20, 2004.

306 Interview with Moseley, July 24, 2003.

307 Interview with Robb, August 30, 2004.

308 Interview with Robb, August 30, 2004.

309 Interview with Nichols, October 13, 2004.

310 Vernon Loeb, "General Defends Tactics in Afghan Battle," *Washington Post*, March 12, 2003.

311 Headquarters United States Air Force AF/XOL, *Operation Anaconda: An Air Power Perspective*, February 7, 2005, pp. 36-37.

312 Anaconda report, p. 39.

313 Franks, *American Soldier*, p. 378.

314 TFEL Interview with Lt. Gen. T. Michael Moseley, Shaw AFB, July 24, 2003.

315 Interview with Taylor, July 23, 2004.

316 Interview with Fitzgerald, July 1, 2004.

317 David Brown, "The Long Haul," *Navy Times*, March 11, 2002.

318 Interview with Zortman, December 20, 2004.

319 Esther Schrader, "Simple Mission Became 18-Hour Fight," *Los Angeles Times*, March 8, 2002.

320 Geoffrey Mohan and Esther Schrader, "Back at Base, Troops Say Afghans Failed Them," *Los Angeles Times*, March 11, 2002.

321 Esther Schrader, "Simple Mission Became 18-Hour Fight," *Los Angeles Times*, March 8, 2002.

322 TFEL Interview with Donnelly, May 20, 2002.

323 Headquarters United States Air Force AF/XOL, *Operation Anaconda: An Air Power Perspective*, February 7, 2005, pp. 69-71.

324 Eric Schmitt and Thom Shanker, "Afghans Retreat Forced Americans to Lead A Battle," *New York Times*, March 10, 2002.

325 Interview with Zortman, December 20, 2004.

326 Interview with Marzano, July 23, 2004.

327 Interview with Marzano, July 23, 2004.

328 Interview with Robb, August 30, 2004.

329 TFEL Interview with Major General John Corley, January 3, 2003.

330 TFEL Interview with Moseley, June 25, 2003.

331 TFEL Interview with Major General John Corley, May 1, 2002.

332 Interviews with Taylor, Marzano July 23, 2004.

333 Interview with Zortman, December 20, 2004.

334 Interview with Marzano, July 23, 2004.

335 Interview with Marzano, July 23, 2004.

336 Headquarters United States Air Force AF/XOL, *Operation Anaconda: An Air Power Perspective*, February 7, 2005, p. 67.

337 DoD Briefing, "Background Briefing on the Report of the Battle of Takur Gar," May 24, 2002.

338 Myers, "Interview with Wolf Blitzer," CNN, March 10, 2002.

339 Rachel Davis, "Kennedy Relieves Roosevelt," *Florida Union-Times*, March 8, 2002.

340 Interview with Taylor, July 23, 2004.

341 Interview with Moseley, July 24, 2004.

342 *Operation Anaconda: An Air Power Perspective*, February 7, 2005, p. 95.

343 Myers, "Interview with Wolf Blitzer," CNN, March 10, 2002.

344 Franks, DoD Press Conference, May 24, 2002.

345 Gulf War Air Power Survey, Volume V.

346 Interview with Marzano, July 23, 2004.

347 Michael Gordon, "Cheney Says Next Goal in US War on Terror is to Block Access to Arms," *New York Times*, March 16, 2002.

CHAPTER 7:
PREPARING FOR IRAQ

348 Michael Evans, "America's Floating Air Base Gets Ready for Battle," *London Times*, January 9, 2003.

349 Sandra Jontz, "US Planning to Reduce Aircraft Carrier Presence in Arabian Gulf", *European Stars and Stripes*, April 9, 2002.

350 Interview with Tomaszeski, August 4, 2004.

351 Rachel Davis, "Kennedy Pilots Cool Jets," *Florida Times-Union Jacksonville*, June 27, 2002.

352 Woodward, *Bush at War*, p. 137.

353 Michael Gordon, "UN Inspectors Prepare for Iraq," *New York Times*, 8 April 2002.

354 Secretary Rumsfeld Interview with Georgie Anne Geyer, United Press Syndicate, November 11, 2001, DoD Transcript.

355 Bob Drogin and Mark Mazzetti, "Only Hussein Had Full Picture," *Los Angeles Times*, October 7, 2004.

356 Franks, *American Soldier*, pp. 355-356.

357 Franks, Testimony to SASC, February 7, 2002.

358 R.W. Rogers, "Combat Ready," *Newport News Daily Press*, May 7, 2002.

359 Franks, *American Soldier*, pp. 348-353.

360 Interview with Keating, October 14, 2004.

361 Franks, *American Soldier*, p. 389.

362 Interview with Moseley, July 24, 2003.

363 Interview with Keating, October 14, 2004.

364 Interview with Moseley, July 24, 2003.

365 Interview with Robb, August 30, 2004.

366 Gordon I. Peterson, "The Real Thing," *Seapower*, June 2002.

367 Interview by Rebecca Grant with Rear Admiral John Kelly, September 9, 2004, Newport, RI.

368 Interview with Kelly, September 9, 2004.

369 Interview with Kelly, September 9, 2004.

370 Interview with Kelly, September 9, 2004.

371 Interview with Nichols, October 13, 2004.

372 Nichols Briefing, October 15, 2004.

373 Interview with Nichols, October 13, 2004.

374 Interview with Robb, August 30, 2004.

375 Interview with Nichols, October 13, 2004.

376 DoD Press Conference, Background briefing by USCENTCOM on Targeting, March 5, 2003.

377 Franks, *American Soldier*, pp. 389-91.

378 USCENTCOM Press Conference, March 22, 2003.

379 Interview with Moseley, July 24, 2003.

380 Interview with Robb, August 30, 2004.

381 Interview with Keating, October 5, 2004.

382 Interview with Nichols, October 13, 2004.

383 Franks, *American Soldier*, p. 475.

384 Interview with Nichols, October 13, 2004.

385 Interview with Kelly, September 9, 2004.

386 Interview with Robb, August 30, 2004.

387 Franks, *American Soldier*, p. 388.

388 DoD News Conference, September 26, 2002.

389 Peter Baker, "Saudis Showcase Cooperation At Air Base with Key Mission," *Washington Post*, November 21, 2002.

390 John A. Tirpak, "Legacy of the Air Blockades," *Air Force Magazine*, February 2003.

391 Interview with Nichols, October 13, 2004.

392 Interview with Keating, October 5, 2004.

393 Interview with Keating, October 5, 2004.

394 Interview with Kelly, September 9, 2004.
395 Interview with Stufflebeem, August 4, 2004.
396 Interview with Nichols, October 13, 2004.
397 DoD Press Conference, October 29, 2001.
398 President George W. Bush, "Rose Garden Remarks," White House Transcript, November 8, 2002.
399 DoD Press Conference, October 29, 2001.
400 Bob Woodward, *Plan of Attack*, (New York: Simon and Schuster, 2004), p. 293.
401 Rick C. Hernitzer, "Anthrax Shots Underway on Kitty Hawk, Lincoln," *Pacific Stars and Stripes*, February 3, 2003.
402 "Iraq: Denial and Deception," Transcript of Secretary of State Colin Powell's Speech to the United Nations Security Council, February 5, 2003, Department of State.
403 Interview with Kelly, September 9, 2004.
404 Interview with Stufflebeem, August 4, 2004.
405 Interview with Stufflebeem, August 4, 2004.
406 Interview with Driscoll, August 4, 2004.
407 Franks, *American Soldier*, p. 473.
408 Interview with Robb, August 30, 2004.
409 Interview with Kelly, September 9, 2004.
410 Woodward, *Plan of Attack*, pp. 316-317.
411 Interview by Rebecca Grant with Air Force Lieutenant General Daniel P. Leaf, June 27, 2003.
412 Interview with Robb, August 30, 2004.
413 Woodward, *Plan of Attack*, pp. 357-358.
414 Remarks by the President in "Address to the Nation," White House Transcript, March 17, 2003.

CHAPTER 8:
OPERATION IRAQI FREEDOM BEGINS

415 Text of Speech by Prime Minister Tony Blair, *The Guardian*, March 18, 2003.
416 Franks, *American Soldier*, p. 436.
417 Interview with Robb, August 30, 2004.
418 Interview with Moseley, July 24, 2003.
419 USCENTCOM Press Conference, March 30, 2003.
420 Franks, *American Soldier*, p. 437.
421 Nichols Briefing, October 15, 2004.
422 Interview with Nichols, October 13, 2004.
423 Interview with Nichols, October 13, 2004.
424 DoD Press Conference, March 21, 2003.
425 Interview with Driscoll, August 4, 2004.
426 Nichols briefing, October 15, 2004.
427 Interview with Nichols, October 13, 2004.
428 Michael R. Gordon, "A Swift, and Risky, Attack By Land, With surprise in Mind," *New York Times*, March 21, 2003. See also Franks, *American Soldier*, p. 467.
429 Franks, *American Soldier*, p. 455.
430 Interview with Nichols, October 13, 2004.
431 Interview with Moseley, July 24, 2003.
432 DoD Press Conference, March 21, 2003.
433 Interview by Rebecca Grant with Commander Kevin F. Greene, July 22, 2004, Lemoore, CA.
434 Interview with Nichols, October 13, 2004.
435 Interview with Moffit, September 17, 2004.
436 Interview with Driscoll, August 4, 2004.
437 Interview with Driscoll, August 4, 2004.
438 Nichols briefing, October 15, 2004.
439 Interview with Nichols, October 13, 2004.
440 Interview with Moseley, July 24, 2003.

441 Interview with Robb, August 30, 2004.

442 Lt Gen Moseley, CFACC, Live Briefing, DoD, April 5, 2003.

443 Interview with Robb, August 30, 2004.

444 Cesar G. Soriano, "Naval, Marine Pilots Soar into 'Epic' Mission," *USA Today*, March 24, 2003.

445 Interview with Nichols, October 13, 2004.

446 Interview with Nichols, October 13, 2004.

447 Interview with Nichols, October 13, 2004.

448 Cesar G. Soriano, "Naval, Marine Pilots Soar into 'Epic' Mission," *USA Today*, March 24, 2003.

449 DoD Press Conference, March 21, 2003.

450 TFEL, *The First 600 Days of Combat: The US Air Force in the Global War on Terrorism,* (Washington, DC: IRIS Press, 2004), pp. 110-111.

451 Thomas Ricks, "Myers Depicts War on Two Fronts," *Washington Post*, March 5, 2003.

452 Interview with Nichols, October 13, 2004.

453 Interview with Robb, August 30, 2004.

454 Interview with Nichols, October 13, 2004.

455 Interview with Robb, August 30, 2004.

456 Interview with Nichols, October 13, 2004.

457 Interview with Nichols, October 14, 2004.

458 Vice Admiral Keating, CFMCC, Live Briefing, DoD, April 12, 2003.

459 Interview with Moseley, July 24, 2003.

460 Interview with Stufflebeem, August 4, 2004.

461 Interview with Lynch, July 22, 2004.

462 Interview with Lynch, July 22, 2004.

463 Interview with Kelly, September 9, 2004.

464 Interview with Moffit, September 17, 2004.

465 Interview with Kelly, September 9, 2004.

466 Brigadier General Vincent Brooks, CENTCOM, March 23, 2003.

467 Cesar G. Soriano, "Naval, Marine Pilots Soar into 'Epic' Mission," *USA Today*, March 24, 2003.

468 Interview with Moffit, September 17, 2004.

469 Interview with Kelly, September 9, 2004.

470 Abizaid, Wall and Brooks, USCENTCOM, March 23, 2003.

471 Bradley Graham, "Air War Targets Enemy Troops," *Washington Post*, March 25, 2003.

472 Interview with Moffit, September 17, 2004.

473 Interview with Driscoll, August 4, 2004.

474 Interview with Nichols, October 13, 2004.

475 Interview with Driscoll, August 4, 2004.

476 Interview with Moffit, September 17, 2004.

477 Interview with Driscoll, August 4, 2004.

478 Charles E. Kirkpatrick, *Joint Fires as They Were Meant to Be: V Corps and the 4th Air Support Operations Group During Operation Iraqi Freedom,* Association of the United States Army: The Institute of Land Warfare, October 2004.

479 Interview with Nichols, October 13, 2004.

480 Williamson Murray and Major General Robert H. Scales, Jr., USA, Ret., *The Iraq War,* (Cambridge, MA: The Belknap Press of Harvard University, 2003), pp. 105-106.

481 United States Army, Center for Army Lessons Learned (CALL) *On Point: The United States Army in Operation Iraqi Freedom,* May 26, 2004, p. 205.

482 Interview with Nichols, October 13, 2004.

483 Rowan Scarborough, "General Tells How Cell Phone Foiled US Attack in Iraq," *Washington Times*, May 8, 2003.

484 *On Point: The US Army in Operation Iraqi Freedom,* Center for Army Lessons Learned, p. 211.

485 Franks, *American Soldier*, p. 498.

486 Interview with Nichols, October 13, 2004.

487 Interview with Nichols, October 13, 2004.

488 Franks, *American Soldier*, p. 499.
489 Interview with Nichols, October 13, 2004.
490 Franks, *American Soldier*, p. 486.
491 DoD Press Conference, December 21, 1998.
492 Michael Gordon, "US Army Starts Push on Republican Guard," *New York Times*, March 24, 2003.
493 Lieutenant General Wallace, V Corps Commander, Live Briefing, DoD, May 7, 2003.
494 Jim Michaels, "Iraqi Tactics Have US Rethinking Strategy," *USA Today*, March 31, 2003.
495 Jim Dwyer, "Troops Endure Blowing Sands and Mud Rain," *New York Times*, March 26, 2003.
496 Franks, *American Soldier*, p. 499.
497 Interview by Rebecca Grant with Commander Jeff Rocha, July 23, 2004, Lemoore, CA.
498 Interview with Kelly, September 9, 2004.
499 Interview with Greene, July 22, 2004.
500 Interview by Rebecca Grant with Lieutenant Michael Rovenholt, July 23, 2004, Lemoore, CA.
501 Interview with Kelly, September 9, 2004.
502 "Interview, Vice Admiral Timothy J. Keating: "This Was a Different War," USNI Proceedings, June 2003.
503 Interview with Moseley, July 24, 2003.
504 *On Point*, p. 232.
505 Franks, *American Soldier*, p. 503.

CHAPTER 9:
DECISIVE COMBAT OPERATIONS

506 "Interview, Vice Admiral Timothy J. Keating: "This Was a Different War," USNI Proceedings, June 2003.
507 *On Point*, pp. 273-274.
508 USCENTCOM Press Conference, March 30, 2003.
509 USCENTCOM Press Conference, March 28, 2003.
510 Lieutenant General James Conway, Commander, I MEF, Briefing From Iraq, DoD, May 30, 2003.
511 *On Point*, p. 218.
512 Interview with Nichols, October 13, 2004.
513 Interview with Hilberer and Annichiarico, March 12, 2004.
514 Interview with Stufflebeem, August 4, 2004.
515 Interview with Stufflebeem, August 4, 2004.
516 Interview with Lynch, July 22, 2004.
517 Interview by Rebecca Grant with Lieutenant Geoffrey Bowman, July 23, 2004, Lemoore, CA.
518 Interview with Bowman, July 22, 2004.
519 USCENTCOM Press Conference, April 2, 2003.
520 Steve Vogel and Karl Vick, "US Reinforces Northern Front," *Washington Post*, March 28, 2003.
521 Steve Vogel, "Paratroopers Move Closer to Defenders," *Washington Post*, April 3, 2003.
522 Interview with Stufflebeem, July 22, 2004.
523 Interview with Stufflebeem, July 22, 2004.
524 Interview with Lynch, July 22, 2004.
525 Interview with Stufflebeem, August 4, 2004.
526 Interview with Bowman, July 22, 2004.
527 Interview with Stufflebeem, August 4, 2004.
528 Interview with Stufflebeem, August 4, 2004.
529 Interview with Bowman, July 22, 2004.
530 Interview with Bowman, July 22, 2004.
531 Interview with Lynch, July 22, 2004.
532 Interview with Bowman, July 22, 2004.
533 Interview with Lynch, July 22, 2004.
534 Interview with Bowman, July 22, 2004.

535 Interview with Lynch, July 22, 2004.
536 DoD Press Conference, April 1, 2003.
537 *On Point*, pp. 283-285.
538 Interview with Bowman, July 22, 2004.
539 DoD Press Conference, December 21, 1998.
540 Anthony Cordesman, *"Key Targets in Iraq,"* CSIS Paper, February 1998.
541 Franks, *American Soldier*, p. 466.
542 Interview with Nichols, October 13, 2004.
543 Interview with Robb, August 30, 2004.
544 USCENTCOM Press Conference, March 30, 2003.
545 Interview with Nichols, October 13, 2004.
546 Moseley, July 24, 2003.
547 Interview with Leaf, June 27, 2003.
548 Interview with Leaf, June 27, 2003.
549 Interview with Nichols, October 13, 2004.
550 *On Point*, p. 340.
551 Interview with Leaf, June 27, 2003.
552 Moseley interview, July 24, 2003.
553 Michael R. Gordon, "Allied Plan Would Encourage Iraqis Not to Fight," *New York Times*, March 11, 2003.
554 Keating, Proceedings
555 Interview with Nekamoto, July 22, 2004.
556 Interview with Nekamoto, July 22, 2004.
557 Interview with Bynum, July 22, 2004.
558 Interview with Moffit, September 17, 2004.
559 Interview with Bynum, July 22, 2004.
560 Interview with Nichols, October 13, 2004.
561 Interview with Moffit, September 17, 2004.
562 Interview with Nichols, October 13, 2004.
563 Interview with Haigler, July 22, 2004.
564 Interview with Kelly, September 9, 2004.
565 Interview by Rebecca Grant with Lieutenant Michael Garcia, July 23, 2004, Lemoore, CA.
566 Interview with Nichols, October 13, 2004.
567 Interview with Moffit, September 17, 2004.
568 Paul Richter, "Bombing is Tool of Choice to Clear Path to Baghdad," *Los Angeles Times*, April 1, 2003.
569 DoD Press Conference, April 1, 2003.
570 DoD Press Conference, April 1, 2003.
571 DoD Press Conference, April 2, 2003.
572 Interview with Haigler, July 22, 2004.
573 Franks, *American Soldier*, pp. 514-515.
574 DoD Press Conference, April 3, 2003.
575 DoD Press Conference, April 3, 2003.
576 Lieutenant General Moseley, CFACC, Live Briefing, DoD, April 5, 2003.
577 DoD Press Conference, April 2, 2003.
578 Interview with Moffit, September 17, 2004.
579 Lieutenant General Moseley, CFACC, Live Briefing, DoD, April 5, 2003.
580 Lieutenant General Moseley, CFACC, Live Briefing, DoD, April 5, 2003.
581 Interview with Nichols, October 13, 2004.
582 Interview with Nichols, October 13, 2004.
583 Moseley interview, July 24, 2003.
584 Interview with Greene, July 22, 2004.
585 Interview with Bynum, July 22, 2004.

586 Interview with Kelly, September 9, 2004.

587 Interview with Robb, August 30, 2004.

588 *On Point*, p. 392.

589 Pace and Wolfowitz interview with NBC Meet the Press, April 6, 2003.

590 Pace, NBC Meet the Press, April 6, 2003.

591 DoD Press Conference, April 7, 2003.

592 Jonathan Finer, "Marines Battle Their Way Toward Central Baghdad," *Washington Post*, April 8, 2003.

593 Myers, DoD Press Conference, April 9, 2003.

594 Interview with Nekamoto, July 22, 2004.

595 Details reported in Nils J. Bruzelius, "Daybook," *Washington Post*, April 10, 2003.

596 Interview with Robb, August 30, 2004.

597 Interview with Kelly, September 9, 2004.

598 Interview with Nichols, October 13, 2004.

599 Interview with Nichols, October 13, 2004.

600 Vice Admiral Tim Keating Briefing from Bahrain, April 12, 2003, DoD Transcript.

601 Vice Admiral Tim Keating Briefing from Bahrain, April 12, 2003, DoD Transcript.

602 Interview with Robb, August 30, 2004.

603 *On Point*, p. 461.

604 Keating, Proceedings

605 Interview with Nichols, October 13, 2004.

606 President George W. Bush, "Remarks by the President from the *USS Abraham Lincoln*," May 1, 2003, White House Transcript.

607 Rumsfeld, DoD Press Conference, April 11, 2003.

CHAPTER 10:
STRATEGIC DIRECTIONS

608 Walter T. Ham IV, "Presence with a Purpose: CNO Explains Fleet Response Plan," *Navy News*, August 18, 2003.

609 Vice Admiral John B. Nathman, "Naval Aviation on Top in Afghanistan," *The Hook*, Spring 2002.

610 Jack Dorsey, "Local Jets Are Flying Over Iraq at Same Pace as Start of War," *Norfolk Virginian-Pilot*, November 10, 2004.

611 Interview with Zortman, December 20, 2004.

612 Interview by Rebecca Grant with Rear Admiral Charles Johnston, January 11, 2005.

613 Interview with Johnston, January 11, 2005.

614 RADM Mark Fitzgerald, "Naval Aviation 'Under the Radar' in Iraq," *The Hook*, Winter 2003.

615 Interview with Kelly, September 9, 2004.

616 Interview with Keating, October 14, 2004.

617 Interview with Keating, October 14, 2004.

618 CFACC April 5 2003 briefing.

619 *On point*, p. 461.

620 CENTAF, *OIF: By the Numbers*, April, 2003.

621 Interview with Nichols, October 13, 2004.

622 Admiral Vern Clark, "Projecting Decisive Joint Capabilities," USNI *Proceedings*, October 2002.

623 Otto Kreisher, "Airwing Built for Two," *Air Force Magazine*, December 2002.

624 Interview with Zortman, December 20, 2004.

625 Interview with Zortman, December 20, 2004.

626 Interview with Rear Admiral Charles Johnston, January 11, 2005.

627 Slobodan Lekic, "Mighty Carriers Remain Key to Naval Warfare," *Washington Times*, April 7, 2003.

628 Michael Evans, "America's Floating Air Base Gets Ready for Battle," *London Times*, January 9, 2003.

629 Interview with Kelly, September 9, 2004.

630 Interview with Zortman, December 20, 2004.

631 Interview with Zortman, December 20, 2004.
632 Interview with Driscoll, August 4, 2004.
633 Interview with Kelly, September 9, 2004.
634 Interview with Moffit, September 17, 2004.
635 William Matthews, "Triumph of Jointness," *Defense News*, April 14, 2003.
636 Reynolds, *The Fast Carriers*, p. 36.
637 Interview with Kelly, September 9, 2004.

Glossary

AAA	Anti-Aircraft Artillery
ADA	Air Defense Artillery
AFB	Air Force Base
AMRAAM	Advance Medium Range Air-to-Air Missile
AOA	Angle of Attack
ASOC	Air Support Operations Center
ATACMS	Army Tactical Missile System
ATO	Air Tasking Order
AWACS	Airborne Warning and Control System
BCD	Battlefield Coordination Detachment
BCT	Battlefield Coordination Team
BDA	Bomb Damage Assessment
CAG	Carrier Air Group
CAOC	Combined Air Operations Center
CAP	Combat Air Patrol
CAS	Close Air Support
CAV	Cavalry
CENTCOM	Central Command
CFACC	Combined Forces Air Component Commander
CFLCC	Combined Forces Land Component Commander
CIA	Central Intelligence Agency
CINC	Commander in Chief
CJCS	Chairman, Joint Chiefs of Staff
CJTF	Combined Joint Task Force
CNO	Chief of Naval Operations
CSAR	Combat Search and Rescue
CTF	Combined Task Force
CVIC	Carrier Intelligence Center
CVN	Nuclear powered aircraft carrier
CVW	Carrier air wing
DASC	Direct Air Support Center (US Marine Corps)
DCA	Defense Communications Agency
DCAG	Deputy Carrier Air Group
DEAD	Destruction of Enemy Air Defenses

DMPI	Designated Mean Point of Impact
EUCOM	European command
FAA	Federal Aviation Administration
FAC	Forward Air Controller
FAC-A	Forward Air Controller – Airborne
FLIR	Forward Looking Infrared Radar
FSCL	Fire Safety Coordination Line
GBU	Guided Bomb Unit
GFAC	Ground Forward Air Control
GPS	Global Positioning System
HARM	High-speed Anti-Radiation Missile
HCS	Helicopter Combat Support
IADS	Integrated Air Defense System
ISR	Intelligence, Surveillance, Reconnaissance
JACE	Joint Aviation Combat Element
JCAS	Joint Close Air Support
JCS	Joint Chiefs of Staff
JDAM	Joint Direct Attack Munition
JFACC	Joint Forces Air Component Commander
JFCOM	Joint Forces Command
JSOA	Joint Special Operations Area
JSTARS	Joint Surveillance and Target Attack Radar System
JTACS	Joint Terminal Attack Controller
KI/CAS	Killbox Interdiction/Close Air Support
KSA	Kingdom of Saudi Arabia
LGB	Laser Guided Bomb
LOC	Line of Communication
MANPAD	Man Portable Air Defense
MEU	Marine Expeditionary Unit
MEZ	Missile Engagement Zone
MOPP	Mission Oriented Protective Posture
NAG	North Arabian Gulf
NALE	Naval Air Liaison Element
NATO	North American Treaty Organization
NAVAIR	Naval Air Systems Command
NEADS	Northeast Air Defense Sector
NORAD	North American Aerospace Defense Command
NSAWC	Naval Strike and Air Warfare Center

NSC	National Security Council
ODA	Operational Detachment Alpha
OEF	Operation Enduring Freedom
OIF	Operation Iraqi Freedom
OSW	Operation Southern Watch
POW	Prisoner of War
PSAB	Prince Sultan Air Base
ROE	Rules of Engagement
RPG	Rocket-Propelled Grenade
SAM	Surface to Air Missile
SAR	Search and Rescue
SATCOM	Satellite Communication
SCAR	Strike Control and Reconnaissance
SEAD	Suppression of Enemy Air Defenses
SEAL	Sea Air Land
SOF	Special Operations Forces
SPINS	Special Instructions
TACAIR	Tactical Air
TF	Task Force
TLAM	Tomahawk Land Attack Missile
TST	Time Sensitive Target
UAV	Unmanned Aerial Vehicle
UN	United Nations
USMC	United States Marine Corps
VFA	Strike-Fighter squadron
VFR	Visual Flight Rules
VMFA	Fighter Attack squadron (US Marine Corps)
VTC	Video Teleconference
WMD	Weapons of Mass Destruction
XCAS	Immediate Close Air Support
XO	Executive Officer

Index